Sixth Workshop on Teaching NLP (TeachNLP 2024)

Bangkok, Thailand
15 August 2024

ISBN: 979-8-3313-0179-8

Printed from e-media with permission by:

Curran Associates, Inc.
57 Morehouse Lane
Red Hook, NY 12571

Association for Computational Linguistics
209 N. Eighth Street
Stroudsburg, Pennsylvania 18360

Phone: 1-570-476-8006
Fax: 1-570-476-0860

acl@aclweb.org

Additional copies of this publication are available from:

Curran Associates, Inc.
57 Morehouse Lane
Red Hook, NY 12571 USA
Phone: 845-758-0400
Fax: 845-758-2633
Email: curran@proceedings.com
Web: www.proceedings.com

TeachNLP 2024

The Sixth Workshop on Teaching NLP

Proceedings of the Workshop

August 15, 2024

The TeachNLP organizers gratefully acknowledge the support from the following sponsors.

Gold Level

Association for Computational Linguistics (ACL)
317 Sidney Baker St. S
Suite 400 - 134
Kerrville, TX 78028
USA
Tel: +1-855-225-1962
acl@aclweb.org

Introduction

Welcome to the Sixth Workshop on Teaching Natural Language Processing (NLP). This hybrid workshop featured an exciting mix of papers, teaching material submissions, panels, talks, and participatory activities.

Educators designing NLP courses and degree programs are facing unique challenges due to the fast-paced progress and growth of the field. This growth has led to the creation and revision of NLP courses, and related programs, as well as new best practices and educational materials focused on emerging subareas. For the sixth edition of the workshop, we were bringing together the communities of NLP research and education to share best practices one can use to share tools and resources for NLP education, as well as to discuss some core challenges, including approaches to facilititating meaningful conversations about language among Computer Science (CS) students, or designing NLP curricula that include user-centered design, while equipping students with the ability to advance responsible and ethical NLP.

We were happy to accept 9 long papers and 9 short papers on teaching materials. The latter were accompanied by exercises and assignments as Jupyter notebooks, software, slides, and teaching guidelines that we hope to make available via a repository created as result of the workshop. Both types of papers cover many topics: course and curriculum design, project-based learning, homeworks and assignments, low-resource languages, and - following NLP trends - Large Language Models.

Our workshop featured **Karën Fort** (LORIA, France) who presented work on teaching ethics in the context of NLP. Our workshop also included a panel discussion featuring **David Adelani** (McGill University, Canada), **Lori Levin** (Carnegie Mellon University (CMU), USA), **Graham Neubig** (CMU), **Aiala Rosá** (University of the Republic, Uruguay), and **Sherry Wu** (CMU).

We thank the Program Committee, who thoughtfully reviewed the submitted papers. We also appreciate the sponsorship funding we received from Apple. Finally, we thank the workshop participants, whose interest in teaching allow us to establish and grow the next generation of NLP researchers and practitioners.

- Sana Sabah Al-azzawi, Laura Biester, György Kovács, Ana Marasović, Leena Mathur, Margot Mieskes, and Leonie Weissweiler (the co-organizers)

Organizing Committee

Organizers

Sana Al-azzawi, Luleå University of Technology
Laura Biester, Middlebury College
György Kovács, Luleå University of Technology
Ana Marasović, University of Utah
Leena Mathur, Carnegie Mellon University
Margot Mieskes, University of Applied Sciences, Darmstadt
Leonie Weissweiler, University of Texas at Austin

Program Committee

Reviewers

Thomas Arnold, Technische Universität Darmstadt
Gábor Berend, University of Szeged
Amanda Bertsch, Carnegie Mellon University
Jason Eisner, Microsoft and Johns Hopkins University
Richard Farkas, University of Szeged
Catherine Finegan-Dollak, University of Richmond
Jennifer Foster, Dublin City University
Annemarie Friedrich, University of Augsburg
Venkata Subrahmanyan Govindarajan, Ithaca College
Amir Hossein Kargaran, Ludwig-Maximilians-Universität München
Brielen Madureira, University of Potsdam
Ted Pedersen, University of Minnesota, Duluth
Alexandra Schofield, Harvey Mudd College
Sofia Serrano, Lafayette College
Shane Storks, University of Michigan
Sowmya Vajjala, National Research Council Canada
Jannis Vamvas, University of Zurich
Veronika Vincze, University of Szeged
Shira Wein, Amherst College
Winston Wu, University of Hawaii at Hilo
Torsten Zesch, Fernuniversität in Hagen

Table of Contents

Documenting the Unwritten Curriculum of Student Research

Shomir Wilson
College of Information Sciences and Technology
Pennsylvania State University
University Park, PA, USA
shomir@psu.edu

Abstract

Graduate and undergraduate student researchers in natural language processing (NLP) often need mentoring to learn the norms of research. While methodological and technical knowledge are essential, there is also a "hidden curriculum" of experiential knowledge about topics like work strategies, common obstacles, collaboration, conferences, and scholarly writing. As a professor, I have written a set of guides that cover typically unwritten customs and procedures for academic research. I share them with advisees to help them understand research norms and to help us focus on their specific questions and interests. This paper describes these guides, which are freely accessible on the web,[1] and I provide recommendations to faculty who are interested in creating similar materials for their advisees.

1 Introduction

Academic research is at the core of many graduate degree programs, and it serves an enrichment activity for high-achieving undergraduates. Students are given graduate-level research problems are expected to produce high-quality results. Even within a supportive environment—including support from a student's advisor, student peers, and the institution—this is challenging for a new researcher. While students likely benefit from the intellectual challenges of research (e.g., *productive struggle* in transformative learning (Murdoch et al., 2020)), basic concepts that enable the activity of research are often left unsaid by mentors. This "hidden curriculum" has been acknowledged in classroom learning (Giroux and Penna, 1979; Andarvazh et al., 2017) but it has received little attention in the realm of mentoring researchers.

I describe a set of guides that I write and maintain to help student researchers learn typically unwritten customs and procedures in academic research. They are part of my advising strategy, as I ask new advisees to discuss them with me after reading them, and to review them at key times during their development as researchers. This approach is similar to a flipped classroom (Akçayır and Akçayır, 2018), but in a one-on-one context. The guides also share the goal of approachability previously explored by Nakai and Guo (2023), who proposed peer-written guides; while I wrote these guides as a professor, I use my perspective as a tool to illustrate how professors' and students' roles differ in research. These guides are also resources that my advisees consult on demand when I am not immediately available. My motivations for providing them include helping students meet expectations, the importance of advising efficiently and fairly, and a desire to focus one-on-one time on topics that matter most to individual advisees. These guides are publicly available on the web, and anecdotally they have received strong positive feedback from the research community.

In the remainder of this paper I describe the guides, explain how I use them, and provide recommendations for other faculty who wish to create similar resources.

2 The Guides

The guides I describe here are a subset of those on my academic advice page (URL in footnote). Some of the information in these guides is specific to academic norms at research universities in the United States, a limitation explicitly acknowledged when applicable. However, most of the content applies to an international audience of student researchers in computing in general and in NLP specifically.

The *Guide for Joining My Lab* describes how students can get involved in research, with separate information for prospective Ph.D. students, prospective M.S. students, and prospective undergraduate researchers. Most of its contents are germane to a

[1] https://shomir.net/advice

Proceedings of the Sixth Workshop on Teaching NLP, pages 1–3
August 15, 2024

large audience, but some items are specific to my lab and advising. In Section 3 below I provide tips to other faculty who wish to create a guide like this as a recruiting tool.

The *Guide for Student Research* focuses on the activities of research in an personal, experiential sense rather than on methods or technical skills. This focus includes descriptions of common high-level tasks, things that tend to surprise students about engaging in research, what people enjoy about it, strategies for productivity, common obstacles and suggestions for overcoming them, and special guidance for undergraduate researchers and graduate students who mentor them.

The *Guide for Research Conferences* covers an arc of activity: deciding when and where to submit to a conference, assembling a manuscript, dealing with acceptance or rejection, and attending a conference. Among these topics, I observe anecdotally that conferences as events are especially obscure to new student researchers. The guide describes common items on a conference program, things to do while attending, and how oral and poster presentations differ, among other topics.

The *Guide for Scholarly Writing* describes some common conventions for writing a research manuscript. These include broad principles (e.g., make writing approachable but formal, and imagine the audience), specific practices (e.g., define jargon, maintain narrative flow), and special guidance for collaborative writing (e.g., follow advice from senior co-authors, explain what changed between revisions).

The *Guide for Citations and References* describes the principles behind citations and references for students who are unfamiliar with them or need a reminder. The guide adopts a *citation positive* tone, focusing on the value these conventions add to a writer's work. While the guide contains warnings about the consequences of plagiarism, I hypothesize a positive tone is more engaging and effective for the audience than a punitive one.

Other guides in the collection cover topics adjacent to research advising, including the expectations faculty have for interacting with students, how to cope with pressure to succeed as a high-achieving student, and the academic job market.

3 Use Cases

These guides are useful in at least four contexts:

- Research Advising: This is the default context. Sharing these guides with advisees helps them to work productively and assimilate otherwise unspoken norms for research.
- Classroom Teaching: I assign some of these guides as readings in courses that have open-ended projects. They tend to be most relevant to graduate-level courses, but undergraduates are sometimes motivated to make substantial contributions and publish their work.
- Recruiting: Prospective research advisees often visit faculty websites. Informally, my impression is these materials encourage prospective students to pursue working with me.
- Public Service: Reactions to these guides on social media suggest their positive impact exceeds the scope of my lab, contributing to public awareness of student research.

The public availability and format of these guides (i.e., as webpages) makes them easily findable and usable for each of these audiences.

4 Recommendations

For faculty who wish to create similar materials, I recommend the following:

First, *assume minimal knowledge from your audience*. Prospective research advisees' eagerness to participate in academic research is easy to mistake for basic knowledge about how it works. For example, when a faculty member writes about advising (such as in an advising statement), they should take care to explain what *research advising* is and its importance in a student researcher's trajectory.

Also, *discard the goal of writing comprehensive guides*. It is easier to produce materials that focus on topics that are not covered by other resources, that are frequently understood, that are specific to the writer's advising, or that particularly motivate the writer. (I note that ease is important, as faculty tend to have many tasks competing for their attention.) Overreach when writing (i.e., writing beyond one's motivation or expertise) is less likely to be productive. Remember it is better to provide something specialized that will assist students with specific tasks than to provide nothing.

Finally, although it may seem challenging, *try to write for all audiences at once*. Whether a guide is targeted undergraduates, graduate students, or others, assume that a subset of each of the other groups will want to read it. This assumption motivates writing in an approachable, unassuming way. When expectations and responsibilities are in scope, this also encourages being open about why they exist.

To further motivate creating similar materials, faculty who are expected to perform *service* duties may ask if this qualifies toward that obligation.

Acknowledgments

This manuscript is based upon work supported by the National Science Foundation under Grant No. 2237574. I also thank my research advisees for inspiring me create these materials.

References

Gökçe Akçayır and Murat Akçayır. 2018. The flipped classroom: A review of its advantages and challenges. *Computers & Education*, 126:334–345.

Mohammad Reza Andarvazh, Leila Afshar, and Shahram Yazdani. 2017. Hidden Curriculum: An Analytical Definition. *Journal of Medical Education*, 16(4). Number: 4 Publisher: Brieflands.

Henry A. Giroux and Anthony N. Penna. 1979. Social Education in the Classroom: The Dynamics of the Hidden Curriculum. *Theory & Research in Social Education*, 7(1):21–42. Publisher: Routledge _eprint: https://doi.org/10.1080/00933104.1979.10506048.

Diana Murdoch, Andrea R. English, Allison Hintz, and Kersti Tyson. 2020. Feeling Heard: Inclusive Education, Transformative Learning, and Productive Struggle. *Educational Theory*, 70(5):653–679. _eprint: https://onlinelibrary.wiley.com/doi/pdf/10.1111/edth.12449.

Kendall Nakai and Philip J. Guo. 2023. Uncovering the hidden curriculum of university computing majors via undergraduate-written mentoring guides: A learner-centered design workflow. In *Proceedings of the 2023 ACM Conference on International Computing Education Research - Volume 1*, ICER '23, page 63–77, New York, NY, USA. Association for Computing Machinery.

Example-Driven Course Slides on Natural Language Processing Concepts

Natalie Parde
Natural Language Processing Laboratory
Department of Computer Science
University of Illinois Chicago
parde@uic.edu

Abstract

Natural language processing (NLP) is a fast-paced field and a popular course topic in many undergraduate and graduate programs. This paper presents a comprehensive suite of example-driven course slides covering NLP concepts, ranging from fundamental building blocks to modern state-of-the-art approaches. In contributing these slides, I hope to alleviate burden for those starting out as faculty or in need of course material updates. The slides are publicly available for external use and are updated regularly to incorporate new advancements.

1 Introduction

Natural language processing is advancing rapidly, making it exciting and difficult to teach. In designing NLP courses, one must build a delicate pedagogical balance between more classical concepts and newer, trendier topics, connecting algorithms to linguistic fundamentals and emphasizing important overlaps with contemporary deep learning. Some material may require frequent updates, and some may grow or shrink in importance over time. Here, I present a comprehensive suite of slides covering classical and modern NLP concepts, designed and iteratively revised over the course of five years at a large, public, minority-serving institution. These slides are primarily based on material from Jurafsky and Martin (2023), and supplemented by material originally published by Pustejovsky and Stubbs (2012), Huyen (2023), and Liu et al. (2023).

2 Intended Use

2.1 Course Structure

These slides were developed for two NLP courses at the University of Illinois Chicago (UIC): *CS 421: Natural Language Processing*, and *CS 521: Statistical Natural Language Processing*. Both are assignment- and project-based courses housed in UIC's Department of Computer Science. Most courses at UIC, including CS 421 and CS 521, are on the semester cycle with 16-week semesters (15 weeks of instructional material and one week reserved only for final exams). Material is delivered via lectures throughout most of CS 421, whereas only five weeks of lectures are included in CS 521 (with the remainder of the course seminar-based). The slides presented within this paper are from the CS 421 and CS 521 lectures during the Fall 2023 (CS 421) and Spring 2024 (CS 521) semesters.

2.2 Student Population

UIC is a large, public university located in Chicago in the United States of America. It is a Minority Serving Institution (MSI), Hispanic Serving Institution (HSI), and Asian American and Native American Pacific Islander Serving Institution (AANAPISI). Fifty percent of undergraduates at UIC receive Federal Pell Grants,[1] and nearly half of first-year students are first-generation college students. UIC's Department of Computer Science includes 2,135 undergraduates, 271 masters students, and 170 PhD students. Nearly 90% of the graduate students in the Department of Computer Science are international students.

CS 421 is classified as a technical elective for the Bachelor of Science (BS) in Computer Science, and it is an option or technical elective for several other CS programs and concentrations. It is required for the BS in CS + Linguistics program (itself housed in the Department of Linguistics). As a result, undergraduates enter the course with broad-ranging technical backgrounds. At the graduate level, CS 421 and CS 521 both count towards the breadth requirement for the CS PhD qualifier exam, meaning that while they are particularly popular for students interested in artificial intelligence research, they are also regularly taken by students from other

[1]These grants are awarded to U.S. undergraduates with exceptional financial need: https://studentaid.gov/understand-aid/types/grants/pell.

Proceedings of the Sixth Workshop on Teaching NLP, pages 4–6
August 15, 2024

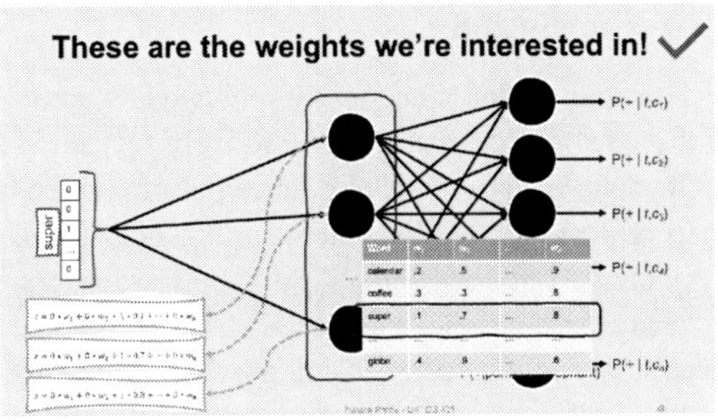

Figure 1: An example CS 421 slide demonstrating how weights are learned using the Word2Vec algorithm.

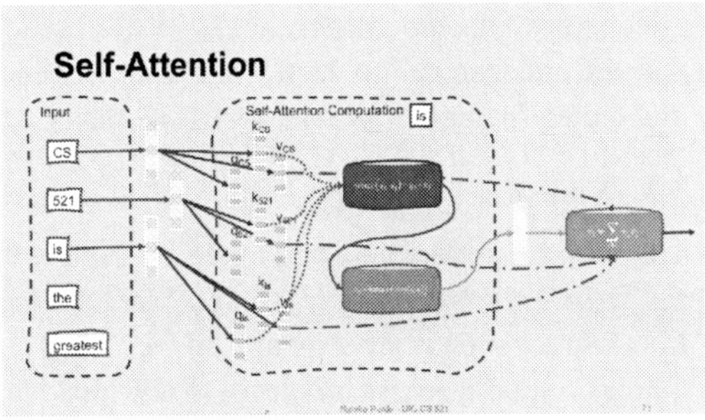

Figure 2: An example CS 521 slide demonstrating how self-attention is computed.

CS subfields. While CS 421 is open to both undergraduate and graduate students (usually slightly more undergraduates than graduate students are enrolled), CS 521 is open only to graduate students and requires CS 421 as a prerequisite. In recent years, CS 421 and CS 521 have had enrollments of approximately 90 and 35 students, respectively. CS 521 is purposely capped at that enrollment size to foster an atmosphere conducive to discussion. CS 421 enrollment caps fluctuate depending on departmental needs and instructional bandwidth.

3 Description of Materials

The slides include many worked-out examples, often drawing from the source textbook(s) and paper(s) but extending or updating them. Videos covering earlier versions of some slides, broken into short segments, are publicly available.[2] Topics covered in the included slides are listed in §3.1. Readings for CS 421 are drawn nearly exclusively from the third edition draft of *Speech and Language Processing* by Jurafsky and Martin (2023). Readings for CS 521 are from *Speech and Language Processing* as well as from *Natural Language Annotation for Machine Learning: A guide to corpus-building for applications* by Pustejovsky and Stubbs (2012), various blogs, and research papers.

3.1 Included Slides

CS 421. Slide decks include: (1) Dialogue Systems and Chatbots; (2) Text Preprocessing and Edit Distance; (3) N-Gram Language Models, Naive Bayes, and Evaluating Text Classifiers; (4) Logistic Regression and Vector Semantics; (5) Word Embeddings and Feedforward Neural Networks; (6) Overview of Deep Learning; (7) Hidden Markov Models and Part-of-Speech Tagging; (8) Constituency Grammars and Constituency Parsing; (9) Dependency Parsing and Logical Representations of Sentence Meaning; (10) Relation and Event Extraction and Temporal Reasoning; (11) Word Senses and WordNet and Semantic Role Labeling; (12) Affective Lexicons and Linguistic Background for Coreference Resolution; and (13) Coreference Resolution and Discourse Coherence. An example slide from the lecture on word embeddings, illustrating how weights are learned using Word2Vec (Mikolov et al., 2013), is provided in Figure 1.

CS 521. Slide decks include: (1) Data Collection; (2) Deep Learning Architectures for Sequence Processing; (3) Machine Translation, Question Answering, and Encoder-Decoder Models; (4) Transfer Learning with Pretrained Language Models and Contextual Embeddings; and (5) Generative AI. An example slide from the lecture on encoder-decoder models, illustrating how self-attention (Vaswani et al., 2017) is computed for language tasks, is provided in Figure 2.

3.2 Slide Organization

Slides in CS 421 can broadly be separated into (1) building blocks of contemporary NLP models, and (2) specific language tasks. The first slide deck falls into neither group but instead was designed to present an exciting application of NLP to students during the first week of class. Building blocks introduce necessary information for completing deliverables throughout the semester, and specific language tasks are presented afterward to enhance understanding of NLP's strong connection to language and ensure familiarity with common terminology and tasks referenced in more advanced NLP classes. Slides in CS 521 build upon one another sequentially. Given the fast-paced nature of NLP research, these are updated more frequently;

[2]https://www.youtube.com/@NatalieParde_NLP

after topics become entrenched in NLP practice, they are either shifted to the CS 421 slide sequence or adapted for more introductory CS 421 use.

3.3 Slide Use and Reuse

The slides discussed here and made available with the *Sixth Workshop on Teaching NLP* are also publicly available on my personal website, which requires no special access privileges to download materials.[3] The slides are made available as PDF files for direct reuse. Source files in Microsoft Powerpoint (.pptx) format are available upon request via email. Slides are shared under a CC BY-NC-SA 4.0 license,[4] which allows non-commercial uses of the work with attribution; any adaptations of the work must be shared under the same licensing terms. All images used in the slides were acquired in one of the following ways: screen captures, images or icons provided via Microsoft Powerpoint or Canva, graphics created by me using shapes and/or other drawing tools in those software applications, or downloads from public domain sources (e.g., `https://commons.wikimedia.org`).

3.4 Slide Updates

Slides will be regularly updated each time that I teach CS 421 or CS 521, and the updated versions will be made available at the same link on my website[3] (older versions of the slides are also available at that link). Given the dynamic nature of the field, updates can be substantial between course iterations. For instance, as large language models (LLMs) loom larger in the public consciousness, they are also likely to be a larger driver for enrollment for CS 421; previously, the more advanced machine learning concepts powering contemporary LLMs were less appropriate and of less interest to individuals fitting the target CS 421 profile. Course topics in CS 421 may correspondingly shift to include more focus on accessible introductory generative AI concepts and more discussion of tradeoffs between general-purpose LLMs and specially designed tools (e.g., syntactic parsers) for the tasks covered. Another topic included in CS 521 that could be ripe for adaptation to CS 421 would be practical guidelines for data development and use, for example through coverage of data sheets, open versus closed data and models, data anonymization, fair use, and data and model release.

[3] `https://www.natalieparde.com/teaching.html`

[4] `https://creativecommons.org/licenses/by-nc-sa/4.0/legalcode.en`

4 Conclusion

This paper described comprehensive, example-driven slides designed and iteratively revised over the span of five years at a large public university to scaffold students' understanding of NLP. The slides are publicly available, and they are regularly updated whenever I teach CS 421 or CS 521; these updates can be accessed via my website.[3] I hope that these materials are useful for new NLP faculty or current faculty looking to update their course content in this fast-paced field.

Acknowledgements

Thank you to the anonymous reviewers, who had excellent ideas for future course lectures; I plan to incorporate these in upcoming semesters. Time spent developing these materials was sponsored in part by a faculty startup grant from the University of Illinois Chicago. CS 421 and CS 521 were both originally conceived by Barbara Di Eugenio, and her syllabi were used as the basis for the first time I taught each of these courses. My own material naturally evolved over time from that starting point. This paper describes only the material included in CS 421 and CS 521 when I teach it personally; content included in course sections taught by other faculty members may vary considerably.

References

Chip Huyen. 2023. Rlhf: Reinforcement learning from human feedback.

Daniel Jurafsky and James H. Martin. 2023. *Speech and Language Processing (3rd Edition)*. Draft.

Pengfei Liu, Weizhe Yuan, Jinlan Fu, Zhengbao Jiang, Hiroaki Hayashi, and Graham Neubig. 2023. Pre-train, prompt, and predict: A systematic survey of prompting methods in natural language processing. *ACM Computing Surveys*, 55(9):1–35.

Tomas Mikolov, Kai Chen, Gregory S. Corrado, and Jeffrey Dean. 2013. Efficient estimation of word representations in vector space. In *International Conference on Learning Representations*.

James Pustejovsky and Amber Stubbs. 2012. *Natural Language Annotation for Machine Learning: A guide to corpus-building for applications*. O'Reilly Media, Inc.

Ashish Vaswani, Noam Shazeer, Niki Parmar, Jakob Uszkoreit, Llion Jones, Aidan N Gomez, Ł ukasz Kaiser, and Illia Polosukhin. 2017. Attention is all you need. In *Advances in Neural Information Processing Systems*, volume 30. Curran Associates, Inc.

Industry vs Academia: Running a Course on Transformers in Two Setups

Irina Nikishina[1*], **Maria Tikhonova**[2,3*], **Viktoriia Chekalina**[4,5], **Alexey Zaytsev**[4], **Artem Vazhentsev**[4,5], **and Alexander Panchenko**[4,5]
[1]Universität Hamburg, [2]HSE University, [3]SaluteDevices, [4]Skoltech, [5]AIRI
irina.nikishina@uni-hamburg.de, a.panchenko@skol.tech

Abstract

This paper presents a course on neural networks based on the Transformer architecture targeted at diverse groups of people from academia and industry with experience in Python, Machine Learning, and Deep Learning but little or no experience with Transformers. The course covers a comprehensive overview of the Transformers NLP applications and their use for other data types. The course features 15 sessions, each consisting of a lecture and a practical part, and two homework assignments organized as CodaLab competitions. The first six sessions of the course are devoted to the Transformer and the variations of this architecture (e.g., encoders, decoders, encoder-decoders) as well as different techniques of model tuning. Subsequent sessions are devoted to multilingualism, multimodality (e.g., texts and images), efficiency, event sequences, and tabular data.

We ran the course for different audiences: academic students and people from industry. The first run was held in 2022. During the subsequent iterations until 2024, it was constantly updated and extended with recently emerged findings on GPT-4, LLMs, RLHF, etc. Overall, it has been ran six times (6 times in industry and 3 times in academia) and received positive feedback from academic and industry students.

1 Introduction

The Transformer (Vaswani et al., 2017) is a versatile neural network model that can be successfully used in various modalities, such as text, images, networks, or sequences of events. Transformer-based models have reached a pinnacle of popularity: they have established state-of-the-art performance in various text processing applications and come with user-friendly wrappers on numerous data science platforms. Therefore, many industrial applications rely on Transformer models.

Figure 1: A course instructor (Maria Tikhonova) gives a lecture for students.

Although current computer science students may study Transformers in their university courses, many machine learning engineers often lack a thorough understanding of the underlying mechanisms of these models. This gap in knowledge can hinder their ability to fully leverage the potential of Transformers, resulting in decreased efficiency and quality in their work.

In this paper, we present an overview of a course on transformer-based models (see Figure 1), which bridges the gap between academic training and industry needs thanks to the balanced program incorporating both theoretical knowledge and a large spectrum of practical use-cases which can be directly used for industrial needs. Therefore, it can be successfully taught in academic and corporate environments. The course seeks to concisely condense and present a vast amount of information on this topic, specifically targeting individuals with ML expertise but limited knowledge of NLP. It aims to provide a comprehensive understanding

[*] Equal contribution.

Proceedings of the Sixth Workshop on Teaching NLP, pages 7–22
August 15, 2024

of the Transformer architectures including the recently emerged topics connected with Large Language Models' (LLMs) theory and their application, enabling students to tackle the challenges that arise when working with them effectively. The course not only gives the theoretical knowledge of this model set but also provides studies with various practical scenarios and use cases they can encounter in industrial applications.

The course was developed and served first in July 2022 and substantially updated in the subsequent runs. Currently, the course has been held six times: 6 times in a corporate environment (data scientists and trained engineers from a large IT company) and 3 times in an academic institution.

The contributions of this paper are as follows:

- We present the syllabus of a modern course on transformer-based models, aimed at broad heterogeneous audiences both in academia and in the industry, which combines deep theoretical knowledge with modern practical applications of the Transformer models;
- We release the materials from the academic course run, which are available in our repo[1];
- We combine recent NLP trends and latest approaches with other best practices, such as fine-tuning of the pre-trained Transformers, multimodality, prompt-tuning, model compression, etc.;
- The course program includes a comprehensive set of Transformer applications, not only the NLP domain but also other modalities.

2 Related NLP Courses

Over the past two decades, dozens of classes on NLP emerged. With the "deep learning revolution" starting around 2017, almost every program in computer science (academic or industrial) features a class on NLP. Modern courses, such as CS224N[2], are focused on the use of deep learning models as the most efficient methodology allowing to obtain state-of-the-art results in a range of tasks. Most currently best-performing models for NLP are based on the Transformer architecture. Besides, Transformer architecture is widely adopted in other domains such as computer vision, tabular data processing, event, and sequence processing. Our course is therefore centered around the Transformer architecture, but in contrast to CS25[3], our course has more focus on NLP, Computer Vision, and applications to tabular and event data while not covering robotics and neuroscience.

The published works on teaching NLP consider different scales and scenarios. Some papers consider the design of extensive programs related to computational linguistics and NLP (Reiter et al., 2017). Other papers describe specific parts of courses, including competitions (Barteld and Flick, 2017; Bozhanov and Derzhanski, 2013). Generally, courses on NLP are either industry- or academia-oriented and target different audiences (Vajjala, 2021), can be held online (Artemova et al., 2021), offline, or in hybrid mode.

We consider a different course objective. Namely, we aim to provide one of the first courses focused on the specifics of Transformer architecture, how it can be applied to solve various problems in NLP, and how it can be used in other domains (e.g., for images, tabular data). The challenge here is how to embed various innovations related to this architecture into a single course. The course can be taken in two scenarios: as part of a computer science master's program or as an additional education course for an industrial audience.

3 Course Overview

The course comprises 15 sessions (two sessions per week) and assignments, which include two homeworks, a final quiz, and bonus lecture quizzes and practical tasks after each session. The course program, presented in Table 1, can be split into two main parts, which cover (i) basic Transformer architectures and models, (ii) the application of Transformers to different modalities, and efficient training procedures.

The course is based on the following prerequisites: (1) **advanced mathematics**: calculus, linear algebra, and statistics; (2) **data science**: classic machine learning methods, basic deep learning methods, and basic knowledge of natural language processing.

Every session consists of a lecture and a practical seminar. Lectures are presented with slides, while practical sessions are real-time coding sessions. The instructor demonstrates code snippets in Jupyter Notebooks and explains them in detail. Both home assignments are started simultaneously

[1]https://github.com/s-nlp/transformers-course

[2]https://web.stanford.edu/class/cs224n

[3]https://web.stanford.edu/class/cs25

Session	Description
1	The Transformer: motivation, original architecture, and attention mechanism.
2	Transformer-based Encoders. Masked language models based on the Transformer architecture. BERT and related models.
3	Classification and sequence tagging with Transformers. Using encoders to generate feature representation for various NLU tasks.
4	Transformer-based Decoders. Generation of text using Transformers. GPT and related decoders.
5	Prompt and instruction tuning. Reinforcement Learning from Human Feedback (RLHF), ChatGPT, and related models.
6	Sequence to sequence tasks: machine translation, text detoxification, question answering, dialogue. Technical tricks for training and inference.
7	Multilingual language models based on the Transformer architecture.
8	Uncertainty estimation for Transformers and NLP.
9	Efficient Transformers.
10	Compression of Transformer models and low-rank approaches.
11	Network encoders with Transformers
12	Multimodal and Vision Transformers.
13	Transformers for event sequences.
14	Transformers for tabular data.
15	Deadline for both assignments. Final quiz.

Table 1: Course structure: each session, except the last one, dedicated to the final quiz, features lecture material and a seminar with code snippets.

from the beginning so that students may plan their time accordingly and try any transformer-based architecture they find applicable to any assignment.

The total score Total is calculated according to the following formula:

$$\mathrm{Total} = 0.4 \cdot A_1 + 0.4 \cdot A_2 + 0.2 \cdot Q + LQ + ST,$$

where A_i is the score for the i-th home assignment, Q is the score for the final quiz, LQ and ST are the extra points for bonus lecture quizzes and practical tasks, respectively. The total score is then uniformly mapped into the grading scale.

As was already mentioned, the course is suitable for both academic and industrial audiences. While the general course program and structure are similar in both environments, the presentation of the material differs, adapting to the audience's needs and objectives. In academic runs, we concentrate more on the theoretical material, giving more mathematical formulas and explanations. In contrast, during the industrial runs, we provide more practical examples, illustrating all methods with as many use cases and business applications as possible.

It is worth noting that the course can be conducted both online and offline. For industrial sessions, the course is delivered online, whereas at the university, we adopt a hybrid approach.

4 Syllabus

The following paragraphs describe each session in more details.

Session 1. The Transformer: motivation, original architecture, and attention mechanism. The first introductory **lecture** is devoted to the vanilla Transformer architecture (Vaswani et al., 2017), introduced for the Machine Translation (MT) task following the traditional approach.

First, we formulate the MT task and present a historical overview of the area. Next, we describe the idea of encoder-decoder or seq2seq architecture, starting with RNN-based models (Sutskever et al., 2014) and then introduce the concept of attention (Bahdanau et al., 2015). That brings us to the Transformer model, which we explain step by step. During the academic runs, we pay special attention to the theoretical background behind the Transformer architecture and its mathematical explanations.

We conclude the lecture with a short recap of the language modeling task and how the idea of attention can be transferred from MT to this field.

The **practical session** is based on Harvard NLP tutorial "Annotated Transformer"[4], that presents the PyTorch[5] implementation of the Transformer architecture. Thus, following the outline of the tutorial, we first go through the Transformer code step by step and then show how it works for WMT14 (Bojar et al., 2014) English-to-French translation task: we train and test the model and allow students to experiment with model training to achieve better scores.

Session 2. Transformer-based Encoders. Masked language models based on the Transformer architecture. BERT and related models. The **lecture** is devoted to the transformer-based Encoders. We begin with discussing most classical encoder-based models, such as BERT (Devlin et al., 2019) and RoBERTa (Liu et al., 2019), and discuss the peculiarities of their architecture and training. For academic students, we pay particular attention to analyzing the results of the original scientific papers, while for the industrial runs, we concentrate

[4]http://nlp.seas.harvard.edu/annotated-transformer

[5]https://pytorch.org

more on the use cases students can encounter in their practice.

The aim of the **practical session** is to teach students how to work with Transformer models using Transformers library[6] and how to utilize pre-trained models and other instruments from HuggingFace Hub[7]. Namely, we show students how to tokenize the data, visualize attention maps, and apply trained models on the example of the BERT model fine-tuned for the sentiment analysis task.

Session 3. Classification and sequence tagging with Transformers. Using encoders to generate feature representation for various NLU tasks. This session focuses on Natural Language Understanding (NLU) applications of Transformers, namely, tasks that need to extract implicit metadata from the text. In the **lecture**, we consider text classification for Sentiment Analysis and Natural Language Inference and the token classification for Named Entity Recognition and Extractive Question-Answering tasks. For the industrial runs, we elaborate more on the practical applications derived from these tasks and the use cases. We study various approaches to sentence encoders in detail and then delve into the realm of dialogue systems.

In the **practical session**, we fine-tune the transformer-based model for entity recognition in the Russian-language drug review corpus (Tutubalina et al., 2020) using a Russian-language compressed version of the BERT[8] for it.

Session 4. Transformer-based Decoders. Generation of text using Transformers. GPT and related decoders. This session is devoted to Generative Pre-trained Transformer (GPT) models based on the Transformer decoders and various text generation strategies.

In the first part of the **lecture**, we briefly recap various types of language models, emphasizing decoder-based Transformer models. Then, we carefully study GPT models (GPT-1,2,3, and 3.5), focusing on GPT-3 (Winata et al., 2021) and introducing the concept of few-shot learning.

Additionally, we explore the strategies for token sampling and text generation (e.g., BeamSearch, Sampling, Nucleus Sampling). For the academic students, we concentrate more on the theoretical aspects, while with the industrial students, we discuss what generation strategies in business applications from their work experience are preferred.

In the second part, we consider examples of controllable text generation where we aim to generate text with specific desired properties at the model level. Then, starting with an additional steering layer (Dathathri et al., 2019), we come to the concept of a Generative Adversarial Network in the model GeDi (Krause et al., 2021).

In the **practical session**, we provide guidance on introductory text generation and sampling strategies and experiment with various methods. Experiments are set on the encoder-based Transformer model sourced from the HuggingFace library (e.g., GPT-2[9]) and aim to analyze the impact of generation hyperparameters on text quality and styling. Upon request, we can develop a straightforward chatbot utilizing the model and explore its practical relevance in industry and startup contexts.

Session 5. Prompt and instruction tuning. Reinforcement Learning from Human Feedback (RLHF), ChatGPT, and related models. This section continues the exploration of advanced text generation models, specifically focusing on the concept of Reinforcement Learning from Human Feedback (RLHF). RLFH involves incorporating human feedback into the learning process to establish an optimal starting point for the further model's training for the given task. As an example, we consider the task of summarization with human feedback (Stiennon et al., 2020) and analyze the concept (Ouyang et al., 2022) of the modern LLM training which underlies the power of such models as ChatGPT[10] or GPT-4[11] models. For the academic runs, we pay special attention to the theory behind the RLHF method and its potential development. In the industrial runs, we discuss the practical difficulties (e.g., data collection, computational resources, cost) of RLHF LLM training.

The next part is devoted to prompt-tuning methods (Li and Liang, 2021; Lester et al., 2021; Liu et al., 2021; Konodyuk and Tikhonova, 2021), for automatically learning language model prompts.

We conclude the lecture by discussing the emerging variety of LLMs (LLaMA-2 (Touvron et al.,

[6]https://pypi.org/project/transformers

[7]https://huggingface.co

[8]https://huggingface.co/cointegrated/rubert-tiny

[9]https://huggingface.co/gpt2

[10]https://openai.com/blog/chatgpt

[11]https://openai.com/gpt-4

2023)[12], Mistral[13], Mixtral[14], etc., their industrial application scenarios, possible downsides connected with their usage, and the overall impact. This list is updated each run with newly released models.

The **practical session** is devoted to prompt-tuning methods. We allow students to experiment with ruPrompts[15], a convenient library for fast language model tuning via automatic prompt search, and use it to solve the Russe Detoxification task (Dementieva et al., 2022).

Session 6. Sequence to sequence tasks: machine translation, text detoxification, question answering, dialogue. Technical tricks for training and inference: infrastructure and performance. During the **lecture**, students' attention is drawn to the models with the standard Transformer Encoder-Decoder architectures, which are aimed at solving sequence-to-sequence tasks such as machine translation, summarization, question answering, etc. In the first part of the lecture, we discuss the existing sequence-to-sequence models such as BART (Lewis et al., 2019), T5 (Raffel et al., 2020a) and PEGASUS (Zhang et al., 2019). With the industrial students, we discuss possible applications of these models in their business practice.

The lecture's second part is devoted to optimizing the Transformers' training process. We discuss such optimization techniques as gradient accumulation, training of only some layers, Adafactor optimizer (Shazeer and Stern, 2018), quantization (Hawks et al., 2021) and mixed precision (Micikevicius et al., 2018), gradient checkpointing (Chen et al., 2016), optimized padding, and ONNX runtime (developers, 2021).

The **practical session** for the sequence-to-sequence Transformers aims to solve the Hypernym Prediction task using the T5 (Raffel et al., 2020b) model. Students are expected to experiment with the zero-shot and few-shot setups and compare them with fine-tuning.

Session 7. Multilingual language models based on the Transformer architecture. This session is devoted to multilingual language modeling. We begin the **lecture** by discussing the specifics of this phenomenon, a short overview of the MT approaches, and methods for parallel corpora creation. Then, we switch to the multilingual transformer models and discuss such models as mBERT[16], XGLM (Newson, 2016), BLOOM (Scao et al., 2022), and mGPT (Shliazhko et al., 2022). In addition, we discuss possible ways to add a new language to the Transformer model (e.g., mBERT).

In the **practical session** we fine-tune XLM-R (Zhuang et al., 2021) for multilingual and cross-lingual word-in-context disambiguation (MCL-WiC), proposed for the SemEval2021 competition (task2) (Martelli et al., 2021).

Session 8. Uncertainty estimation for Transformers and NLP. This session aims to provide a general introduction to the uncertainty estimation (UE) field and methods and their application to NLP, especially transformer-based models.

The **lecture** begins with highlighting the importance of uncertainty estimation and introducing standard and well-established methods, such as Softmax Response (Geifman and El-Yaniv, 2017) and Monte-Carlo (MC) Dropout (Gal, 2016). We also cover various regularization techniques (Xin et al., 2021), density-based methods (Lee et al., 2018), and also state-of-the-art UE methods for the classification task (Yoo et al., 2022). Next, we show the importance of uncertainty estimation for LLMs, e.g., to avoid hallucinations. We discuss the most advanced techniques, including both white-box methods (Kuhn et al., 2023), applicable for any open-sourced model, and black-box methods (Lin et al., 2023), which are useful for closed-sourced models available via API. We conclude the lecture by discussing the practical application of uncertainty estimation for active learning (Settles, 2009), out-of-distribution (OOD) detection, etc.

In the **practical session**, we implement several UE methods, such as Mahalanobis distance (Lee et al., 2018), MC Dropout, and HUQ (Vazhentsev et al., 2023), and apply them for the selective classification and OOD detection tasks. In addition, we study two baseline methods (Sequence Probability and Lexical Similarity) (Fomicheva et al., 2020) for UE of LLMs and use them to detect factual errors in the summarization task.

Session 9. Efficient Transformers. LLMs impose high memory requirements, and this, consequently, leads to substantial energy costs and noteworthy CO_2 emissions (Rae et al., 2021) through-

[12]https://ai.meta.com/research/publications/llama-2-open-foundation-and-fine-tuned-chat-models

[13]https://mistral.ai/news/announcing-mistral-7b

[14]https://ollama.com/library/mixtral

[15]https://github.com/ai-forever/ru-prompts

[16]https://huggingface.co/bert-base-multilingual-cased

out the training and inference process.

In the **lecture**, we explore various approaches to reduce the model size without compromising quality. We delve into pruning (Sanh et al., 2020), (Lagunas et al., 2021), quantization (Hawks et al., 2021), (Wang et al., 2022b), and distillation (Hinton et al., 2015). In the academic runs, we spend more time on the theory behind these methods, while in the industrial runs, we concentrate more on the practical applications of these methods.

We also examine methods that aim to reduce the computational complexity of the attention layer (Tay et al., 2020). It includes approaches that simplify the calculation procedure, such as the kernel method, techniques that decrease the input sequence size, and techniques for selecting a subset of tokens for attention computation (learnable or fixed patterns).

Finally, we overview two approaches to parallelism during training: model- and data-level parallelism. Using the examples of the Megarton (Shoeybi et al., 2019) and Varuna (Athlur et al., 2021) pipelines, we explore options for distributed computing across multiple GPU cards and nodes and the concomitant challenges. We touch upon the topic of the impact of model training processes on the environment and methods for its evaluation, which is relevant to the industry.

During the **practical session**, students will construct their own layer, based on *torch.nn.Linear* incorporating a quantization mechanism. The objective is to minimize the total memory footprint of the model by representing several layers in a compressed bit format.

Session 10. Compression of Transformer models and low-rank approaches. In this session, we explore methods for decreasing the number of parameters by representing layer weights in a more compressed way. Focusing on the representation by SVD, Kronecker decomposition, and Tensor Train Matrix (TTM) (Oseledets, 2011) decomposition; we study the peculiarities of the structure of such layers and the propagation of signals within them.

For the **practical session**, students are offered a layer implementation based on SVD and TTM decomposition. The objective is to assess the performance of a compressed model achieved by substituting fully connected layers with algebraic structures based on the compression rank.

Session 11. Network encoders with Transformers This **lecture** starts with a short recap of graph theory. Then we introduce Graph Convolutional Networks (GCNs) (Kipf and Welling, 2016) and analyze those that are related to Transformers: GAT (Yun et al., 2022), Graph BERT (Zhang et al., 2020), and GreaseLM (Zhang et al., 2022). We also discuss how such models could be applied and for which NLP tasks.

In the **practical session**, we discuss the Taxonomy Enrichment task using Graph Transformers (GCN, GAT, and Graph-BERT). We also revise the code of GAT-v2 (Brody et al., 2022) and make a quick overview of the OpenHGNN library[17] with the implementation of Graph-based models.

Session 12. Multimodal and vision Transformers. Multimodal Transformer architectures are significant as they generate representations of language concepts by leveraging textual data and information from diverse sources such as images, videos, and knowledge bases.

We start the **lecture** with the CLIP (Radford et al., 2021) model architecture analysis, which provides a joint embedding for words and pictures representing this word. Then go through all the most important and relevant multimodal models (DALLE, DALLE-2 (Ramesh et al., 2022), VQ-VAE (van den Oord et al., 2017), Rudolph (AIRI, 2022), Fromage (Koh et al., 2023), Flamingo (Alayrac et al., 2022), OFA (Wang et al., 2022a), Kandinsky (Razzhigaev et al., 2023), ImageBind (Girdhar et al., 2023)). We discuss the possible use cases of these models with the industrial students in their work practice.

During the **practical session**, we made a zero-shot classifier with CLIP and implemented a visual saliency map. We also studied how Kandindky[18] works for generating images by text.

Session 13. Transformers for event sequences. Another essential data modality in modern applications is event sequences. We consider a sequence of events with features or marks provided for each event. The model can be used end-to-end or as an encoder to get embeddings of a sequence (Zhuzhel et al., 2021; Babaev et al., 2022). We also note that in this topic, we describe a connection between these models and temporal point random processes (Shchur et al., 2021). During the **lecture**, we study the adaptation of the Transformer architecture to this problem and compare it to other

[17]https://github.com/BUPT-GAMMA/OpenHGNN
[18]https://huggingface.co/ai-forever/Kandinsky3.1

approaches. During the **practical session**, we train from scratch a Transformer model (Zuo et al., 2020) for processing open-sourced financial transactions data (Fursov et al., 2021), a modality that is widely used in major banks (Babaev et al., 2022).

Session 14. Transformers for tabular data. In this session, we step aside from classical Transformer applications and discuss their use for tabular data. It is a new but quite promising area.

The **lecture** is based on three papers devoted to this subject. We start with (Huang et al., 2020), which proposes the TabTrasformer model, applying the attention mechanism for categorical feature embeddings. Then, we walk through (Gorishniy et al., 2021), which extends the idea of the attention mechanism to numerical features by embedding them via linear transformation and subsequently applying the Transformer block. We also study various embedding types for numerical features proposed in (Gorishniy et al., 2022) and how they can be combined with the Transformer block. Finally, we discuss practical applications and how the architectures can be adapted to industrial needs (we pay special attention to this part of the lecture during industrial runs).

In the **practical session**, we study the described transformer-based tabular models implemented in PytorchTabular[19] Python library and apply them for one of the classical tabular datasets (e. g., Bank Marketing Data Set[20]).

Session 15. Deadline for both assignments. Final quiz. During the final session, students are expected to share their feedback on the course and discuss their solutions for the home assignments. We first discuss each task's strengths, weaknesses, and difficulties and the time spent developing the method that outperforms the baseline. Afterward, we split students into groups to discuss the developed methods and to share their experiences. Each group is asked to present one method for each task to share with other groups.

5 Assessment

5.1 Home assignments

We provide two home assignments for the course described in sub-subsections 5.1.1 and 5.1.2.

For both tasks, students are expected to provide a technical report (max 10 points) and code (max 10 points) and submit the results of the best-performing model to the CodaLab competition leaderboard (max 15 points) (see Appendix A for the detailed grading criteria). They should also write a technical report in the provided IPynb template describing the method used in their solution and the analysis of the obtained results. In the code section, students are expected to develop a solution and provide a reproducible code in the provided template. Then, the (best) model output is expected to be submitted to the CodaLab platform[21] with the name of the user for evaluation.

There is no formal difference in assignments or grading criteria for the academic and industrial runs. However, during the academic runs, we stimulate students to concentrate more on the theoretical analysis of their results and the scientific conclusions they can draw from them, while in industrial runs, we ask students to elaborate more on practical effects that can be inferred from the results they obtained in the assignments.

We chose these assignments since they cover the two most widespread tasks in NLP: classification and generation. In the classification task, we ask to perform sequence tagging which is a token classification task using any Encoder Transformer model, while text detoxification assignment is one of the text generation tasks to be solved with Decoder or Encoder-decoder models.

Each assignment involves a deep dive into the task, offering the opportunity to try several different approaches to solving it, carefully considering and discussing their advantages, disadvantages, and possible modifications. Such an assignment closely models the process of solving real-world problems and takes at least a month to complete. Therefore, the number of assignments is selected given the course's total length and ability to cover the basic use cases for Transformers.

5.1.1 Assignment 1: Semantic Role Labelling

The first assignment is to perform semantic role labelling for comparisons. Task is formulated as a classical sequence tagging organized in the form of CodaLab competition[22]. The main goal is identifying objects, aspects, and predicates given an input sentence. For instance: [Python=OBJECT] is [better=PREDICATE] than [Matlab=OBJECT] for [Deep Learning=ASPECT]. Such kind of semantic role labelling is usually applied for comparative argument

[19] https://github.com/manujosephv/pytorch_tabular

[20] https://archive.ics.uci.edu/ml/datasets/bank+marketing

[21] https://codalab.lisn.upsaclay.fr

[22] https://codalab.lisn.upsaclay.fr/competitions/531

mining (Schildwächter et al., 2019).

Students are required to train a sequence labeling model on a provided labeled dataset. For this task, they can use any transformer-based model and experiment with different types of embedding initialization and the fine-tuning procedure. The provided data files are in CoNLL-U format. Each line contains one word, and its label is in BIO format for predicting "Objects", "Aspects" and "Predicates in the sentence".

In the latest edition of the course, this task was replaced by the KGQA task which is a binary classification, so, in principle the new assignment can nicely complement the sequence tagging task.[23]

5.1.2 Assignment 2: Text Detoxification

For the second assignment, students participate in the competition of automatic text detoxification (Dementieva et al., 2022). This task is seq2seq style transfer task: its required to paraphrase a sentence from the toxic (i.e. rude) to the non-toxic (ie. neutral) style while preserving its meaning. Such textual style transfer can be used to process toxic content on social media.

In the assignment context, students need to train a model and submit its output to the CodaLab competition[24]. They are free to use any methods and/or models for style transfer or pre-trained models for text generation (GPT (Radford et al., 2019), T5 (Raffel et al., 2020a), etc.). The competition provides baselines that may be improved. Otherwise, the students are allowed to rely on them when composing their own solutions.

In the last edition of the course, the students were asked to participate in the multilingual text detoxification shared task at CLEF 2024 (Bevendorff et al., 2024) where 9 languages to be supported instead of a single one.[25]

5.2 Final Quiz

The final session is followed by a comprehensive quiz covering all topics studied. It consists of 26 multiple-choice questions (1 point for each question). Each topic covered in the course is presented in the quiz with one or two questions. We keep the list of questions closed to avoid revealing them to the current running of the course.

[23] https://codalab.lisn.upsaclay.fr/competitions/18214

[24] https://codalab.lisn.upsaclay.fr/competitions/642

[25] https://codalab.lisn.upsaclay.fr/competitions/18243

5.3 Bonus Lecture Quizzes and Practical Tasks

After each session, students are given a lecture quiz consisting of ten multiple-choice questions on the topic and a short practical task, which usually includes several simple experiments. Such activities allow students to revise the material and gain small extra points (1 point maximum for each lecture quiz or practical task).[26]

6 Expected Outcomes

First, we expect the students to acquire a comprehensive understanding of the transformer-based models and the underlying mechanisms and to get acquainted with a diverse set of Transformer architectures. Second, we expect them to learn how to train and apply Transformers to multiple NLP tasks and how to adapt them to other domains. Third, we anticipate that the students will be able to use pre-trained models from the HuggingFace library and to employ other tools or datasets from the HuggingFace project.

7 Formal Course Evaluation

At the end of each running of the course, we collect feedback by asking students to complete a short survey. Figure 2 presents the aggregated results for all industrial runs. We can see that most students are satisfied with the course and find it quite engaging. The average rating is 8.5 out of 10, and the highest grade of 10 accounts for 44 percent of all ratings. The feedback from the academic run is also strongly positive (See Appendix B); all students note clear objectives and explanations, challenging enough content, and grading criteria. Both industry (94%) and academia (100%) respondents note the usefulness of practical skills and the quality of the course organization and teaching (87% for industry and 89% for academia).

8 Academic vs Industrial Students

We summarize qualitative differences in expectations of the course between students from industry and academia below (based on obtained feedback and evaluation comments):

- Students from industry demand more practical programming materials and sessions, being

[26] We provide free access to quizzes and tasks upon a request from an academic email to professors, lecturers, and teachers.

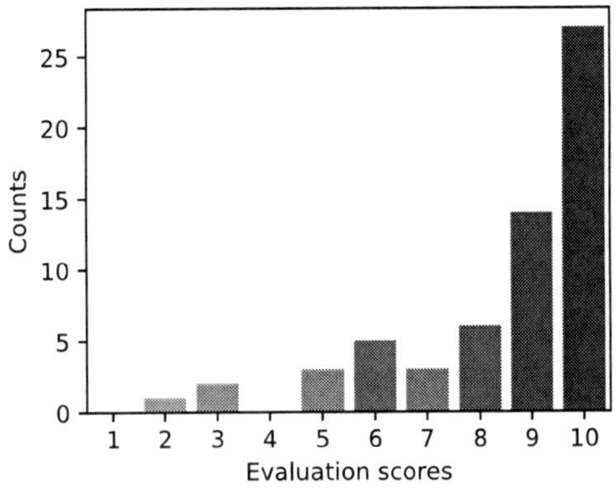

Figure 2: Students feedback for the course in the industrial setup. 10 is the maximum, 1 is the minimum score.

less happy with dense lectures than academic students who are used to such format.

- Professionals asked for a translation of terms and materials to their native language, while academics didn't mind English.
- Industrial students were asking more questions during lectures and chat discussions.
- In competition results (e.g., for the shared task on text detoxification), the leaderboard was a mixture of industrial and academic students with no apparent leader.
- Attendance in percentage was more significant for industrial students (while industrial sessions were in the working days afternoon, 18-21 time slot while for academic students were during the day, usually 16-19 time slot), indicating overall greater motivation/commitment of professionals.
- Industrial students often are determined and specifically seeking for application of a particular task (e.g., motivated by the job project). In contrast, academic students do not have such "extra" learning goals, with a few exceptions where it is required for their research.
- For both types of students, not as much the topic matter so much its presentation. Even "hottest" lecture on how ChatGPT works may get very variable levels of student involvement, depending on the instructor.

9 Conclusion

This paper describes a course on Transformer models, initially designed in early 2022 and updated in the subsequent runs. During lectures and practical sessions, we present a comprehensive overview of transformer-related concepts and a variety of Transformer applications, including practical industrial use cases, covering both NLP and language modeling, as well as other domains, such as computer vision and processing of event sequences. The course was run several times for both academic and industrial audiences.

The theoretical outcome of the course for the students is a deep understanding of the Transformer architecture, the attention mechanism, and knowledge of a diverse set of transformer-based models and their adaptations for various domains. As a practical outcome, the students acquire diverse skills in working with all types of transformer-based models and using Transformers for other modalities and domains. The feedback about the course from the students from both industry and academia was generally positive yet different in various aspects, such as the desired balance between theory and practice (with industrial learners being more proactive and demanding hands-on skills).

In the future, we plan to add lectures related to newer Transformer models and more applications to other modalities and domains.

10 Acknowledgements

First, we thank David Dale, who prepared and delivered about half of the lectures and seminars in the first run of the industrial course (partially based on materials from the Skoltech course on Neural NLP, among other sources). Indeed, without David, this course would not seen the light.

Second, we would like to acknowledge Anton Razzhigaev's essential contribution to the lecture and seminar related to multimodal and vision Transformers.

Finally, we acknowledge contributions of Ilyar Alimova and Vladislav Zhuzhel, who were instructors of several sessions in some runs of the industrial part of the course. Finally, we would like to acknowledge the TAs of the academic part of the course: Mikhail Salnikov, Maria Lysuyk, Sergey Petrakov, Daniil Moscovskiy, and Daniil Larionov.

References

AIRI. 2022. Rudolph: One hyper-tasking transformer can be creative as dall-e and gpt-3 and smart as clip. `https://github.com/ai-forever/ru-dolph`.

Jean-Baptiste Alayrac, Jeff Donahue, Pauline Luc, Antoine Miech, Iain Barr, Yana Hasson, Karel Lenc, Arthur Mensch, Katherine Millican, Malcolm Reynolds, Roman Ring, Eliza Rutherford, Serkan Cabi, Tengda Han, Zhitao Gong, Sina Samangooei, Marianne Monteiro, Jacob L. Menick, Sebastian Borgeaud, Andy Brock, Aida Nematzadeh, Sahand Sharifzadeh, Mikolaj Binkowski, Ricardo Barreira, Oriol Vinyals, Andrew Zisserman, and Karén Simonyan. 2022. Flamingo: a visual language model for few-shot learning. In *Advances in Neural Information Processing Systems 35: Annual Conference on Neural Information Processing Systems 2022, NeurIPS 2022, New Orleans, LA, USA, November 28 - December 9, 2022*.

Ekaterina Artemova, Murat Apishev, Veronika Sarkisyan, Sergey Aksenov, Denis Kirjanov, and Oleg Serikov. 2021. Teaching a massive open online course on natural language processing. *CoRR*, abs/2104.12846.

Sanjith Athlur, Nitika Saran, Muthian Sivathanu, Ramachandran Ramjee, and Nipun Kwatra. 2021. Varuna: Scalable, low-cost training of massive deep learning models. *CoRR*, abs/2111.04007.

Dmitrii Babaev, Nikita Ovsov, Ivan Kireev, Mariya Ivanova, Gleb Gusev, Ivan Nazarov, and Alexander Tuzhilin. 2022. Coles: Contrastive learning for event sequences with self-supervision. In *SIGMOD '22: International Conference on Management of Data, Philadelphia, PA, USA, June 12 - 17, 2022*, pages 1190–1199. ACM.

Dzmitry Bahdanau, Kyunghyun Cho, and Yoshua Bengio. 2015. Neural machine translation by jointly learning to align and translate. In *3rd International Conference on Learning Representations, ICLR 2015, San Diego, CA, USA, May 7-9, 2015, Conference Track Proceedings*.

Fabian Barteld and Johanna Flick. 2017. LEA - linguistic exercises with annotation tools. In *Proceedings of the Workshop on Teaching NLP for Digital Humanities (Teach4DH) 2017, Berlin, Germany, September 12, 2017*, volume 1918 of *CEUR Workshop Proceedings*, pages 11–16. CEUR-WS.org.

Janek Bevendorff, Xavier Bonet Casals, Berta Chulvi, Daryna Dementieva, Ashaf Elnagar, Dayne Freitag, Maik Fröbe, Damir Korenčić, Maximilian Mayerl, Animesh Mukherjee, Alexander Panchenko, Martin Potthast, Francisco Rangel, Paolo Rosso, Alisa Smirnova, Efstathios Stamatatos, Benno Stein, Mariona Taulé, Dmitry Ustalov, Matti Wiegmann, and Eva Zangerle. 2024. Overview of pan 2024: Multi-author writing style analysis, multilingual text detoxification, oppositional thinking analysis, and generative ai authorship verification. In *Advances in Information Retrieval*, pages 3–10, Cham. Springer Nature Switzerland.

Ondrej Bojar, Christian Buck, Christian Federmann, Barry Haddow, Philipp Koehn, Johannes Leveling, Christof Monz, Pavel Pecina, Matt Post, Herve Saint-Amand, Radu Soricut, Lucia Specia, and Ales Tamchyna. 2014. Findings of the 2014 workshop on statistical machine translation. In *Proceedings of the Ninth Workshop on Statistical Machine Translation, WMT@ACL 2014, June 26-27, 2014, Baltimore, Maryland, USA*, pages 12–58. The Association for Computer Linguistics.

Bozhidar Bozhanov and Ivan Derzhanski. 2013. Rosetta stone linguistic problems. In *Proceedings of the Fourth Workshop on Teaching NLP and CL*, pages 1–8, Sofia, Bulgaria. Association for Computational Linguistics.

Shaked Brody, Uri Alon, and Eran Yahav. 2022. How attentive are graph attention networks?

Tianqi Chen, Bing Xu, Chiyuan Zhang, and Carlos Guestrin. 2016. Training deep nets with sublinear memory cost. *CoRR*, abs/1604.06174.

Sumanth Dathathri, Andrea Madotto, Janice Lan, Jane Hung, Eric Frank, Piero Molino, Jason Yosinski, and Rosanne Liu. 2019. Plug and play language models: A simple approach to controlled text generation. *CoRR*, abs/1912.02164.

Daryna Dementieva, Irina Nikishina, Varvara Logacheva, Alena Fenogenova, David Dale, Irina Krotova, Nikita Semenov, Tatiana Shavrina, and Alexander Panchenko. 2022. Russe-2022: Findings of the first russian detoxification task based on parallel corpora. In *Computational Linguistics and Intellectual Technologies*, pages 114–131.

ONNX Runtime developers. 2021. Onnx runtime. `https://onnxruntime.ai/`. Version: x.y.z.

Jacob Devlin, Ming-Wei Chang, Kenton Lee, and Kristina Toutanova. 2019. BERT: Pre-training of deep bidirectional transformers for language understanding. In *Proceedings of the 2019 Conference of the North American Chapter of the Association for Computational Linguistics: Human Language Technologies, Volume 1 (Long and Short Papers)*, pages 4171–4186, Minneapolis, Minnesota. Association for Computational Linguistics.

Marina Fomicheva, Shuo Sun, Lisa Yankovskaya, Frédéric Blain, Francisco Guzmán, Mark Fishel, Nikolaos Aletras, Vishrav Chaudhary, and Lucia Specia. 2020. Unsupervised quality estimation for neural machine translation. *Transactions of the Association for Computational Linguistics*, 8:539–555.

Ivan Fursov, Matvey Morozov, Nina Kaploukhaya, Elizaveta Kovtun, Rodrigo Rivera-Castro, Gleb Gusev, Dmitry Babaev, Ivan Kireev, Alexey Zaytsev, and Evgeny Burnaev. 2021. Adversarial attacks on deep models for financial transaction records. In *KDD '21: The 27th ACM SIGKDD Conference on Knowledge Discovery and Data Mining, Virtual Event, Singapore, August 14-18, 2021*, pages 2868–2878. ACM.

Yarin Gal. 2016. *Uncertainty in Deep Learning*. Ph.D. thesis, University of Cambridge.

Yonatan Geifman and Ran El-Yaniv. 2017. Selective classification for deep neural networks. In *Proceedings of the 31st International Conference on Neural Information Processing Systems*, NeurIPS 2017, page 4885–4894, Red Hook, NY, USA. Curran Associates Inc.

Rohit Girdhar, Alaaeldin El-Nouby, Zhuang Liu, Mannat Singh, Kalyan Vasudev Alwala, Armand Joulin, and Ishan Misra. 2023. Imagebind one embedding space to bind them all. In *IEEE/CVF Conference on Computer Vision and Pattern Recognition, CVPR 2023, Vancouver, BC, Canada, June 17-24, 2023*, pages 15180–15190. IEEE.

Yury Gorishniy, Ivan Rubachev, and Artem Babenko. 2022. On embeddings for numerical features in tabular deep learning. In *NeurIPS*.

Yury Gorishniy, Ivan Rubachev, Valentin Khrulkov, and Artem Babenko. 2021. Revisiting deep learning models for tabular data. In *Advances in Neural Information Processing Systems 34: Annual Conference on Neural Information Processing Systems 2021, NeurIPS 2021, December 6-14, 2021, virtual*, pages 18932–18943.

Benjamin Hawks, Javier M. Duarte, Nicholas J. Fraser, Alessandro Pappalardo, Nhan Tran, and Yaman Umuroglu. 2021. Ps and qs: Quantization-aware pruning for efficient low latency neural network inference. *Frontiers Artif. Intell.*, 4:676564.

Geoffrey E. Hinton, Oriol Vinyals, and Jeffrey Dean. 2015. Distilling the knowledge in a neural network. *CoRR*, abs/1503.02531.

Xin Huang, Ashish Khetan, Milan Cvitkovic, and Zohar S. Karnin. 2020. Tabtransformer: Tabular data modeling using contextual embeddings. *CoRR*, abs/2012.06678.

Thomas N. Kipf and Max Welling. 2016. Semi-supervised classification with graph convolutional networks. *CoRR*, abs/1609.02907.

Jing Yu Koh, Ruslan Salakhutdinov, and Daniel Fried. 2023. Grounding language models to images for multimodal inputs and outputs. In *International Conference on Machine Learning, ICML 2023, 23-29 July 2023, Honolulu, Hawaii, USA*, volume 202 of *Proceedings of Machine Learning Research*, pages 17283–17300. PMLR.

Nikita Konodyuk and Maria Tikhonova. 2021. Continuous prompt tuning for russian: How to learn prompts efficiently with rugpt3? In *Recent Trends in Analysis of Images, Social Networks and Texts - 10th International Conference, AIST 2021, Tbilisi, Georgia, December 16-18, 2021, Revised Supplementary Proceedings*, volume 1573 of *Communications in Computer and Information Science*, pages 30–40. Springer.

Ben Krause, Akhilesh Deepak Gotmare, Bryan McCann, Nitish Shirish Keskar, Shafiq Joty, Richard Socher, and Nazneen Fatema Rajani. 2021. GeDi: Generative discriminator guided sequence generation. In *Findings of the Association for Computational Linguistics: EMNLP 2021*, pages 4929–4952, Punta Cana, Dominican Republic. Association for Computational Linguistics.

Lorenz Kuhn, Yarin Gal, and Sebastian Farquhar. 2023. Semantic uncertainty: Linguistic invariances for uncertainty estimation in natural language generation. In *The Eleventh International Conference on Learning Representations, ICLR 2023, Kigali, Rwanda, May 1-5, 2023*. OpenReview.net.

François Lagunas, Ella Charlaix, Victor Sanh, and Alexander M. Rush. 2021. Block pruning for faster transformers.

Kimin Lee, Kibok Lee, Honglak Lee, and Jinwoo Shin. 2018. A simple unified framework for detecting out-of-distribution samples and adversarial attacks. In *Advances in Neural Information Processing Systems 31: Annual Conference on Neural Information Processing Systems 2018, NeurIPS 2018, December 3-8, 2018, Montréal, Canada*, volume 31, pages 7167–7177.

Brian Lester, Rami Al-Rfou, and Noah Constant. 2021. The power of scale for parameter-efficient prompt tuning. In *Proceedings of the 2021 Conference on Empirical Methods in Natural Language Processing, EMNLP 2021, Virtual Event / Punta Cana, Dominican Republic, 7-11 November, 2021*, pages 3045–3059. Association for Computational Linguistics.

Mike Lewis, Yinhan Liu, Naman Goyal, Marjan Ghazvininejad, Abdelrahman Mohamed, Omer Levy, Veselin Stoyanov, and Luke Zettlemoyer. 2019. BART: denoising sequence-to-sequence pre-training for natural language generation, translation, and comprehension. *CoRR*, abs/1910.13461.

Xiang Lisa Li and Percy Liang. 2021. Prefix-tuning: Optimizing continuous prompts for generation. In *Proceedings of the 59th Annual Meeting of the Association for Computational Linguistics and the 11th International Joint Conference on Natural Language Processing (Volume 1: Long Papers)*, pages 4582–4597, Online. Association for Computational Linguistics.

Zhen Lin, Shubhendu Trivedi, and Jimeng Sun. 2023. Generating with confidence: Uncertainty quantification for black-box large language models. *CoRR*, abs/2305.19187.

Xiao Liu, Yanan Zheng, Zhengxiao Du, Ming Ding, Yujie Qian, Zhilin Yang, and Jie Tang. 2021. GPT understands, too. *CoRR*, abs/2103.10385.

Yinhan Liu, Myle Ott, Naman Goyal, Jingfei Du, Mandar Joshi, Danqi Chen, Omer Levy, Mike Lewis, Luke Zettlemoyer, and Veselin Stoyanov. 2019. Roberta: A robustly optimized BERT pretraining approach. *CoRR*, abs/1907.11692.

Federico Martelli, Najla Kalach, Gabriele Tola, Roberto Navigli, et al. 2021. Semeval-2021 task 2: Multilingual and cross-lingual word-in-context disambiguation (mcl-wic). In *Proceedings of the 15th International Workshop on Semantic Evaluation (SemEval-2021)*, pages 24–36.

Paulius Micikevicius, Sharan Narang, Jonah Alben, Gregory F. Diamos, Erich Elsen, David García, Boris Ginsburg, Michael Houston, Oleksii Kuchaiev, Ganesh Venkatesh, and Hao Wu. 2018. Mixed precision training. In *6th International Conference on Learning Representations, ICLR 2018, Vancouver, BC, Canada, April 30 - May 3, 2018, Conference Track Proceedings*. OpenReview.net.

Roger Newson. 2016. Xglm: Stata module to extend glm.

Ivan V. Oseledets. 2011. Tensor-train decomposition. *SIAM J. Sci. Comput.*, 33(5):2295–2317.

Long Ouyang, Jeffrey Wu, Xu Jiang, Diogo Almeida, Carroll L. Wainwright, Pamela Mishkin, Chong Zhang, Sandhini Agarwal, Katarina Slama, Alex Ray, John Schulman, Jacob Hilton, Fraser Kelton, Luke Miller, Maddie Simens, Amanda Askell, Peter Welinder, Paul F. Christiano, Jan Leike, and Ryan Lowe. 2022. Training language models to follow instructions with human feedback. In *NeurIPS*.

Alec Radford, Jong Wook Kim, Chris Hallacy, Aditya Ramesh, Gabriel Goh, Sandhini Agarwal, Girish Sastry, Amanda Askell, Pamela Mishkin, Jack Clark, Gretchen Krueger, and Ilya Sutskever. 2021. Learning transferable visual models from natural language supervision. *CoRR*, abs/2103.00020.

Alec Radford, Jeffrey Wu, Rewon Child, David Luan, Dario Amodei, Ilya Sutskever, et al. 2019. Language models are unsupervised multitask learners. *OpenAI blog*, 1(8):9.

Jack W. Rae, Sebastian Borgeaud, Trevor Cai, Katie Millican, Jordan Hoffmann, H. Francis Song, John Aslanides, Sarah Henderson, Roman Ring, Susannah Young, Eliza Rutherford, Tom Hennigan, Jacob Menick, Albin Cassirer, Richard Powell, George van den Driessche, Lisa Anne Hendricks, Maribeth Rauh, Po-Sen Huang, et al. 2021. Scaling language models: Methods, analysis & insights from training gopher. *CoRR*, abs/2112.11446.

Colin Raffel, Noam Shazeer, Adam Roberts, Katherine Lee, Sharan Narang, Michael Matena, Yanqi Zhou, Wei Li, and Peter J. Liu. 2020a. Exploring the limits of transfer learning with a unified text-to-text transformer. *J. Mach. Learn. Res.*, 21:140:1–140:67.

Colin Raffel, Noam Shazeer, Adam Roberts, Katherine Lee, Sharan Narang, Michael Matena, Yanqi Zhou, Wei Li, and Peter J Liu. 2020b. Exploring the limits of transfer learning with a unified text-to-text transformer. *Journal of machine learning research*, 21(140):1–67.

Aditya Ramesh, Prafulla Dhariwal, Alex Nichol, Casey Chu, and Mark Chen. 2022. Hierarchical text-conditional image generation with CLIP latents. *CoRR*, abs/2204.06125.

Anton Razzhigaev, Arseniy Shakhmatov, Anastasia Maltseva, Vladimir Arkhipkin, Igor Pavlov, Ilya Ryabov, Angelina Kuts, Alexander Panchenko, Andrey Kuznetsov, and Denis Dimitrov. 2023. Kandinsky: An improved text-to-image synthesis with image prior and latent diffusion. In *Proceedings of the 2023 Conference on Empirical Methods in Natural Language Processing: System Demonstrations*, pages 286–295, Singapore. Association for Computational Linguistics.

Nils Reiter, Sarah Schulz, Gerhard Kremer, Roman Klinger, Gabriel Viehhauser, and Jonas Kuhn. 2017. Teaching computational aspects in the digital humanities program at university of stuttgart - intentions and experiences. In *Proceedings of the Workshop on Teaching NLP for Digital Humanities (Teach4DH) 2017, Berlin, Germany, September 12, 2017*, volume 1918 of *CEUR Workshop Proceedings*, pages 43–48. CEUR-WS.org.

Victor Sanh, Thomas Wolf, and Alexander M. Rush. 2020. Movement pruning: Adaptive sparsity by fine-tuning.

Teven Le Scao, Angela Fan, Christopher Akiki, Ellie Pavlick, Suzana Ilić, Daniel Hesslow, Roman Castagné, Alexandra Sasha Luccioni, François Yvon, Matthias Gallé, et al. 2022. BLOOM: A 176b-parameter open-access multilingual language model. *CoRR*, abs/2211.05100.

Matthias Schildwächter, Alexander Bondarenko, Julian Zenker, Matthias Hagen, Chris Biemann, and Alexander Panchenko. 2019. Answering comparative questions: Better than ten-blue-links? In *Proceedings of the 2019 Conference on Human Information Interaction and Retrieval*, pages 361–365.

Burr Settles. 2009. Active learning literature survey. Computer Sciences Technical Report 1648, University of Wisconsin–Madison.

Noam Shazeer and Mitchell Stern. 2018. Adafactor: Adaptive learning rates with sublinear memory cost. In *Proceedings of the 35th International Conference on Machine Learning, ICML 2018, Stockholmsmässan, Stockholm, Sweden, July 10-15, 2018*, volume 80 of *Proceedings of Machine Learning Research*, pages 4603–4611. PMLR.

Oleksandr Shchur, Ali Caner Türkmen, Tim Januschowski, and Stephan Günnemann. 2021. Neural temporal point processes: A review. In

Proceedings of the Thirtieth International Joint Conference on Artificial Intelligence, IJCAI 2021, Virtual Event / Montreal, Canada, 19-27 August 2021, pages 4585–4593. ijcai.org.

Oleh Shliazhko, Alena Fenogenova, Maria Tikhonova, Vladislav Mikhailov, Anastasia Kozlova, and Tatiana Shavrina. 2022. mgpt: Few-shot learners go multilingual. *CoRR*, abs/2204.07580.

Mohammad Shoeybi, Mostofa Patwary, Raul Puri, Patrick LeGresley, Jared Casper, and Bryan Catanzaro. 2019. Megatron-lm: Training multi-billion parameter language models using model parallelism. *CoRR*, abs/1909.08053.

Nisan Stiennon, Long Ouyang, Jeff Wu, Daniel M. Ziegler, Ryan Lowe, Chelsea Voss, Alec Radford, Dario Amodei, and Paul F. Christiano. 2020. Learning to summarize from human feedback. *CoRR*, abs/2009.01325.

Ilya Sutskever, Oriol Vinyals, and Quoc V. Le. 2014. Sequence to sequence learning with neural networks. In *Advances in Neural Information Processing Systems 27: Annual Conference on Neural Information Processing Systems 2014, December 8-13 2014, Montreal, Quebec, Canada*, pages 3104–3112.

Yi Tay, Mostafa Dehghani, Dara Bahri, and Donald Metzler. 2020. Efficient transformers: A survey. *CoRR*, abs/2009.06732.

Hugo Touvron, Louis Martin, Kevin Stone, Peter Albert, Amjad Almahairi, Yasmine Babaei, Nikolay Bashlykov, Soumya Batra, Prajjwal Bhargava, Shruti Bhosale, et al. 2023. Llama 2: Open foundation and fine-tuned chat models. *arXiv preprint arXiv:2307.09288*.

Elena Tutubalina, Ilseyar Alimova, Zulfat Miftahutdinov, Andrey Sakhovskiy, Valentin Malykh, and Sergey I. Nikolenko. 2020. The russian drug reaction corpus and neural models for drug reactions and effectiveness detection in user reviews. *CoRR*, abs/2004.03659.

Sowmya Vajjala. 2021. Teaching NLP outside linguistics and computer science classrooms: Some challenges and some opportunities. *CoRR*, abs/2105.00895.

Aäron van den Oord, Oriol Vinyals, and Koray Kavukcuoglu. 2017. Neural discrete representation learning. In *Advances in Neural Information Processing Systems 30: Annual Conference on Neural Information Processing Systems 2017, December 4-9, 2017, Long Beach, CA, USA*, pages 6306–6315.

Ashish Vaswani, Noam Shazeer, Niki Parmar, Jakob Uszkoreit, Llion Jones, Aidan N. Gomez, Lukasz Kaiser, and Illia Polosukhin. 2017. Attention is all you need. In *Advances in Neural Information Processing Systems 30: Annual Conference on Neural Information Processing Systems 2017, December 4-9, 2017, Long Beach, CA, USA*, pages 5998–6008.

Artem Vazhentsev, Gleb Kuzmin, Akim Tsvigun, Alexander Panchenko, Maxim Panov, Mikhail Burtsev, and Artem Shelmanov. 2023. Hybrid uncertainty quantification for selective text classification in ambiguous tasks. In *Proceedings of the 61st Annual Meeting of the Association for Computational Linguistics (Volume 1: Long Papers)*, pages 11659–11681, Toronto, Canada. Association for Computational Linguistics.

Peng Wang, An Yang, Rui Men, Junyang Lin, Shuai Bai, Zhikang Li, Jianxin Ma, Chang Zhou, Jingren Zhou, and Hongxia Yang. 2022a. OFA: unifying architectures, tasks, and modalities through a simple sequence-to-sequence learning framework. In *International Conference on Machine Learning, ICML 2022, 17-23 July 2022, Baltimore, Maryland, USA*, volume 162 of *Proceedings of Machine Learning Research*, pages 23318–23340. PMLR.

Zheng Wang, Juncheng B. Li, Shuhui Qu, Florian Metze, and Emma Strubell. 2022b. Squat: Sharpness- and quantization-aware training for BERT. *CoRR*, arXiv:2210.07171.

Genta Indra Winata, Andrea Madotto, Zhaojiang Lin, Rosanne Liu, Jason Yosinski, and Pascale Fung. 2021. Language models are few-shot multilingual learners. In *Proceedings of the 1st Workshop on Multilingual Representation Learning*, pages 1–15, Punta Cana, Dominican Republic. Association for Computational Linguistics.

Ji Xin, Raphael Tang, Yaoliang Yu, and Jimmy Lin. 2021. The art of abstention: Selective prediction and error regularization for natural language processing. In *Proceedings of the 59th Annual Meeting of the Association for Computational Linguistics and the 11th International Joint Conference on Natural Language Processing (Volume 1: Long Papers)*, pages 1040–1051, Online. Association for Computational Linguistics.

KiYoon Yoo, Jangho Kim, Jiho Jang, and Nojun Kwak. 2022. Detection of adversarial examples in text classification: Benchmark and baseline via robust density estimation. In *Findings of the Association for Computational Linguistics: ACL 2022*, pages 3656–3672, Dublin, Ireland. Association for Computational Linguistics.

Seongjun Yun, Minbyul Jeong, Sungdong Yoo, Seunghun Lee, Sean S. Yi, Raehyun Kim, Jaewoo Kang, and Hyunwoo J. Kim. 2022. Graph transformer networks: Learning meta-path graphs to improve gnns. *Neural Networks*, 153:104–119.

Jiawei Zhang, Haopeng Zhang, Congying Xia, and Li Sun. 2020. Graph-bert: Only attention is needed for learning graph representations. *CoRR*, abs/2001.05140.

Jingqing Zhang, Yao Zhao, Mohammad Saleh, and Peter J. Liu. 2019. Pegasus: Pre-training with extracted gap-sentences for abstractive summarization. *Preprint*, arXiv:1912.08777.

Xikun Zhang, Antoine Bosselut, Michihiro Yasunaga, Hongyu Ren, Percy Liang, Christopher D. Manning, and Jure Leskovec. 2022. Greaselm: Graph reasoning enhanced language models for question answering. *CoRR*, abs/2201.08860.

Liu Zhuang, Lin Wayne, Shi Ya, and Zhao Jun. 2021. A robustly optimized bert pre-training approach with post-training. In *Proceedings of the 20th chinese national conference on computational linguistics*, pages 1218–1227.

Vladislav Zhuzhel, Rodrigo Rivera-Castro, Nina Kaploukhaya, Liliya Mironova, Alexey Zaytsev, and Evgeny Burnaev. 2021. COHORTNEY: deep clustering for heterogeneous event sequences. *CoRR*, abs/2104.01440.

Simiao Zuo, Haoming Jiang, Zichong Li, Tuo Zhao, and Hongyuan Zha. 2020. Transformer hawkes process. *CoRR*, abs/2002.09291.

A Assessment criteria

A.1 Technical Report Grading Criteria

The technical report is evaluated via the two criteria:

- Methodology (5 points): description of all methods they try and the best method. Here, students can include some tricks with pre-processing, a description of the models and motivation of their usage, and details of the training process (train-test split, cross-validation, etc.).
- Discussion of results (5 points): here, we expect the final comparison table. Even if some methods did not bring students to the top of the leaderboard, they should nevertheless indicate this result and a discussion of why, in their opinion, some approaches work while others fail.

A.2 Code Grading Criteria

The code of the students is graded according to the following criteria:

- Readability (5 points): code should be well-structured, preferably with indicated parts of your approach (Pre-processing, Model training, Evaluation, etc.).
- Reproducibility (5 points): code should be reproduced without any mistakes with the "Run all" mode (obtaining experimental part).

A.3 CodaLab Competition Grading Criteria

Students get points for participating in the corresponding CodaLab competition. For example, a student receives 5 points for outperforming the baseline, an additional 5 points for being in the top 20% on the leaderboard, or an additional 10 points for being top-1. As a result, students may get 0-15 points depending on their performance.

B Feedback

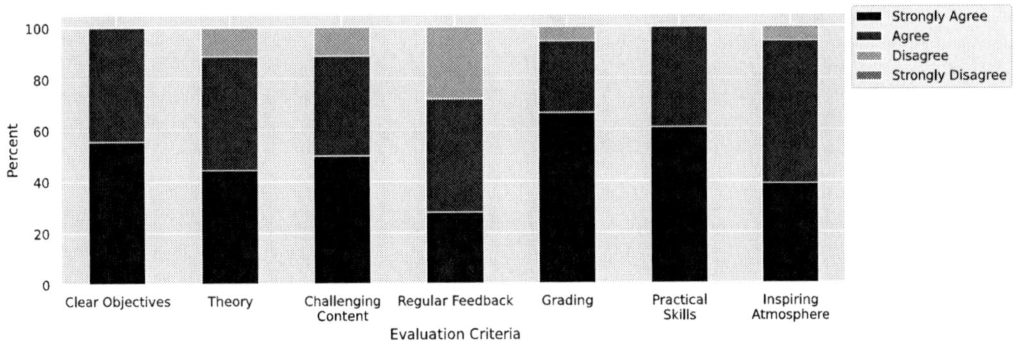

Figure 3: Students feedback for the course in academic setup.

After the academic running of the course (2023), students were asked to provide feedback. Figure 3 demonstrates the statistics of students' feedback for each question, which are listed below:

1. Course objectives were clear to me.
2. Key concepts and theories were well explained by the Course instructor(s).
3. Course content was difficult enough to be challenging.
4. I regularly received feedback on my performance.

5. Grading criteria were well explained, and I understood what action was required to achieve each of the performance levels.
6. The course was useful in developing practical skills.
7. The Course atmosphere was inspiring for active learning.

Striking a Balance between Classical and Deep Learning Approaches in Natural Language Processing Pedagogy

Aditya Joshi[1], **Jake Renzella**[1], **Pushpak Bhattacharyya**[2], **Saurav Jha**[1], **Xiangyu Zhang**[1]
[1] University of New South Wales, Sydney, Australia
[2] Indian Institute of Technology Bombay, Mumbai, India
{aditya.joshi,jake.renzella,saurav.jha,xiangyu.zhang2}@unsw.edu.au
pb@cse.iitb.ac.in

Abstract

While deep learning approaches represent the state-of-the-art of natural language processing (NLP) today, classical algorithms and approaches still find a place in NLP textbooks and courses of recent years. This paper discusses the perspectives of conveners of two introductory NLP courses taught in Australia and India, and examines how classical and deep learning approaches can be balanced within the lecture plan and assessments of the courses. We also draw parallels with the objects-first and objects-later debate in CS1 education. We observe that teaching classical approaches adds value to student learning by building an intuitive understanding of NLP problems, potential solutions, and even deep learning models themselves. Despite classical approaches not being state-of-the-art, the paper makes a case for their inclusion in NLP courses today.

1 Introduction

Transformer-based models are the state-of-the-art in natural language processing (NLP). They represent a new era of deep learning approaches[1] for NLP. From early work in word representations to recent approaches in instruction tuning, deep learning approaches have significantly transformed NLP and many other areas of artificial intelligence. Universities around the world have incorporated deep learning approaches in their introductory NLP courses, arguably with varying speed, and to different extents, as evidenced to an extent, in Table 2). This puts under question the relevance of classical approaches, *i.e.*, those pre-dating deep learning approaches, in NLP curricula. This reflection from academics/faculty members may also be based on questions from students taking the course who wonder why they should learn about classical approaches, as seen in pre-course feedback received by the authors of this paper.

Therefore, we analyse the role of classical approaches in the context of modern university-based courses in NLP. We focus on introductory NLP courses offered to students of computer science & engineering or equivalent degrees, and investigate the question:

"How can an introductory NLP course balance between the content covering classical and deep learning approaches?"

We address the question in two parts: (a) how others do it, and (b) how we do it. With respect to (a), we describe summaries of NLP textbooks and publicly available courses in the context of the question. As for (b), we draw insights from our experience teaching NLP courses at two large, research-intensive universities in Australia and India. We introduce and discuss our motivations, considerations and decisions in the lectures, tutorials and projects of NLP courses. Authors of this paper represent two *personas* of NLP educators: (a) an early-career educator who introduced a new NLP course in the beginning of 2024; and (b) a seasoned educator with two-decade experience of teaching and research experience. The novelty of this paper is as follows:

1. There have been papers in the past on specific aspects (tutorials, lecture content, etc.) of individual NLP courses (Plank, 2021; Foster and Wagner, 2021; Gaddy et al., 2021). This paper is novel in its comparison of two NLP courses taught by educators with significantly different experience in NLP research and pedagogy.

2. We also draw parallels to the age-long objects-first or -later debate in computer science education, to highlight that the classical approaches in NLP courses can benefit from lessons in computer science education.

[1]The phrase 'deep learning approaches' is expected to refer to the broad spectrum including but not limited to dense word representations, Transformer and Transformer-based models used in NLP.

Proceedings of the Sixth Workshop on Teaching NLP, pages 23–32
August 15, 2024 ©2024 Association for Computational Linguistics

3. We hope that the paper serves as a useful resource for NLP educators to examine the role of classical methods in their curricula now and in the future.

The rest of the paper is described as follows. We first introduce the context in terms of the two courses being compared in Section 2. Following that, we discuss an analogous objects first- and objects-later- debate in computer science education in Section 3. We describe how NLP textbooks and NLP courses (as per publicly available course outlines) cover classical approaches in Section 4. We then proceed to compare the lecture plan, and coding assessments involved in the two courses in Sections 5 and 6 respectively. Section 7 puts it all together to make our case for the relevance of classical approaches in NLP courses. Finally, Section 8 concludes the paper.

2 Context

The two NLP courses we compare are run at two large universities in Australia and India, both titled 'Natural Language Processing'. We refer to these as **NLP-UNSW** and **NLP-IITB**[2]. NLP-UNSW is the first offering of the course with 60 enrolled students, while NLP-IITB is the ninteenth offering of the course with 150 enrolled students. While NLP-UNSW is the only NLP-focussed course at UNSW at the time of writing this paper, NLP-IITB is accompanied with a 'Deep learning for NLP' course which often follows NLP-IITB. Both courses were offered as an undergraduate/postgraduate elective as a part of the computer science and engineering programme, and were introductory courses to NLP. The cohorts consisted of undergraduate (nearly 50%) and postgraduate students. Postgraduate students included those enrolled in Masters by Coursework or Masters by Research programmes, and early PhD students.

The course components of NLP-UNSW and NLP-IITB, along with the course conveners' reasons behind covering classical approaches, are shown in Figures 1 and 2 respectively. Generally speaking, an exposition to classical approaches allowed the students to solve problems and understand deep learning approaches vis-á-vis their predecessors. NLP-UNSW insisted that the group project compare deep learning methods with their predecessors. NLP-IITB allowed the students to choose an appropriate method. In contrast, the individual assignment in NLP-UNSW only involved using black-box NLP libraries while NLP-IITB used multiple assignments covering both statistical as well as deep learning models.

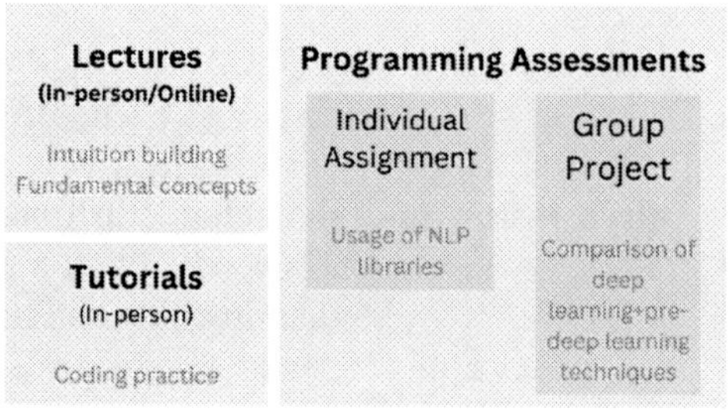

Figure 1: Course Structure for NLP-UNSW.

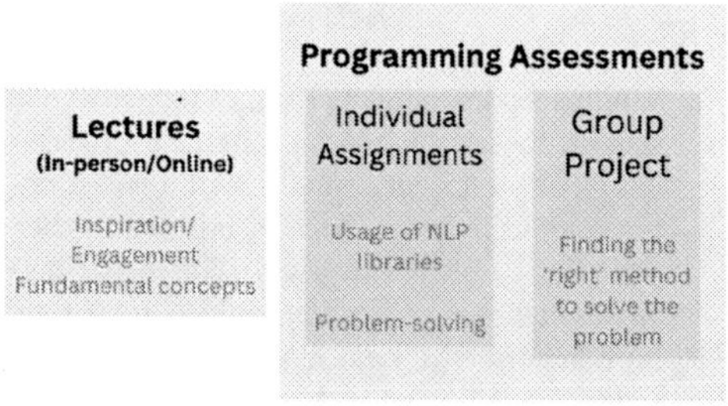

Figure 2: Course Structure for NLP-IITB.

3 Parallels to Computer Science Education

As NLP educators grapple with Classical-first, -later, or perhaps -interleaved approaches to curricula, it is helpful to draw upon empirical research and lessons learned by CS1 educators (introductory programming) who have grappled with a similar dilemma: the age-long objects-first or -later debate. For decades, introductory programming students learned imperative-style programming in languages such as C, Pascal, and Fortran. In the early 2000s, educators started incorporated object-oriented programming concepts into their curriculum as object-oriented programming took hold in industry (Cooper et al., 2003). Where the objects-first community may begin immediately with concepts of composition, inheritance, and abstraction, the objects-later community instead focus on simpler, foundational programs and concepts such as sequence and control flow.

The primary criticism of objects-first approaches surrounds the added complexity necessary to dis-

[2]UNSW: University of New South Wales, Sydney, Australia; IITB: Indian Institute of Technology Bombay, Mumbai, India.

cuss object-oriented concepts (Proulx et al., 2002). Objects-first must tackle objects, classes, encapsulation, and access modifiers to discuss even the most basic object-oriented concepts. Of course, objects-first educators will retort that this extra effort is worth it, with students reporting a solid sense of program design and contextualisation of object oriented concepts (Cooper et al., 2003).

These criticisms of object-first approaches are not unfounded. We can apply cognitive load theory, the theory of human cognition and how learning occurs, to inform instructional design in computing and NLP. The theory, backed by many empirical studies, finds that limited amounts of secondary information (such as computing tasks) can be processed at any given time (Sweller, 2011). Put simply, human cognitive architecture lends itself to learning best when concepts are minimally introduced. This reduces the cognitive overload that can hinder the assimilation of new information.

Cognitive load theory has been applied in introductory programming contexts, finding that cognitive load measures and tools can be applied to computing education to inform curriculum and instructional design (Morrison et al., 2014).

While cognitive load theory may, at first glance, support an objects-later approach due to the reduction of concepts required, approaches to reduce cognitive load when delivering objects-first curriculum may be preferable if it aligns with its goals.

Empirical studies of learning outcomes between objects-first and -later seek to focus on measurable evaluations of student learning outcomes. Ehlert and Schulte (2009) found no differences in learning gain between objects-first and objects-later courses; however, they did find that students in objects-later courses reported lower perceived difficulty and higher comfort levels. (Tew et al., 2005) compared objects-first/later at the same institution and found that students performed comparatively by the end of their second term. A more recent, large-scale systematic literature review on Introductory Programming seems to support this nuanced take on programming paradigms (Luxton-Reilly et al., 2018). The authors find that there is still active research on programming paradigms, and surmise with: "after full consideration of all the papers it is by no means clear that any paradigm is superior to any other for the teaching of introductory programming". We may glean from this comparison to CS1 education design that many dimensions are involved in curriculum design. Empirical studies have found that the goals of the program and the institution itself, perspectives of educators, and quality of instruction and instructional materials are more critical than an objects-first or -later design.

Unlike CS1 education, however, NLP may often be available as a single elective in a computer science program. Therefore, NLP educators are forced to balance providing practical, deep learning skills to students while also providing solid foundations in classical NLP in a shorter time-frame, perhaps supporting an interleaved approach to NLP curricula.

4 Observations from NLP textbooks and courses

Table 1 presents a summary of some NLP textbooks, in terms of layouts and their deep learning focus. The books were identified using a search on the UNSW library. The focus was identified using the content plan of the book, along with a surface analysis of the chapters. We observe that nearly all textbooks cover classical approaches, primarily in terms of statistical models. We describe two textbooks in particular. The textbook by Jurafsky-Martin [3] divides its chapters into fundamental algorithms and NLP applications. The first five chapters introduce regular expressions, one-hot vectors and statistical algorithms like support vector machines and logistic regression. In the subsequent chapters, the book covers word embeddings, then begins to combine LSTM with CRFs in the context of POS tagging. Following that, the book covers Transformer, fine-tuning and prompting/prompt learning Transformer. Bhattacharyya and Joshi (2023) use a different approach. They cover fundamental algorithms for representation learning: computational grammar, probabilistic language modeling, and word2vec/LSTM-based representations. The book visualizes NLP as three generations: rule-based, statistical and neural. Following that, the book introduces Transformer. The subsequent chapters alternate between the approaches in the three generations.

Table 2 illustrates how some NLP courses cover classical topics. We only use examples of courses whose course outlines are publicly available on the internet. Similarly, this is not a complete list either. In universities where there is a deep learning-focused course for NLP, topics such as syntactic

[3]https://web.stanford.edu/~jurafsky/slp3/

Authors; Publisher	Year	Chapter Layout	Deep learning focus
Speech and Language Processing; Dan Jurafsky, James H Martin; -	2024	Fundamental Algorithms (Statistical Models, Neural Models, RNNs, LSTMs.) followed by NLP applications and linguistic tasks.	Techniques first. classical: Yes.
A Course in Natural Language Processing; Yannis Haralambous; Springer	2024	Layers of NLP: Phoneme, Grapheme, Morpheme. Last chapter: Going Neural.	Neural Models (RNNs, Transformers)
Natural Language Processing; Pushpak Bhattacharyya, Aditya Joshi; Wiley	2023	Fundamental techniques first. Then neural. Significant focus on NLP problems.	Interleave classical and neural both. Three generations.
Real-World Natural Language Processing; Masato Hagiwara; Manning	2022	Neural-focussed. Embeddings, Sentence-Clasification, Seq2Seq, Transformer, etc.	Neural-focussed.
Deep Learning for Natural Language Processing; Stephan Raaijmakers; Manning Publications	2022	Text embeddings, sequential NLP, attention, multitask learning, last chapter: Transformers and using Transformers. Lots of code examples	Neural focussed.
Practical Natural Language Processing; Sowmya Vajjala, Bodhisattwa Majumder, Anuj Gupta, Harshit Surana; O'Reilly	2020	NLP Primers: Quick introduction to primary NLP concepts. Very task driven: Classification, IE, Chatbots, Applications to domains	Cover deep learning Early. Focus on applications and tasks
Introduction to Natural Language Processing; Jacob Eisenstein; MIT Press	2019	Learning: Classification (Tasks and approaches); Sequences (Tasks and approaches); Semantics. Word embeddings, parsing, reference resoluton	Pre-deep learning first. Then neural.

Table 1: Deep learning focus in some NLP textbooks listed in the reverse-chronological order.

parsing or statistical classification are covered in substantial detail. Even for courses that cover little classical content, n-gram language modeling is a topic that is included. The table also shows 'when is Transformer taught' which may be viewed as a turning point when deep learning-based approaches assume focus in the course. We view Transformer as a transformative technology in NLP, and do not claim that all of deep learning is Transformer.

5 Lecture Plan

NLP-UNSW: In the NLP-UNSW course which is spread over 10 weeks, we adopt a hybrid methodology where we interleave deep learning approaches with statistical/rule-based approaches. The hybrid methodology is illustrated in Figure 3. In the first week, we introduce NLP via black-boxes such as spacy, nltk, and HuggingFace pipelines. The students are introduced to NLP tasks with demonstrations of the three libraries. This is to help the students develop an understanding of the task. Similarly, if students aim to only 'use' NLP in their projects (which may be sufficient for interdisciplinary projects), these libraries are sufficient. The focus here is also to help them understand the input and output of NLP systems, which we believe is the starting point to understanding NLP.

In week 2, we cover representations of text via one-hot vectors and probabilistic language modeling (statistical approach), and word representation learning as in word2vec and GloVe (deep learning approach). This not only allows students to appreciate the value addition of deep learning approaches but also identify situations in which non-deep learning approaches may be sufficient. In week 3, we focus on Transformer architecture: exposing the students to the architectural details, pseudocode, and code implementations. This is followed by Transformer-based models (encoder, decoder, and encoder-decoder models) in week 4. With this background in neural NLP models, we switch gears and focus on one NLP task every week. Every task is covered using the following steps: the linguistic task and associated challenges, classical approaches, deep learning approaches, and recent advances in the area. The first two allow the students to gain a foundational understanding of the problem, followed by the state-of-the-art in deep learning. The recent advances are catered to students who might be interested in future research in NLP without going into too much depth - to ensure that the content is accessible. The NLP tasks we cover are: sentiment analysis (representing sequence classification), named entity recognition (representing token classification), machine translation (representing sequence-to-sequence tasks), summarization (modified sequence-to-sequence tasks) and bias mitigation.

In NLP-UNSW, we experience a recurring challenge when discussing NLP tasks every week. Foundation models (both encoder-only and decoder-only models) are versatile in their utility for different tasks. Therefore, we structure each neural section in three steps: (a) fine-tuning BERT, (b) one or more advanced methods relevant for the task. This serves two purposes. It allows us to teach different fine-tuning techniques. In addition, it also permits us to ground them in specific NLP tasks. We remember to remind students that the method is applicable in other NLP tasks.

NLP-IITB: NLP-IITB starts with a focus on sequence labeling via HMM-based POS tagging, followed by tree extraction via probabilistic parsing. In both cases, the mathematical details (driven by probability) go hand in hand with the algorithms (explained through the code). Then, machine translation is introduced, which makes way for an introduction to Transformer and large language models. The subsequent weeks discuss sentiment analysis as a specific NLP task and evaluation metrics in NLP. It must be noted that NLP-IITB is the introductory NLP course while there is a deep learning-specific NLP course at IITB which is often a follow-up to the introductory NLP-IITB. This is not the case for NLP-UNSW (being the only NLP-centric course). As a result, the course needs to balance between the two. This comparison shows how educators may make different choices, depending on the length of the teaching period. As a result, the lecture plan of NLP-IITB uses the spectrum shown in Figure 4. classical approaches allow focusing on the linguistic phenomenon which is captured using a model. The data provides the parameters of the model.

Comparison: In both NLP-UNSW and NLP-IITB, however, we observe that the foundational material serves as a good basis to introduce terminology (for example, types of summarization are abstractive and extractive summarization) and tag sets (as in the case of named entity recognition). The classical approaches build an intuitive understanding of building computational models for the

University	Year	Examples of pre-deep-learning topics	When is Transformer taught?
UMAss Amherst[4]	2023	N-gram language modeling	Week 2 of 11
CMU[5]	2024	Representing words	Week 3 of 16
IIT Delhi[6]	2022	Finite state automata, statistical parsing	End of month 2 out of 3.5
University of Edinburgh[7]	2024	Lexical, syntactic and semantic parsing, etc.	This only covers algorithmic fundamentals; separate course for neural models
University of Washington[8]	2024	N-gram language modeling	Week 2 of 11
NYU [9]	2023	Feature-based classification, N-gram language modeling	Week 3 of 15

Table 2: Examples of the coverage of deep learning in NLP courses.

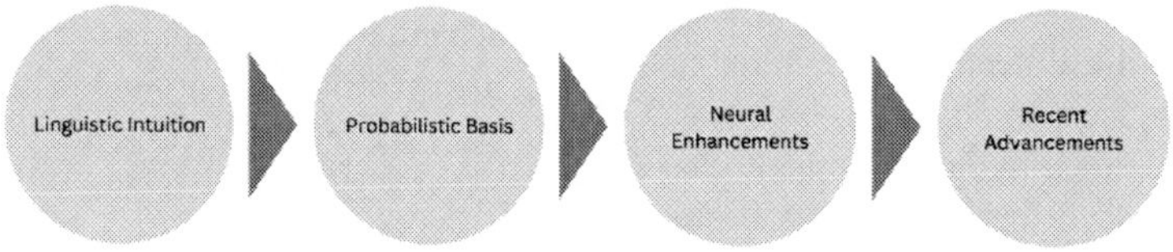

Figure 3: Lecture Plan for NLP-UNSW.

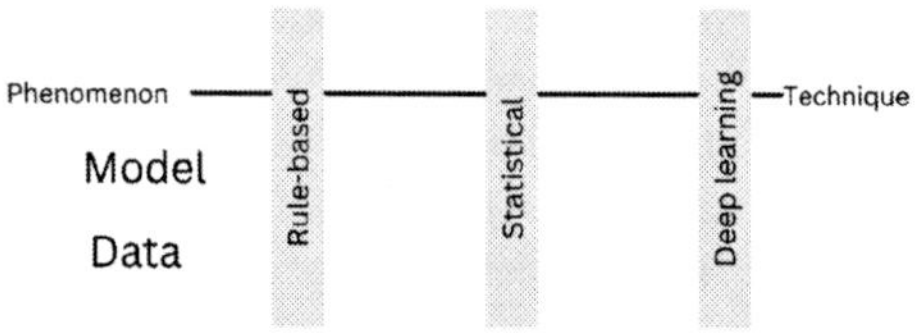

Figure 4: Lecture Plan for NLP-IITB.

specific NLP task. Appreciating the challenges in the classical approaches leads the students to the need for deep learning approaches. Through handwritten examples in the lecture, we highlight the relationships between the mathematics of classical approaches and Transformer-based approaches (for example, alignment model in statistical MT with cross-attention in Transformer).

6 Coding Assessments

Both NLP-UNSW and NLP-IITB have individual and group coding assessments. NLP-UNSW has one of each, while NLP-IITB has two individual and one group assessment(s).

6.1 Course Assignment

NLP-UNSW: The first coding assessment in NLP-UNSW is an individual coding assignment completed by students by the end of week 3. The coding assessment is run in a competition-like environment. The students are given a document defining the problem definition, and a template code that also contains stubs for testing. The students are required to add to the template. Closer to the submission, the students are given test cases to evaluate their code. The topic of the individual assignment needed deliberation. Until that point, we have only started discussing Transformer in the lectures. Therefore, we utilize the individual assignment to assess the classical skills of the students. In the case of this offering, the task was to extract skills from job ads, based on a skills ontology. The assignment was designed in two parts: the first part required the students to use the spacy matcher, while the second part required them to use embedding similarities. The former tests them for their ability to use a classical library while the latter requires them to use HuggingFace models. As a result, the assessment covers the students' ability to 'use' NLP models. Marking the assignment includes an automatic marking component with test cases and manual marking by the tutors. Being a rule-based system, the evaluation of test cases is found to return low precision. Therefore, rather than scoring on individual test cases, we mark the students on precision thresholds.

NLP-IITB: NLP-IITB follows a similar strategy although there are multiple individual assignments.

The course convener found it useful to give classical assignments on topics such as POS tagging, parsing and so on. An innovative assignment was also tried out, which met with good student feedback. Given a large dataset of names of cities, the task was to identify a preferred suffix in the name of a city. Students reported multiple deep learning/non-deep learning approaches.

6.2 Course Project

Running in its first year, NLP-UNSW provides detailed guidelines for the course project. In contrast, NLP-IITB provides less guidelines but involves periodic consultation with the course team.

NLP-UNSW: The group project is a centerpiece of the NLP-UNSW course, allowing students to explore diverse topics within NLP. Teams of four to five students are encouraged to select a specific area of interest, ranging from NLP topics of active research such as prompt recovery in large language models to purely applied topics like developing a virtual learning assistant using Retrieval Augmented Generation (Lewis et al., 2020). To guide students effectively, we provide a detailed scope guideline document. The document outlines the following key aspects alongside their respective credits (cr):

1. Problem definition: Must be an NLP problem (5 cr) with a text-based source/domain (5 cr);

2. Dataset selection: Use an existing dataset (10 cr), create your own labelled dataset (20 cr) and use an existing lexicon (10 cr);

3. Modelling: Implement a rule-based/statistical baseline (50 cr), use an existing pre-trained model (5 cr), fine-tune your own model (50 cr), and integrate a language model with external tools (20 cr);

4. Evaluation: Quantitative (10 cr), qualitative (5 cr), command-line testing (5 cr) and demonstration (10 cr).

Project teams are expected to cover a minimum of 100 credits. The aspects show that, while deep learning-based techniques, carry a significant focus, students are encouraged to experiment with simpler models.

Project evaluation. The submission evaluation is structured around specific questions that capture the essence of a well-rounded NLP project pipeline. These include the evaluation of the project report – for scope: architectural, methodological, and analytical details; group presentation – for quality: architectural details, presentation format/style; codebase – for code style: readability, scope, errors, and structure, and individual effort of group members. For the lattermost evaluation, each group is to submit an individual contribution file enlisting the technical contributions of each member.

Findings. The diversity of modeling algorithms is particularly interesting across the submissions (see Fig. 5). We note that classical techniques such as such as lexicon-based systems, traditional machine learning algorithms (e.g., SVM, Naive Bayes), and feature engineering-based techniques serve towards foundation building, interpretable analyses, and resource efficiency all while allowing the students to appreciate the advancements brought about by deep learning in NLP by benchmarking against them. Deep learning models (Fig. 5a), on the other hand, help achieve complex pattern recognition, state-of-art performance, and end-to-end learning while helping the students understand the laws of scalability on large-scale datasets.

(a) Deep-learning (b) classical

Figure 5: Word clouds showing the key deep learning and classical methods explored in the group projects.

NLP-IITB: In NLP-IITB, we list a few topics for students to choose from, while being open to new ideas. Providing topics helps to streamline project ideas while giving student teams a headstart. The projects are evaluated using a combination of demonstration and presentation, including an in-person discussion with the course team. The focus is the selection of the 'right' algorithm. The difference in the level of detail appears to reflect the experience of the two academics running the courses.

6.3 Tutorials

Tutorials are a weekly activity in NLP-UNSW (while not a part of NLP-IITB). In a typical tutorial, we first cover a focused review of the content covered in the lectures. We initially provide a brief overview of classical methods, as these approaches often greatly assist students in understanding the task. Among the classical topics, students show interest in learning about POS tagging and HMM-related algorithms. In the tutorial, we emphasize the mathematical derivation of HMM itself to improve the student's understanding. Subsequently, we extend the discussion by integrating the latest research related to the lecture topics. This part is focused on expanding on the lecture content to cover recent, trending papers that are not included in the syllabus. For instance, when discussing Parameter-Efficient Fine-Tuning (PEFT), we incorporate a paper-reading session of the paper by (He et al., 2021), explaining its essence from a unified perspective and how it can be generally summarized. This allows us to meet the expectations of students who may be interested in advanced topics. Next, we utilize code demonstrations to illustrate the concepts presented in the lectures, facilitating a deeper understanding for the students. Following this, we explain and demonstrate the coursework requirements, such as homework assignments. Finally, we conclude by addressing student questions, which may pertain to projects or other assignments. Particularly in the tutorials, the students show less interest in the classical sections, focusing more on deep learning-based methods that are perceived as more employable. Students who actively participate and show interest in the derivation of various model principles are often also interested in research.

7 Making the Case for Classical Approaches

Based on the considerations discussed so far, we are now able to make several arguments that may influence the inclusion of classical approaches in NLP courses. Designing a curriculum based on course expectations along these arguments may help determine the 'balance' that is the focus of this paper.

7.1 Intuition-building

The conveners of NLP-UNSW and NLP-IITB find that rule-based and statistical approaches are great for intuition building and also appreciate that NLP is challenging. Classroom exercises where students describe rules for a particular NLP task enable them to see why a good rule-based system would be laborious due to the well-known high-precision-low-recall setup. Statistical approaches help to highlight

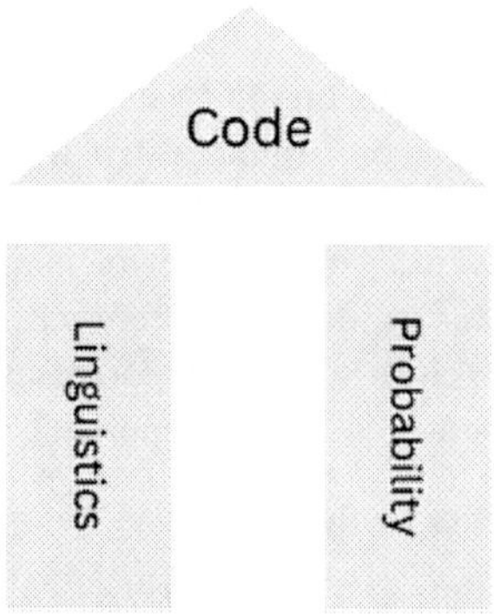

Figure 6: Intuition-building using classical approaches.

the importance of probability in NLP. Probability is the cornerstone of NLP models, including modern models. Softmax being the center of Transformer-based models is an example of that. Starting with Bayes theorem, a teacher can effectively tease out dependencies between different variables, serving to be a great explanation to lead to attention and related concepts, especially during lectures.

A pre-course survey done in NLP-IITB revealed that, out of 150 students, 80% preferred that the course build intuition as opposed to providing information. Information refers to providing a suite of approaches and methods, while intuition refers to the motivation (linguistic or mathematical, etc.) underlying the methods. In fact, both courses combine the pillars illustrated in 6. Linguistics motivates the problem, probability and code run as common threads allowing a comparison between the two kinds of approaches. This motivation is highlighted by the instructor of NLP-IITB, by leveraging examples from his rich research experience. In contrast, the instructor of NLP-UNSW prefers to give examples from industry applications, given their professional experience in the tech industry.

7.2 Student Motivation

Several blog articles on NLP are available online. A clear differentiator in a university-based course is inspiring students using blended learning (Deng and Yuen, 2010). Towards this, classical approaches are effective in inspiring students to take up NLP projects. The conveners of NLP-UNSW and NLP-IITB observe that the challenges of rule-based systems are clear with some examples, during lectures. Covering classical approaches serves as a good motivator for students to see why deep learning approaches have been revolutionary to the field. This feeling of inspiration is often reported in NLP-IITB.

7.3 Popular classical approaches

Classical approaches have done well for linguistic tasks, particularly at the lower levels of the NLP hierarchy. Approaches like HMM and CRF work well for POS tagging and other token classification tasks. We observe that past courses also tend to cover classical methods as an introduction to deep learning methods. Comparison of popular classical approaches with deep learning approaches can aid learning during projects and assignments, as described in Section 6.

7.4 Annotation

Classical techniques, particularly in terms of annotation, are the benchmark for modern NLP models since tag sets used in classical approaches are still useful for their linguistic rigour. An example is the POS tagset. Nuances in Penn TreeBank about tags for "JJ" versus "JJR" (adjectives and comparative adjectives) help the students understand why they were designed in a certain way. The pre-course survey in NLP-IITB revealed that 67% students preferred fundamental approaches versus state-of-the-art. The course covered a combination of the two.

7.5 Cognitive load theory

Classical techniques often involve explicit, well-defined rules and simpler models that can be more transparent and interpretable than their neural counterparts. This clarity can reduce extraneous cognitive load for learners by providing simpler examples of how inputs are transformed into outputs. For instance, a decision tree for language processing allows learners to see the exact paths through which decisions are made, thus aligning with the segmenting principle of cognitive load theory.

8 Conclusion

Classical approaches for NLP refer to those prior to the predominant use of neural networks and deep learning. This paper investigated the role of classical approaches in an introductory NLP course, by comparing perspectives from two courses: one which was offered for the first time and another which has been running for nineteen years while being continually revised. We discussed key considerations and reasons why classical approaches may be helpful, in terms of the past textbooks, lectures, and assessments. An understanding of classical NLP not only builds a strong foundation for the students but also enables them to look back at some of these methods to develop new techniques. We hope that the analyses presented in the paper will allow NLP educators and students alike to find the right balance between the classical and deep learning approaches.

Limitations

The books and courses described in the paper are a subset curated only as an example. It does not represent a complete list. Similarly, the sections derive from insights teaching the two courses covered in the paper, and are not necessarily prescriptive.

Ethical Considerations

The paper describes summary statistics of student surveys without identifying individual students or student cohorts. The assessment section provides only a high-level view of the assignments and lectures, and may not result in implications to academic integrity in the future versions of the courses.

Acknowledgment

The authors thank Dipankar Srirag, UNSW Sydney, for his feedback on a near-camera-ready draft of the paper.

References

Pushpak Bhattacharyya and Aditya Joshi. 2023. *Natural Language Processing*. Wiley.

Stephen Cooper, Wanda Dann, and Randy Pausch. 2003. Teaching objects-first in introductory computer science. *ACM SIGCSE Bulletin*, pages 191–195.

Liping Deng and Allan HK Yuen. 2010. Exploring the role of academic blogs in a blended community: An integrative approach. *Research and Practice in Technology Enhanced Learning*, 5(02):53–71.

Albrecht Ehlert and Carsten Schulte. 2009. Empirical comparison of objects-first and objects-later. *ICER'09 - Proceedings of the 2009 ACM Workshop on International Computing Education Research*, pages 15–26.

Jennifer Foster and Joachim Wagner. 2021. Naive Bayes versus BERT: Jupyter notebook assignments for an introductory NLP course. In *Proceedings of the Fifth Workshop on Teaching NLP*, pages 112–114, Online. Association for Computational Linguistics.

David Gaddy, Daniel Fried, Nikita Kitaev, Mitchell Stern, Rodolfo Corona, John DeNero, and Dan Klein. 2021. Interactive assignments for teaching structured neural NLP. In *Proceedings of the Fifth Workshop on Teaching NLP*, pages 104–107, Online. Association for Computational Linguistics.

Junxian He, Chunting Zhou, Xuezhe Ma, Taylor Berg-Kirkpatrick, and Graham Neubig. 2021. Towards a unified view of parameter-efficient transfer learning. In *International Conference on Learning Representations*.

Patrick Lewis, Ethan Perez, Aleksandra Piktus, Fabio Petroni, Vladimir Karpukhin, Naman Goyal, Heinrich Küttler, Mike Lewis, Wen-tau Yih, Tim Rocktäschel, et al. 2020. Retrieval-augmented generation for knowledge-intensive nlp tasks. *Advances in Neural Information Processing Systems*, 33:9459–9474.

Andrew Luxton-Reilly, Simon, Ibrahim Albluwi, Brett A. Becker, Michail Giannakos, Amruth N. Kumar, Linda Ott, James Paterson, Michael James Scott, Judy Sheard, and Claudia Szabo. 2018. *Introductory programming: A systematic literature review*. ACM.

BB Morrison, B Dorn, M Guzdial of the tenth annual conference on ..., and undefined 2014. 2014. Measuring cognitive load in introductory cs: adaptation of an instrument. *Proceedings of the tenth annual conference on International computing*, pages 131–138.

Barbara Plank. 2021. From back to the roots into the gated woods: Deep learning for NLP. In *Proceedings of the Fifth Workshop on Teaching NLP*, pages 59–61, Online. Association for Computational Linguistics.

Viera K. Proulx, Jeff Raab, and Richard Rasala. 2002. Objects from the beginning - with guis. *Proceedings of the 7th annual conference on Innovation and technology in computer science education*, pages 65–69.

John Sweller. 2011. Cognitive load theory. *Psychology of Learning and Motivation - Advances in Research and Theory*, 55:37–76.

AE Tew, WM McCracken, M Guzdial Proceedings of the first, and undefined 2005. 2005. Impact of alternative introductory courses on programming concept understanding. *dl.acm.orgAE Tew, WM McCracken, M GuzdialProceedings of the first international workshop on Computing education research, 2005•dl.acm.org*.

Co-Creational Teaching of Natural Language Processing

John P. McCrae
Data Science Institute
University of Galway
Galway, Ireland
john@mccr.ae

Abstract

Traditional lectures have poorer outcomes compared to active learning methodologies, yet many natural language processing classes in higher education still follow this outdated methodology. In this paper, we present, co-creational teaching, a methodology that encourages partnership between staff and lecturers and show how this can be applied to teach natural language processing. As a fast-moving and dynamic area of study with high interest from students, natural language processing is an ideal subject for innovative teaching methodologies to improve student outcomes. We detail our experience with teaching natural language processing through partnership with students and provide detailed descriptions of methodologies that can be used by others in their teaching, including considerations of diverse student populations.

1 Introduction

Co-creational teaching is a methodology that involves an active collaboration between students and teachers in the learning process. Natural Language Processing (NLP) is a fast-moving area and it is my experience that students are increasingly demanding that the latest cutting-edge technologies are taught in the classroom. This presents a fundamental challenge to the teaching of NLP in that the teacher must deliver content that satisfies students' demands while providing them with skills that will remain useful throughout their careers. This can also help to support students' interest and the need to balance between cutting-edge neural NLP techniques and traditional statistical techniques. In this paper, we discuss the use of co-creational methods to enable students to explore the subject of natural language processing alongside the teacher, acting as subject matter expert, in a manner that co-creates the learning material.

Such a style of teaching provides several key benefits by encouraging students to engage in hands-on examples of dealing with NLP challenges. It brings diverse perspectives into the classroom, representing the diversity of backgrounds and also reflecting the interdisciplinary nature of natural language processing. Co-creational teaching is a form of *active learning* (Felder and Brent, 2009) that has been shown to improve the retention of knowledge and deepen the comprehension in the subject area. This is achieved through activities where the teacher and student work together in group discussions, peer teaching and project-based learning activities. In a co-creational teaching environment, students provide feedback to each other and to the instructor throughout the learning process, which further leads to more effective learning outcomes. As NLP is a rapidly evolving field with new techniques emerging rapidly, this teaching methodology encourages experimentation and the sharing of findings with peers and teachers. In this way, such a teaching methodology builds a community within the classroom where everyone feels valued and encouraged to participate actively.

In this paper, we will discuss co-creational methods and how they can be applied to teaching natural language processing in higher education. These methods will act as an illustrative guide for other teachers applying these methodologies. We will also consider the challenge of evaluating students in such a co-creational environment, which has become a major issue in higher education due to the increasing adoption of generative AI technologies by students. We will demonstrate how these were applied in teaching a class of about fifty MSc students in a University of Galway course. Finally, we will reflect and discuss on the promise of co-creational teaching and how this can be applied across other settings in higher education.

2 Methods

Student participation in teaching has been described as a ladder (Martens et al., 2019) from

Proceedings of the Sixth Workshop on Teaching NLP, pages 33–42
August 15, 2024

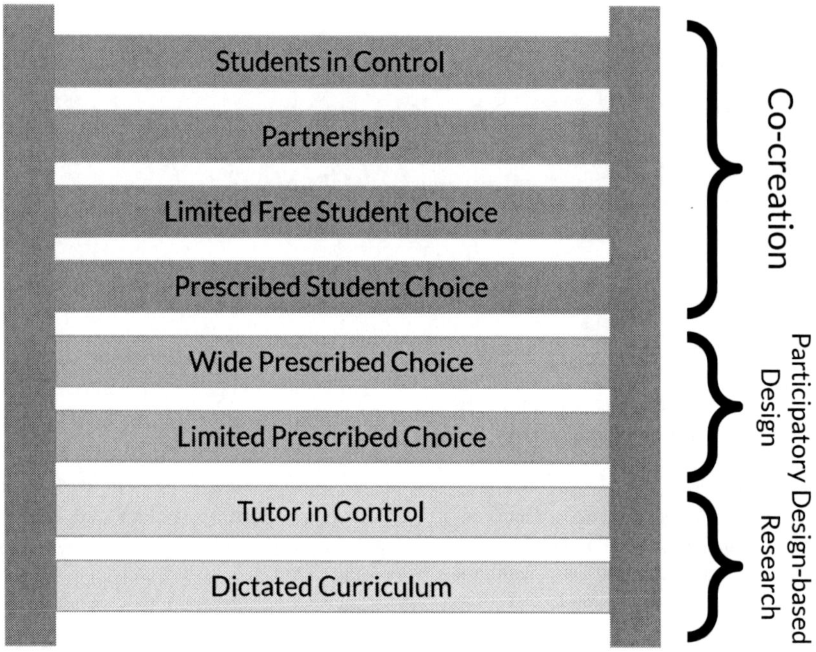

Figure 1: Ladder of student participation as model from Martens et al. (2019) and Bovill and Bulley (2011)

a fully dictated curriculum up to the level of students being fully in control as described in Figure 1. The ladder proposes a number of levels of student engagement:

Dictated Curriculum This is a traditional model of lecturing where the teacher dictates all content in the course

Tutor in control Students may be involved in a limited way, for example through quizzes or discussion groups, but the teacher retains full control over the content of the course

Limited Prescribed Choice In this case, the students can make some choices over the content of the course, however these are from a limited set of options provided by the teachers

Wide Prescribed Choice Similar to the above case, however in this model the teacher provides a wide range of options for the students to choose from.

Prescribed Student Choice Here the students are free to choose their own content, however, the teacher still has editorial control over the content.

Limited Free Student Choice Some areas of the content of a course are created without the teacher's control, while other areas are still at lower levels of this ladder

Partnership In this case, all areas of the course are created by discussion and negotiation between the teachers and the students

Student Control The teacher has no control over the curriculum and all areas are selected by the students

These levels describe a transition from a traditional lecture model of teaching towards full student control. As more control is given to the students, this will encourage more active participation and thus more engagement and better learning outcomes (Martens et al., 2019). However, as the teacher's control is reduced it becomes harder to ensure that the curriculum is appropriate and topical and can be assessed effectively in the context of a university degree. We will now look at the methodologies that can be applied to teaching natural language processing and specific constraints or opportunities with this subject matter.

2.1 Co-design of Curriculum

Natural language processing is a rapidly changing area and the transition of knowledge from initial research proposals to teachable material in the classroom is very short. Further, due to the wide coverage in the media and societal impacts of natural language processing research, I have observed that students are often highly knowledgeable about the subject area. As an example of this, a term like 'language models' has moved in the last few years from a term that was not familiar to many NLP researchers into a term that is now widely discussed in the media[1]. Due to the popularity and rapid speed of change of the subject area, natural language processing is an area that can benefit from the co-creational design of curricula.

There are a number of ways that students can be involved in the creation of a curriculum. Involving students from the initial stages is vital and this could be done by creating a pre-course survey that students could complete ahead of starting the course and could be administered through a learning management system. The first lecture within a course should be used to discuss the topics that could be chosen for the course and brainstorm and design the course syllabus. This provides students with opportunities to suggest topics, resources, projects, and assignments that align with their interests and career goals. Such a process can often be dominated by the most enthusiastic and motivated students in the class and thus in order to represent the class and to provide support for non-neurotypical students, asynchronous methods of feedback can also be implemented. One way of doing this is to create a poll that allows students to vote on the topics that will be covered as part of the course. This poll can be structured by the lecturer such that fundamental introductory material is covered earlier in the course.

Once, the curriculum of the course has been decided it is vital that this does not become fixed, as the students will learn more about natural language processing during the course and so their preferences will update with their learning. The teacher should create mechanisms for ongoing feedback throughout the course, such as anonymous surveys after each module or regular class discussions where students can voice their opinions and suggestions for improvement. Finally, this process should be repeated for every instance of the course in order to remain flexible and open to incorporating changes based on student feedback and evolving trends in the field of NLP. This can result in a curriculum that is dynamic and responsive to the needs of students and the rapidly changing landscape of NLP technology.

A key method for achieving this is *backwards design* (Wiggins and McTighe, 2005), where the students and teacher work together to identify desired learning outcomes and thus ensure that the educational goals align with the needs and interests of the learners. Throughout the course, it is important to continuously gather feedback from students by encouraging open communication and being flexible.

2.2 Peer Teaching

In order to achieve co-creational teaching, the teaching should move from a model where the lecturer leads all the content. In this way, the teaching methodology is similar to flipped classroom (Bergmann and Sams, 2012) approaches. Teaching through a flipped classroom generally leads students to score higher on both general and critical thinking exams (Talley and Scherer, 2013; Missildine et al., 2013; Mortensen and Nicholson, 2015). The standard way of delivering a flipped classroom teaching is through videos that the students watch in advance of the class, however, videos are not the only way to achieve this outcome (Uskoković, 2018). For a topic such as natural language processing, there is already a large amount of material available on sites such as YouTube and in many cases, this is of higher quality and more instructive than material that could be developed by a single lecturer. Thus, it is a great idea to incorporate this material in combination with material developed by the lecturer. Although, it is important to note that videos on YouTube often vary substantially in terms of the length and the assumed background knowledge of the viewers.

Further to enable a truly co-creational approach to teaching, the content to be taught should be developed in collaboration and ideally even by the students. In this way, the students achieve ownership over the material and gain a deeper understanding of the material. This *jigsaw technique* (Aronson et al., 1978) divides the content into smaller parts with each part assigned to a different group of students. In this way, each group becomes an expert on a part of the topic and can teach this to the overall group.

[1]According to OpenAlex, 8.5% of papers that mentioned 'natural language processing' also mentioned 'language models' in 2003, by 2023 this had increased to 28.7%. Google n-gram reports a decline in the usage of the term 'language model' during the period 2005-2014

A particular challenge with this kind of teaching is that students can be unwilling to engage with this kind of teaching. As such, it is often the case that students are more keen to contribute in a textual form rather than in front of the class (Uskoković, 2018). Thus, the topic can be presented by each student developing a slide summarising the main ideas of the topic and in this way providing an opportunity for students to take ownership of their learning.

2.3 Group Work

Group work is one of the most important methods for enabling co-creational learning as groups by their nature involve students teaching each other and developing educational material. However, simply assigning students to groups and assigning a traditional project to them does not necessarily engender positive co-creational teaching outcomes. Instead, the teacher must develop a culture that encourages this form of co-creational teaching. One way to achieve this is through *controversy theory* which "posits that when students are confronted with opposing points of view, ... [it] results in more refined and thoughtful conclusions" (Johnson et al., 1998). In the case of cutting-edge fields such as natural language processing, there is plenty of room to discuss opposing approaches to tasks and the merits of different methods (e.g., LSTMs vs transformers). Other ways in which the group work can be structured for better outcomes include providing a joint reward for the group alongside an individual score and defining complementary roles within the group so that each student is clear about what they will achieve in the group. In this way, the problem of *social loafing* (Karau and Williams, 1993) (where one or more students in the group make little contribution) can be minimised as each student is responsible for a part of the project and thus the overall success of the project. Another idea can be to make sure that each student has to explain what they have worked on and learned to the other students and require this in the assessment of the group project.

While the students can be largely autonomous in the design and implementation of the group work, the role of the teacher is vital in setting the scope and in ensuring the effectiveness of such a project. For group work, Nokes-Malach et al. (2015) propose a theory of the *Zone of Proximal Facilitation* (ZPF), which hypothesises that collaborative success depends on the relation between the task's complexity and competence of the group and individuals. That is, if the task is so simple, that an individual in the group could do it by themselves, then group learning is unlikely to be effective. Conversely, if the task has too much *cognitive load* (Kirschner, 2002) for the whole group then the task will fail. As such, it is important that the teacher can orchestrate the task and intervene appropriately. This can be achieved by a specific orchestration tool, such as the one developed by Lawrence and Mercier (2019), which would allow the teacher to examine the progress of each group. However, for more open-ended co-creational projects a simpler method such as a weekly journal entry would be of value. Further, it is important that when the teacher intervenes in the work of the group this provides concrete help to the group and is not simply an interruption of the group's work. As such, teachers must carefully review the orchestration and or journal to identify problems in the group work.

Working in groups is one of the most effective ways to promote active learning and it has been shown that cooperative learning promotes higher individual learning outcomes (Johnson et al., 1998). In particular, solving problems collaboratively increases engagement in STEM subjects (Freeman et al., 2014)[2].

2.4 Disadvantages

While there are many advantages to this approach, there are some drawbacks to this approach. Firstly, these methods require a more spontaneous and dynamic approach to scheduling than would be required in a traditional course. This can clash with timetabling constraints at the institution and also make advanced planning more difficult, for example, with respect to exam questions. This may pose challenges for students, especially those from non-neurotypical backgrounds, who are more comfortable with planned lecture content. Secondly, the role of the lecturer is redefined in a way that changes the lecturer's role. On the one hand, there is less need to prepare formal content, however, on the other hand, content must be prepared anew for each year that this course runs. As such, this kind of teaching may require more work from the

[2] As natural language processing is a subject requiring mathematics and programming, its teaching is more influenced by STEM, although we note that it is often delivered in linguistics departments at some universities

lecturer and certainly requires flexibility in terms of adapting to a new topic. Finally, while these methodologies should lead to more engagement from students, many students will not be engaged and responsive and as such there is a risk that these methods may produce poorer outcomes for less engaged students.

3 Assessment

One specific challenge with co-creational teaching is the assessment of the student work especially when the educational institute will require individual assessment of learners. When much of the work is done in groups, it can be difficult to assess the individual contributions. However, there are also opportunities for peer assessment in such environments to provide feedback beyond what would be possible by the teaching team of a lecture course.

3.1 Individual Assessment

Individual assessment of students is a particular challenge and the rise of generative AI has led to a crisis of academic integrity (Eke, 2023), that is still going on. The nature of teaching natural language processing requires that students interact with large language models and generative AI, as this is at the core of the subject. However, the temptation among students to use such methods for any continuous assessment is great and methods to reliably detect the use of such tools do not exist and may never exist (Dalalah and Dalalah, 2023). As such, many educational institutes are increasing the use of in-person exams to ensure academic integrity is maintained. However, these methods as well as being stressful for students, fail to produce objective assessments (Curzon, 2003) or provide feedback for students. Instead, co-creational methods would involve the students in the design of assessment materials and in the setting of goals that demonstrate learning. As such, continuous assessment should remain an important part of teaching and it is important that we find ways to continue this in the era of generative AI, including by allowing students to use these systems. For example, by structuring the assessment around the activities in the classroom, rather than essays or survey articles written separately, students must connect the assessment with their learning.

Some specific challenges that may be encountered are the requirements from professional bodies that certify courses, which may put certain restrictions on the way a course can be evaluated and these can make it hard to apply co-creational teaching methodologies. Further, the exam timetable of the institute may require that an exam is submitted before the curriculum has been fully developed in collaboration with the students, and this may also complicate the development of assessment material for the course.

3.2 Peer Assessment

An alternative to traditional, individual assessment that should be applied, as much as possible, to teaching is peer assessment. This model provides for a highly interactive method of assessment (Kollar and Fischer, 2010), that provides feedback and increases engagement with the material. It is important that the teacher scaffolds this correctly so that students gain valuable opportunities to learn from and support each other. Clear assessment that aligns with the learning objectives and expectations of the assignment or activity should be defined and, where possible, students should be given guidance on how to give constructive feedback to minimize bias and promote fairness. These guidelines should emphasize the importance of providing both strengths and areas for improvement, and encourage students to offer suggestions for how their peers can enhance their work. This can even be incorporated into the grading process such that students receive marks not only based on the feedback from their peers but also on the feedback they provide. The teachers' role is also important and they must follow up with students after the peer assessment process to discuss the feedback they received, address any questions or concerns they may have, and provide additional support or guidance as needed.

4 Experience

We applied these methods of co-creational teaching to a lecture course on 'Advanced Topics in Natural Language Processing' (CT5121) taught at the University of Galway in the second semester of the academic year 2023/24. Students had already taken a one-semester introductory course on natural language processing and so had a broad familiarity with the area and this helped in terms of choosing topics for the course. The course was taken by 47 students in MSc programmes on Artificial Intelligence, Data Analytics and Cybersecurity over the course of 12 weeks. These students were mainly

1. Machine Learning for NLP
2. Recurrent Neural Networks
3. Transformers
4. Zero-shot/few-shot Learning
5. Multimodal NLP
6. Named Entity Recognition
7. Question Answering
8. Recommender Systems
9. Machine Translation
10. Evaluation of Machine Translation

Figure 2: The syllabus developed in co-creation with students in the CT5121 course

graduates of computer science and other STEM programmes and were predominantly international students. The course was delivered through flipped classroom lectures, where the lecturer and the students worked together to define topics, and through open-ended group projects.

The syllabus was defined through discussions with the class. The lecturer suggested an initial list of topics that were then discussed in the class and updated based on student feedback. The lecturer organised these into three classes of theories (e.g., 'Recurrent Neural Networks'), methodologies (e.g., 'Named Entity Recognition') and applications (e.g., 'Question Answering') and the polls initially contained only theoretical topics and the later polls introduced more methodology and application topics and removed theoretical topics (based on receiving fewer votes in the earlier polls). The topics for each week were presented to the class and discussed and this in a few instances led to updates in the topics from the selection chosen by the lecturer. No specific material was provided to help choose the topics, but the lecturer guided the class discussion of the topics to encourage new suggestions. The class suggested a number of topics and these were then put to the class through an open vote on the learning management system Blackboard. The final resulting syllabus is shown in Figure 2, and this process was repeated for the first five weeks of the semester[3], and the final five topics were fixed by a single poll. This was due to constraints on the assessment of the material by means of a written exam. Each lecture was prepared by the teacher finding appropriate video material on YouTube, as well as writing some outline notes on GitHub [4]. The students were instructed to review these materials before the lecture and the classes were then structured around open discussion and interactive exercises on the topics. For example, in one lecture the students were divided into four groups and competed to implement various few-shot and zero-shot methodologies on a single dataset.

The other main component of the course was an open project, that the students completed in groups of their own choosing, with groups ranging in size from one to five participants. The students discussed these projects with the teaching team and this feedback was taken by the teaching team and used to adjust the content continuously throughout the semester. An end-of-module survey was deployed through the learning management system, however, participation was poor and this did not provide any useful information on the success of the teaching methodology. The students were encouraged to find their own topics and to structure their own learning. The project work was assessed by two written essays and a final presentation. The two written assignments were approximately 1,000-1,200 words and they were marked by the primary lecturer, with feedback given to the students. A flexible policy was applied to the submission deadline for these assignments and the majority of the class submitted these assignments later than would be planned in order to provide constructive feedback. The presentation was made to the lecturer and two teaching assistants and consisted of a 10-minute presentation or demo, as the groups saw fit, the mark was agreed between the lecturer and teaching assistants. Groups were encouraged to discuss among themselves and with other groups and provide feedback. Finally, the course had a final written exam, due to institutional requirements.

4.1 Lessons learned

Overall, the course received strong positive feedback in terms of student engagement and the overall outcomes of the students were strong in the written exam, showing that they had benefited from choosing their own teaching and the active learn-

[3] Due to public holidays in Ireland, two lectures were cancelled during the semester

[4] https://github.com/jmccrae/2024-CT5121

ing provided through the course. Still, there were some issues, especially related to the engagement of students with the material that will be improved in future iterations of the course. Firstly, from the lecture sessions, it was clear that the video material was not generally being watched by students ahead of the lectures. This may in part be due to the content being available on another platform than our learning management system and the variability in the length of the material selected. Further, feedback throughout the course was not taken advantage of by many students, who only engaged with the project near deadlines. This was particularly notable in the peer group assessment which was very infrequently used. In future instances of this course, a weekly journal and formal marks being assigned by peer assessment will encourage more engagement. Finally, several students chose to work in groups of one (e.g., alone), and these students were much less engaged with the teaching, so in future groups of two will be the minimum group size. In summary, this experience focused on the techniques of co-designing the curriculum and the use of group work and did not apply some of the peer teaching techniques discussed above, but this will be a goal for future instances of this course. Student choice, in this case, was limited but free in the topics, however, students in most cases accepted the lecturer's suggestions regarding topics leading to a curriculum that was more prescribed, yet still quite different than the curriculum that would have been chosen by the lecturer. The next instance of the course will focus on improving peer instruction and applying some of the techniques discussed in this paper.

5 Discussion

It has been widely concluded that the traditional lecture is the least effective way to communicate with learners (Laurillard, 2013; Bligh, 1985). For this reason, there has been an increasing focus on active learning approaches which can processes and outcomes in higher education (Kuh, 2008). Further, it has been noted that students learn best when they become their own teachers (Hattie, 2008) and this is one of the key objectives of co-creational teaching and learning.

A number of methods have been proposed to encourage student participation in teaching. Firstly, *design-based research* is a methodology that involves iterative cycles of design and implementation emphasizing co-design and co-implementation with stakeholders. This represents the lower rungs of the co-creation ladder as depicted in Figure 1. *Participatory design* (Scheer et al., 2012) involves students to a higher degree, where they play a central role in defining the curriculum. *Co-creation* involves educators and learners working as equal partners in the education process to create learning experiences that meet the needs of all participants. All three terms have been used for active collaborative learning practices but differ in the focus and degree of participation of the students in their learning. In fact, methods that focus on participation are not novel and can be seen in the dialogic methods of Aristotle or the progressive education movement of the late 19th and early 20th century (Dewey, 1916)

One of the key goals of co-creational learning is to generate critical thinkers (Freire, 2000) who take responsibility for their own learning (hooks, 2014). As such co-creational teaching empowers students to collaborate with their teachers. However, co-creation is an open-ended model requiring teachers to give up "complete creative control" (Uskoković, 2018). This can be challenging and can be seen as almost 'counter-cultural' (Cook-Sather et al., 2014) in modern higher education environments. The goal of teaching in this manner is to promote equality and partnership between lecturers and students. In this way, it is important to see the teachers as learners as well, and in fact, the syllabus selected by the students in the course described above went beyond the lecturer's (and lead author of this article's) expertise in several areas of natural language processing. As such co-creational teaching reframes education where very often the students are seen as problems to solved (Sambell et al., 2012), into a space where equality is natural. However, it is important to understand that student participation does not replace teachers' expertise (Breen and Littlejohn, 2000), and there is naturally an imbalance of knowledge between the lecturer, who is often a subject matter expert, and the students who have limited knowledge of the subject area. As such, the teacher should retain executive control and work with the students to direct them into areas that are interesting and valuable to study. Finally, it is important to note that co-creational methods can often threaten students as well (Bovill et al., 2011), as it breaks from the usual passive consumption of material that they have experienced in their studies so far. As such, this can lead to poorer engagement for some students who see active and collaborative methods as merely extra effort. It is important to make the benefits of such teaching methods clear to students and not to compel any students to take part in these methods. Further, many aspects of co-creational teaching can be conducted in liminal spaces that do not affect the main delivery of teaching but support the teaching. The results of this can lead to student testimonies such as "I am finding myself being more understanding of my professor's struggles" (Bovill et al., 2011), illustrating the value of this approach.

In the particular context of natural language processing, the role of co-creation is important as this is a subject for which there is wide interest and thus a wide amount of educational information available on the web. As such, to connect with the 'YouTube Google-eyed generation' (Ashraf, 2009), it is important to situate the teaching within this context and thus to help students find their ways to valuable material. We find that students will consult YouTube anyway and this can lead to conflicts with attempts to impose a top-down curriculum. Further, providing students with suitable recorded material as well as summary notes can help substantially with their learning of the topic.

Finally, students with Autistic Spectrum Disorders (ASD) and other neurodivergent traits are particularly attracted to STEM subjects (Wei et al., 2013) and can be expected to be seen in higher proportions in classrooms teaching natural language processing. Many of the characteristics of people with ASD can be in conflict with the collaborative and participatory methods proposed in this paper. In particular, many students with ASD have issues with personal interaction and do not like learning through videos and social situations. As such, it is also important to allow these students to interact through text reports or prepared material where possible. Further, clear guidance and instruction (Stuurman et al., 2019) are vital to ensure that all members of a class understand the task as some students do not learn well by examples. In group work, which is a key method of co-creational teaching, students with ASD can perform well by focusing on specific tasks (Wareham and Sonne, 2008), especially those that focus on details such as testing. Conversely, the co-creational method can act as a key method for involving students with ASD in the classroom, by allowing them input over the structure of the programme, including not just only the curriculum but also the teaching methods, and by assisting in the development of collaboration guidelines that can outline how all students interact in the course of their study of natural language processing.

6 Conclusion

This paper has presented the co-creational methodology for teaching and focused on how it can be applied to the teaching of natural language processing in a higher education setting. We defined three key pillars of teaching: curriculum co-design, peer teaching and group work and showed how partnership with students can be achieved through these methods. We also considered how student performance can be evaluated using such approaches, especially in the current academic integrity crisis. This approach was tested in an MSc course and the results showed good engagement, with several key areas that can be improved. We also considered how these approaches can be adapted to students in particular those with neurodiversity.

Limitations

This work focuses on a teaching methodology and is primarily a theoretical work. This work has only been evaluated in a single setting and further application of this methodology and quantitative analysis would support this work.

Ethics Statement

The anonymity of all students has been preserved in this report. We do not see any other ethical issues with this work

Acknowledgements

This work has been supported by Science Foundation Ireland under Grant Number SFI/12/RC/2289_P2 Insight_2, Insight SFI Centre for Data Analytics and the ADAPT Centre for Digital Content Technology (grant number 13/RC/2106 P2).

References

Elliot Aronson et al. 1978. *The jigsaw classroom.* Sage.

Bill Ashraf. 2009. Teaching the Google-eyed YouTube generation. *Education+ Training*, 51(5/6):343–352.

Jonathan Bergmann and Aaron Sams. 2012. *Flip your classroom: Reach every student in every class every day*. International Society for Technology in Education.

Donald Bligh. 1985. What's the use of lectures? *Journal of Geography in Higher Education*, 9(1):105–106.

Catherine Bovill and Cathy J Bulley. 2011. A model of active student participation in curriculum design: exploring desirability and possibility. In C. Rust, editor, *Improving Student Learning (ISL) 18: Global Theories and Local Practices: Institutional, Disciplinary and Cultural Variations*, pages 176–188. Oxford Brookes University: Oxford Centre for Staff and Learning Development.

Catherine Bovill, Alison Cook-Sather, and Peter Felten. 2011. Students as co-creators of teaching approaches, course design, and curricula: implications for academic developers. *International Journal for Academic Development*, 16(2):133–145.

Michael P Breen and Andrew Littlejohn. 2000. *Classroom decision-making: Negotiation and process syllabuses in practice*. Cambridge University Press.

Alison Cook-Sather, Catherine Bovill, and Peter Felten. 2014. *Engaging students as partners in learning and teaching: A guide for faculty*. John Wiley & Sons.

Leslie Basil Curzon. 2003. *Teaching in further education: An outline of principles and practice*. A&C Black.

Doraid Dalalah and Osama MA Dalalah. 2023. The false positives and false negatives of generative AI detection tools in education and academic research: The case of ChatGPT. *The International Journal of Management Education*, 21(2):100822.

John Dewey. 1916. *Democracy and Education: An Introduction to the Philosophy of Education*. Macmillan.

Damian Okaibedi Eke. 2023. ChatGPT and the rise of generative AI: Threat to academic integrity? *Journal of Responsible Technology*, 13:100060.

Richard M Felder and Rebecca Brent. 2009. Active learning: An introduction. *ASQ Higher Education Brief*, 2(4):1–5.

Scott Freeman, Sarah L Eddy, Miles McDonough, Michelle K Smith, Nnadozie Okoroafor, Hannah Jordt, and Mary Pat Wenderoth. 2014. Active learning increases student performance in science, engineering, and mathematics. *Proceedings of the national academy of sciences*, 111(23):8410–8415.

Paulo Freire. 2000. *Pedagogy of the oppressed*. Bloomsbury. 30th Anniversary Edition.

John Hattie. 2008. *Visible learning: A synthesis of over 800 meta-analyses relating to achievement*. Routledge.

bell hooks. 2014. *Teaching to transgress*. Routledge.

David W Johnson, Roger T Johnson, and Karl A Smith. 1998. Cooperative learning returns to college what evidence is there that it works? *Change: the magazine of higher learning*, 30(4):26–35.

Steven J Karau and Kipling D Williams. 1993. Social loafing: A meta-analytic review and theoretical integration. *Journal of personality and social psychology*, 65(4):681.

Paul A Kirschner. 2002. Cognitive load theory: Implications of cognitive load theory on the design of learning.

Ingo Kollar and Frank Fischer. 2010. Peer assessment as collaborative learning: A cognitive perspective. *Learning and instruction*, 20(4):344–348.

George D Kuh. 2008. High-impact educational practices. *Peer Review*, 10(4):30–31.

Diana Laurillard. 2013. *Rethinking university teaching: A conversational framework for the effective use of learning technologies*. Routledge.

LuEttaMae Lawrence and Emma Mercier. 2019. Co-design of an orchestration tool: Supporting engineering teaching assistants as they facilitate collaborative learning. *Interaction Design and Architecture*, 42:111.

Samantha E Martens, Stephanie NE Meeuwissen, Diana HJM Dolmans, Catherine Bovill, and Karen D Könings. 2019. Student participation in the design of learning and teaching: Disentangling the terminology and approaches. *Medical teacher*, 41(10):1203–1205.

Kathy Missildine, Rebecca Fountain, Lynn Summers, and Kevin Gosselin. 2013. Flipping the classroom to improve student performance and satisfaction. *Journal of Nursing Education*, 52(10):597–599.

Christopher J Mortensen and Angie M Nicholson. 2015. The flipped classroom stimulates greater learning and is a modern 21st century approach to teaching today's undergraduates. *Journal of animal science*, 93(7):3722–3731.

Timothy J Nokes-Malach, J Elizabeth Richey, and Soniya Gadgil. 2015. When is it better to learn together? insights from research on collaborative learning. *Educational Psychology Review*, 27:645–656.

Kay Sambell, Liz McDowell, and Catherine Montgomery. 2012. *Assessment for learning in higher education*. Routledge.

Andrea Scheer, Christine Noweski, and Christoph Meinel. 2012. Transforming constructivist learning into action: Design thinking in education. *Design and Technology Education*, 17(3):8–19.

Sylvia Stuurman, Harrie JM Passier, Frédérique Geven, and Erik Barendsen. 2019. Autism: Implications for inclusive education with respect to software engineering. In *Proceedings of the 8th Computer Science Education Research Conference*, pages 15–25.

Cheryl P Talley and Stephen Scherer. 2013. The enhanced flipped classroom: Increasing academic performance with student-recorded lectures and practice testing in a "flipped" STEM course. *Journal of Negro Education*, 82(3):339–347.

Vuk Uskoković. 2018. Flipping the flipped: the co-creational classroom. *Research and Practice in Technology Enhanced Learning*, 13(1):11.

Jonathan Wareham and Thorkil Sonne. 2008. Harnessing the power of autism spectrum disorder. *Innovations*, 3(1):11–27.

Xin Wei, Jennifer W Yu, Paul Shattuck, Mary McCracken, and Jose Blackorby. 2013. Science, technology, engineering, and mathematics (STEM) participation among college students with an autism spectrum disorder. *Journal of autism and developmental disorders*, 43:1539–1546.

Grant P Wiggins and Jay McTighe. 2005. *Understanding by design*. ASCD.

Collaborative Development of Modular Open Source Educational Resources for Natural Language Processing

Matthias Aßenmacher[1,2], Andreas Stephan[3,4], Leonie Weissweiler[2,5], Erion Çano[3,6], Ingo Ziegler[5,7], Marwin Härttrich[5], Bernd Bischl[1,2], Benjamin Roth[3], Christian Heumann[1], Hinrich Schütze[2,5]

[1]Department of Statistics, LMU Munich, [2]Munich Center for Machine Learning (MCML),
[3]Faculty of Computer Science, University of Vienna,
[4]UniVie Doctoral School Computer Science, Vienna, Austria,
[5]Center for Information and Language Processing (CIS), LMU Munich,
[6]Department of Computer Science, Paderborn University,
[7]Department of Computer Science, University of Copenhagen

Correspondence: matthias@stat.uni-muenchen.de

Abstract

In this work, we present a collaboratively and continuously developed open-source educational resource (OSER) for teaching natural language processing at two different universities. We shed light on the principles we followed for the initial design of the course and the rationale for ongoing developments, followed by a reflection on the inter-university collaboration for designing and maintaining teaching material. When reflecting on the latter, we explicitly emphasize the considerations that need to be made when facing heterogeneous groups and when having to accommodate multiple examination regulations within one single course framework. Relying on the fundamental principles of OSER developments as defined by Bothmann et al. (2023) proved to be an important guideline during this process. The final part pertains to open-sourcing our teaching material, coping with the increasing speed of developments in the field, and integrating the course digitally, also addressing conflicting priorities and challenges we are currently facing.

1 Introduction

The rapid acceleration of developments in natural language processing (NLP) research, starting with the introduction of the Transformer (Vaswani et al., 2017) in 2017, also poses a challenge to designing appropriate curricula for formal education in this area. Numerous longstanding paradigms have been replaced by new technologies enabled by a new class of (autoregressive) large language models (LLM; OpenAI, 2022, 2023; Anil et al., 2023; Touvron et al., 2023; AI@Meta, 2024) alongside massively increased computational capacities. The curriculum of deep learning (DL) courses for NLP before 2017 mostly consisted of teaching different types of word embedding models (e.g. Mikolov et al., 2013; Pennington et al., 2014; Bojanowski et al., 2017) as building blocks within specialized neural network architectures. This often pertained to employing and tuning recurrent neural networks (RNN) for solving various kinds of token- or sequence-level tasks. With the advent of transformer-based transfer learning models (Radford et al., 2018; Devlin et al., 2019; Raffel et al., 2020) developments sped up, the field has become a lot more diverse,[1] and hence course curricula require significant updates/enhancements more and more frequently. We believe that collaboration across and within universities (across different faculties and departments) can be one way to combat the resulting challenges. Furthermore, bringing together researchers with multifaceted backgrounds and different levels of seniority for co-creating lecture material can help create a more inclusive course suitable for a broad audience of undergraduate and graduate-level students from various fields.

2 Related work

Open Educational Resources. The number of Massive Open Online Courses has been rapidly increasing over the past decade, be it in machine learning (ML; Ng, 2021; Google, 2023) in general or in NLP specifically. Probably one of the most notable *applied* NLP courses is courtesy of Hugging Face (Hugging Face, 2022). It provides a hands-on introduction to the state-of-the-art (SOTA) software package for NLP, but in doing so it does not discuss the theoretical foundations in much detail. Other popular and very well-taught courses,

[1]This refers to both the kind of problem statements tackled with NLP technology and the academic audience of students and researchers interested in taking NLP-related courses.

Proceedings of the Sixth Workshop on Teaching NLP, pages 43–53
August 15, 2024

like e.g. the Stanford CS224N lecture (Stanford NLP Group, 2024) or the `deeplearning.ai` NLP course (DeepLearning.AI, 2023) provide great theoretical (and applied) introductions to NLP, but are not truly *open source*: Neither do any of these courses provide open and modifiable sources of their lectures, nor do they explicitly specify the license(s) under which their material is released. The latter even requires registering at a platform and only provides the material as videos, not even releasing versions of their lecture material as PDFs. So while these courses can be considered open, they are unfortunately not fully *open-source* (Bothmann et al., 2023).

Open *Source* Educational Resources. According to Bothmann et al. (2023), open source educational resources (OSER) are characterized by a set of core principles (which also served as guidelines for the development of our course) motivated by best practices from open source software development. This is very well reflected in the following principles:

- Develop course material collaboratively.
- Make your sources open and modifiable and use open licenses.
- Release well-defined versions and maintain change logs.

Other principles Bothmann et al. (2023) define in their work are more focussed on pedagogical aspects and on the goal of enabling as many people as possible to learn from the developed material in their own way and at their own speed:

- Modularization: Structure the material in small chunks and disentangle theory and implementation
- Define prerequisites and learning goals
- Foster self-regulated learning and enable feedback from everyone

A notable NLP OSER is the course created for the software library *spaCy* (Montani, 2019), where developers comply with most of the OSER principles. A drawback of this course, however, is its high entanglements with one specific software library (spaCy), severely limiting the modular reuse of the resources. Further, "Deep Learning for Coders with Fastai and PyTorch" (Howard and Gugger, 2020) presents a fully open-source and modifiable online course (fast.ai, 2020) with extensive coverage of various DL applications, it focuses on NLP in just one chapter. Consequently, it falls short of delivering the comprehensive depth expected from a university-level NLP lecture series.

Course creation: Machine Learning vs. NLP. Further challenges going along with working on creating/teaching courses for NLP compared to ML pertain to the rapid speed of developments. In typical ML courses, there is a more or less agreed-upon set of topics being taught in most of the introductory/basic courses, including supervised learning methods (classification/regression), unsupervised learning, tree-based methods as well as approaches for hyperparameter tuning or resampling strategies. Building upon this foundation, various special topics such as, e.g., boosting, gaussian processes, or even neural networks can be flexibly added/exchanged, depending on the focus of the respective target audience or tailored to a certain program of studies. A prime example is the "Introduction to Machine Learning (I2ML)" course by Bischl et al. (2022), a collection of three ML courses taught at LMU Munich. The creators rely on the stable content of their undergraduate-level course, build up two M.Sc. level courses on top of this foundation, and open-source everything on one central platform.[2] This course perfectly shows the stability of the fundamentals for teaching ML while simultaneously stressing the modular extensions one can build upon these fundamentals. In NLP, however, the fundamentals are to some extent subject to change, since new training techniques and new model capabilities are constantly emerging, given the fluid fast-moving nature of the field. In the subsequent chapters, we will thus describe the rationale behind our design choices, try to make the underlying thought processes transparent, and illustrate the resulting OSER we created.

3 Course Design Principles

The design of our OSER relies on a set of principles laid out in greater detail in the following subchapters: First, we want the course to be created as a modular system allowing every partnering institution to adjust the teaching material to their specific needs and to change it between different iterations of the course. This encompasses a set of *core modules* (e.g. the Transformer) as well as a multitude

[2] `https://slds-lmu.github.io/i2ml/`

of more elaborated, rather optional, and audience-specific modules (e.g. Multilinguality). Second, we intend to provide the students with a set of challenging (programming) assignments while trying to balance the trade-off of the following question: What are longstanding and established concepts that need to be taught to students, and which are just of short-term importance?

Additionally, we want the students to be well-prepared for our course and to have the right expectations: Figure 1 shows our "Module 0", directing the students to several core chapters of the I2ML course (Bischl et al., 2022) for getting familiar with the machine learning basics.

3.1 Modularity of Teaching Material

Bringing together different universities or study programs for a joint teaching project inherently requires building a modular system. This enables every party involved in this endeavor ("inside use"), as well as everyone else ("outside use") to pick out the parts that are relevant for this specific party in specific situations. For the inside use, we further define a set of *core modules* taught at every institution allowing for sharing the work when creating exams. This most likely results in (a) more comparable examinations ensuring (b) a higher quality of the exam questions while (c) gaining time efficiency during the creation of the exams. The second part of the *optional modules* pertains to topics that are either just targeted at a specific subgroup of the target audience or that are considered "hot topics" that need(ed) to be addressed at a certain point in time. This leads to a larger and more stable set of core modules, while the pool of optional ones is (a) smaller (but potentially growing over time) and (b) more fluid than the former (some modules might be deprecated over time). The second form of modularity pertains to disentangling theoretical concepts and implementation details (Bothmann et al., 2023). The slide sets we provide the audience with contain explanations and mathematical formulas, but rarely Python code. All programming-related tasks and explanations are outsourced to the programming assignments and the corresponding exercise sessions (cf. Sec. 3.3). This modular composition allows the audience to also use our slides alongside other, more software-centric tutorials (e.g. Hugging Face, 2022), to extract suitable parts for combining it with their own teaching material (without having to disentangle it with our code chunks or similar), and helps us in maintaining the material as we do not run into problems with dependencies or debugging ("Do not use literate programming systems everywhere", Bothmann et al., 2023).

3.2 Lecture Content

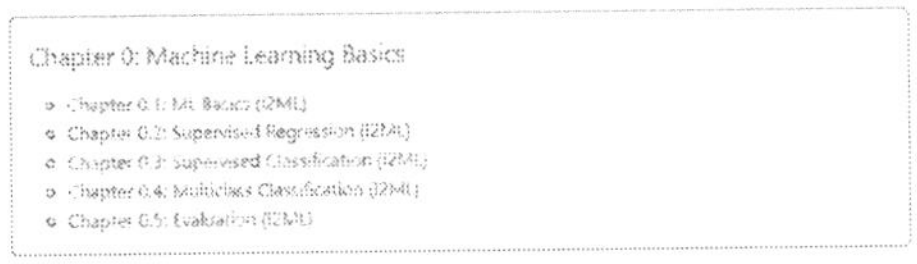

Figure 1: Referencing the prerequisites for the course.

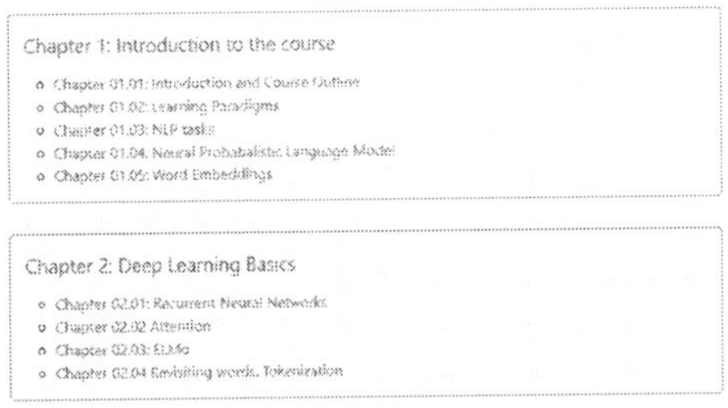

Figure 2: First lecture block – Providing the heterogenous target group with a unified foundation.

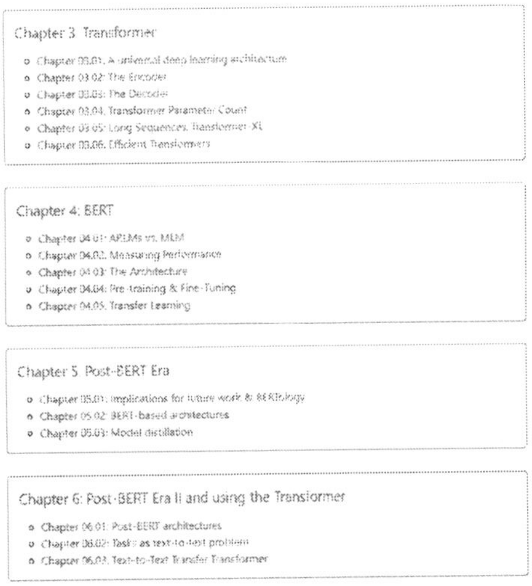

Figure 3: Second lecture block – Introducing important conceptualizations and architectural milestones.

The first block of the lecture material (equivalent to two 90-minute lectures) encompasses two modules for providing the quite heterogenous groups of students (cf. Sec. 4.1) with a unified knowledge base to start with (cf. Fig. 2): First, general NLP-specific topics are introduced before in the second lecture important conceptual topics regarding neural networks are dealt with. Building on this foundation, the next lecture block (cf. Fig. 3; equivalent to four 90-minute lectures) starts by covering the Transformer architecture in-depth since it is the focal methodological topic the students need to understand every tiny detail of. The next module is of similarly central importance, as it introduces BERT as one major cornerstone of the developments leading up to contemporary LLMs. It further deals with important concepts of transfer learning from a birds-eye perspective, the components of pre-training LLMs (objectives, hyperparameters, data), the implications of architectural choices (encoder-only, decoder-only, encoder-decoder), and the (efficient) fine-tuning of such models. The third (and final) central building block of the current version of the lecture is centered around decoder-only LLM architectures (cf. Fig. 4; equivalent to three 90-minute lectures). After having learned how to comprehend *all potential tasks* as a text-to-text problem in the previous block, the students will be introduced to alternative concepts of learning (zero-/few-short learning) before more elaborated alignment techniques (instruction fine-tuning, reinforcement learning from human feedback) are covered.

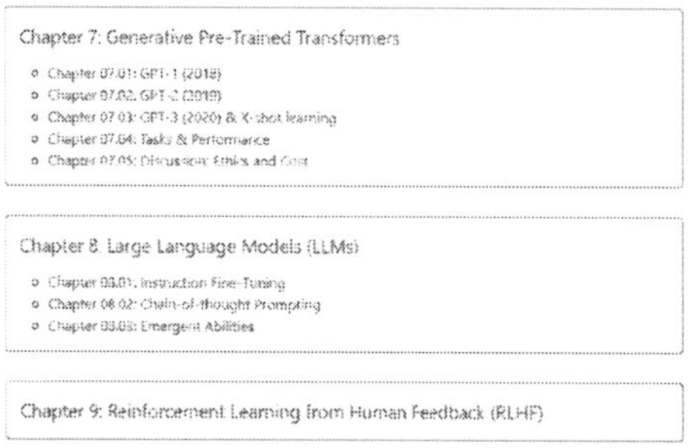

Figure 4: Third lecture block – Discussing the capabilities and the inner workings of contemporary LLMs.

These three central building blocks can be flexibly extended using optional modules based on (a) the needs of the target audience, (b) the fit with the surrounding curriculum of studies, and (c) what is of particular interest based on how current research is developing. The subsequent list of lecture blocks has been employed over the past semesters:

0. *Machine Learning Basics:* Before Module 1 to bring everyone up to speed (if required, cf. Fig. 1).

4. *Multilinguality:* Multilingual alignment techniques for embeddings/pre-trained models, mostly taught at LMU for the computational linguistics (CL) students (cf. Fig. 5).

5. *LLMs in Practice:* Considerations regarding hardware, parameter counts, and scaling (including a guest lecture from industry, cf. Fig. 5).

We will continuously monitor future developments in the field and adjust the course accordingly. This allows us to react flexibly to newly emerging or newly established methods/topics which can be added as further modules whenever we see fit.

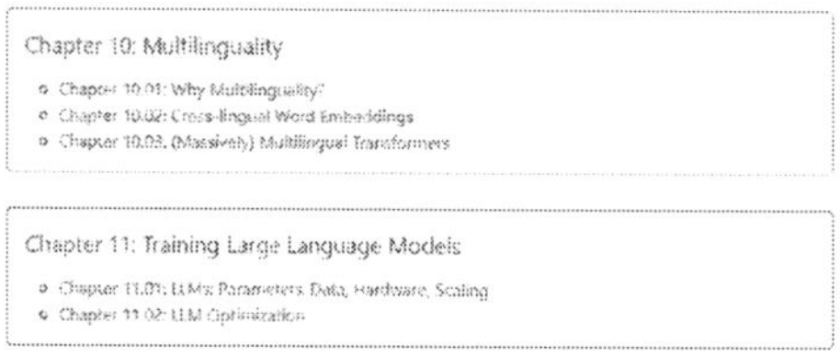

Figure 5: Optional lecture blocks – Multilinguality and further insights into contemporary LLMs.

3.3 Programming Questions

The current design of our programming assignments tries to carefully balance basic understanding, i.e. bringing every student from this heterogeneous group up to speed, against novelty, i.e. conveying (sufficiently) interesting new content that is of interest to the majority of the students. At the same time, the degree of difficulty of the assignments is a further crucial consideration since they partly influence the grading of the students (cf. Sec. 4.2). Trying to get this interplay right, we designed the following five two-week assignments for the iteration in the winter term of 2023.

Assignment 1: Building, Tuning and Evaluating an RNN Model. The goal of the first assignment is to familiarize all the students with the general setup of the training loop for a DL model. We expect the students to be familiar with embeddings and the basic concepts of DL, and with the basic functionalities of Python on a technical side. The intended outcome is that the students become familiar with working with using PyTorch (Paszke et al., 2019) and learn how to set up everything from scratch, so they know what is happening behind the scenes once they start using high-level frameworks like Hugging Face (Wolf et al., 2020) later.

Contentwise, the students are tasked with loading, splitting, and formatting datasets from hosted places, such as Hugging Face, to gain hands-on experience with data preparation. They then learn to build parallelized dataloaders using the PyTorch API to efficiently handle datasets of varying sizes. Following that, students are asked to design a custom RNN model layer-by-layer and to write the training and evaluation processes by hand. This exposes them to the inner workings of PyTorch modules and helps them understand how to connect their own modules to the core "Autograd" functionality. Enhancing their understanding of model evaluation is another goal of this assignment. Consequently, they need to implement a classification metric tracking system and plot and document their results. The assignment provides the class with three hyperparameter configurations intended to produce an underfitted, overfitted, and well-fitted model, lastly prompting them to pinpoint and discuss notable training moments on their plots.

Assignment 2: Building the "Vanilla" Transformer from Scratch. The next important milestone in our curriculum is implementing the vanilla Transformer *from scratch*. We deem this task to be of extremely high didactic importance, as later on students will most likely use the Hugging Face libraries to train or to interact with transformer-based models. Obtaining a proper understanding of the model's inner workings is crucial, as the Transformer itself might be replaced in the future, but in general large, complex models with many hyperparameters are still likely to persist.

Since various well-known teaching-oriented implementations of the vanilla Transformer exist, notably "The Annotated Transformer" (Rush, 2018; Huang et al., 2022) and a chapter of "Deep Learning Notebooks" (Lippe, 2022), we refrain from asking the class to simply implement a working Transformer model. Instead, we provide specific instructions to break down the task into smaller sub-tasks, with clear expectations for intermediate results. This has two key benefits: First, it enables students to identify and debug issues early on, by checking their sub-results against expected outputs and tensor shapes. Second, it encourages students to engage deeply with the paper and code, making it difficult to simply copy from existing online resources. Even if students tried to copy, they would need to make significant changes to fit our instructions, ensuring a contribution to the implementation. To strike a balance between realism and learning value, we fit our assignment requirements into input and output specifications for each module, along with `assert` statements to verify intermediate results in `init` and `forward` methods of each module.

Assignment 3: The Hugging Face Ecosystem. As one central objective of the assignments is to convey hands-on practical knowledge to the students, the third assignment is centered around the Hugging Face ecosystem. The Hugging Face ecosystem has become a de facto standard in the NLP community, providing a unified interface for a wide range of SOTA models and datasets. By working with it, students can gain experience with a powerful tool that simplifies the process of building, training, and distributing NLP models, while facilitating reproducibility and collaboration.

Students were tasked with fine-tuning the encoder-only BERT (Devlin et al., 2019) for classification and the encoder-decoder T5 (Raffel et al., 2020) for text summarization. Through this exercise, students gain hands-on experience with tokenizers, loading, and preparing models from the Hugging Face hub for different tasks. A key focus is on the `Trainer` and its `TrainingArguments` class, where students are supposed to experiment with various techniques to reduce GPU memory usage, including batch size, gradient accumulation steps, gradient checkpointing, and 16-bit floating point data types. Taking it a step further, students are also introduced to the concept of reversing the abstractions provided by Hugging Face, for instance, by inheriting from the `Trainer` class and customizing the loss calculation logic according to our requirements. In the second part, we focus on approaching problems as text-to-text tasks, including the pre-/post-processing steps for summarization. Again, while models might change, implementing the whole pipeline (data-to-model; task description; GPU utilization) is a vital skill for the future.

Assignment 4: Interpretability and Decoding. As the parameter count of NLP models continues to grow, it has become increasingly important to understand the inner workings of these models. Currently, there are many ways to analyze models. The fourth assignment examines the topics of employing a simple interpretability method and investigating decoding strategies, both of which are essential for understanding the models' behavior/biases and improving the trustworthiness of models.

To gain insight into the attention mechanism, students explore the attention patterns of various heads in pre-trained models. By visualizing and comparing the patterns of BERT and GPT-2 (Radford et al., 2019) for the same sentence, students observe how BERT's bidirectional attention differs from GPT-2's left-to-right attention. They then quantify their observations by calculating and visualizing the entropy per head and layer, revealing how individual heads distribute their attention. Next, students implement and calculate importance scores (Michel et al., 2019) per head, visualize their results, and finally use them for pruning, i.e. removing heads below a certain importance score threshold. In the decoding part of the assignment, students load GPT-2 and compare its outputs for a single input prompt using different decoding strategies. They begin by implementing beam search (Vijayakumar et al., 2016) and contrasting it with standard greedy decoding, and then progress to more advanced strategies like top-k (Fan et al., 2018) or top-p (Holtzman et al., 2019) sampling and temperature scaling.

Assignment 5: LLMs and Prompting. Language-to-language is a promising paradigm, likely to persist, as it resonates with human interaction. Therefore, it is central for students to learn how to work with this paradigm. The fifth assignment covers this and showcases key prompting strategies to accomplish various tasks and structured, parseable output formats. Students begin by loading LlaMA-2 (Touvron et al., 2023) and familiarizing themselves with the concept and formatting the system prompt. By modifying the system prompt while keeping the downstream instruction equal, students observe how the model's behavior changes in response to different meta-instructions. Subsequently, students explore zero-shot inference (Radford et al., 2019) and investigate the model performance in a multi-class classification task without structured output. They learn to address the difficulties of parsing errors caused by varying model outputs and format errors, before repeating the same task while employing a batched, JSON input- and output structure. This makes it possible to implement formatting checks and parsing rules to reject certain outputs before encountering unknown outputs. Lastly, the assignment incorporates the few-shot learning paradigm (Brown et al., 2020) by solving a relation extraction problem while enforcing a custom, parseable output style while providing in-context examples in the desired format.

3.4 Grading

Two common approaches to grading coding assignments are automated evaluation through test suites and manual checks. While the benefits of automated test suits are fully automated autonomous testing in little time and certainly unbiased grading, the disadvantages are the requirement of precise task descriptions and little to no variance in allowed outcomes, partially solved or nonexecutable submissions may not be testable or it might require additional effort to define those tests. Manual evaluation, on the other hand, results in time-intensive corrections per submission and can introduce biases during grading. The benefits and disadvantages need to be considered beforehand and should also be considered during the task creation. The optimal approach toward grading depends on the expected number of submissions, the available (human) resources for (a) assignment preparation and (b) correction over the course of the semester, and the probable reuse in future iterations of the course.

Due to our design choice of integrating open-ended interpretations of results and observations, we have opted for a hybrid approach: We leverage the benefits of automated tests for the subset of well-defined tasks with clear expected outcomes while resorting to manual evaluation and grading of the more open-ended parts. This allows us to manually handle cases where the automated tests failed within the second pass. To allow the seamless combination of both grading approaches, textual mistake descriptions alongside their resulting point deductions are collected in one text file per submission. The automated tests log mistakes to this file as predefined textual statements, while mistakes encountered during manual inspection are added in the corresponding format. That way both the final grade of the assignment and the encountered mistakes can be reported back to the student, offering insightful feedback via comments. This allows the student to comprehend the grade and reflect on his/her solution, and misapprehension.

4 Collaboration Across Universities

4.1 Target groups and their prerequisites

The initial target group of the course was third-semester master's students in CL from LMU Munich for whom the compulsory module has been the first touching point with DL. Opening the course to master's students of statistics and data science (Stats+DS) by collaboratively improving and teaching it in 2020 brought in a group with a different background for whom this is contrarily the first touching point with linguistics. Students eligible to take the course at the University of Vienna (UNIVIE) have a multi-faceted background as well: While the majority of the students are enrolled in computer science (CS), there is also a share of students from business analytics in the target group of this course. This leaves us with students that can be (coarsely) categorized into three groups:[3]

- Strong CL background, but not much experience with ML, DL, and programming
- High level of technical and theoretical expertise in ML, DL, and programming, but (presumably) no knowledge about linguistics.
- Some affinity to digital tools and programming, but neither an in-depth formal education in ML/DL nor linguistics.

4.2 Examination requirements

While the modularization of the course makes it relatively straightforward to collaborate in creating the material, differences in examination regulations and grading requirements between universities are a stumbling block. Rules at LMU require us to assess a student's performance via one final examination at the end of the semester, whereas at UNIVIE it is strictly necessary to do 50% of the overall performance assessment during the semester. We manage these discrepancies by introducing three types of (self-)assessments, two of which happen continuously over the semester while the last one pertains to a written test at the end of the semester:

(A) Moodle Quizzes: Multiple-Choice/Cloze-style questions (*on a weekly basis*).

(B) Assignments: Advanced programming tasks (*on a bi-weekly basis*, cf. Sec. 3.3).

(C) Written exam (*90min, end of the semester*).

Despite the strict requirements regarding performance assessment at LMU, it is possible to use assessment types **(A)** and **(B)** for awarding bonus points to the students who complete them successfully. The students were able to achieve a maximum of 9 bonus points (10% of the total points of the 90-minute exam) weighted by the share of the quizzes/assignments they were able to solve correctly. Employment of the bonus points was restricted by one condition: The bonus only counted if a student had passed the exam already without the bonus. Table 1 shows the proportions of the students at LMU who were able to achieve a bonus when entering the written examination[4], highlighting the effectiveness of this type of incentive for working on the intra-semester assessments.[5]

year	2020	2021	2022	2023
# students	52	48	64	38
w/ bonus	57.7%	68.8%	98.4%	81.6%
bonus > 50%	57.7%	54.2%	54.7%	60.5%

Table 1: Relative frequencies of students with bonus points among all students who took the exam at LMU.

There is an important breakpoint to be addressed when looking at the numbers in Table 1: From 2020 – 2022 there were ten assignments (to be completed on a weekly basis) with relatively easy tasks to be completed by the students, i.e. filling in some blanks in otherwise complete Jupyter notebooks. Starting in 2023, the assignments became significantly harder: The number was reduced to five, students were given two weeks to work on each of them and the task was to write the complete code by themselves. While this led to a substantial decrease in the share of students with bonus points among those who took the exam compared to 2022[6], the share of students who achieved over 50% of the bonus remained relatively constant over the whole observation period. For 2023, however, we observe a slight increase in the latter figure (plus 6 percentage points compared to 2022), hinting at the effectiveness of the more challenging assignments. We do not show similar numbers for students from

[3]One can argue that Stats+DS and CS students represent two distinct groups, but we believe that they are sufficiently similar concerning their prerequisites for this course.

[4]Unfortunately it is hard to calculate the share of students dropping out before the exam, since typically many more students enroll to the moodle course just to check out the material compared to the actual number of participating students.

[5]Note, that we only include students who actually took the exam here. Students with a bonus who did not register for the exam (or did not show up to it) are not counted in.

[6]Since the assignments were not substantially changed between 2020 and 2022 there was some "leakage", i.e. more senior students (presumably) passing on the solutions to their successors and thus leading to more students completing (some of) the tasks. This suspicion is supported by the rising numbers (until 2022) in the second row of Table 1.

UNIVIE, as they are obliged to successfully submit the assignments to pass the course. Hence a direct comparison does not make much sense here.

5 Open-Sourcing the Material

A core building block of this course is its public website alongside the complete source code for both website and slides. This differentiates the course from other open teaching resources (cf. Sec. 2) as it enhances its reusability. People are not only able to use the material as-is, but also to modify, extend, and enhance it. An important side effect of this policy is the potential feedback loop that we might hopefully enter at some point in time: Instead of only developing and improving the material ourselves, other parties re-using the material could reach out and become collaborators by contributing via issues or pull requests. The technical setup is kept pretty simple: We use two separate repositories on GitHub for the source code of the material and the source code of the website. We believe this separation helps interested third parties in finding what they are looking for and it also eases the whole development process. Using GitHub as a platform is motivated by its focal nature to the CS and NLP community, hence lowering the barrier for collaboration between the co-developers as well as for interested third parties.

The following list contains links to (i) the material, (ii) the website, and (iii) its source code for the interested reader and for potential collaborators:

(i) `https://github.com/slds-lmu/lecture_dl4nlp`

(ii) `https://slds-lmu.github.io/dl4nlp/`

(iii) `https://github.com/slds-lmu/dl4nlp`

6 Future Challenges and Next Steps

Open-source *everything*? An important case of conflicting priorities pertains to the goal of open-sourcing everything and the interest of providing the students with fair and challenging quizzes/assignments. While open-sourcing the solutions to the coding assignments perfectly aligns with the goal of open-sourcing, it contradicts the secondary goal to some extent as it could discourage students from working on the assignments and incentivize checking out the readily available solutions. Further, it would hinder re-using the same assignments for rewarding bonus points (LMU) or grading the performance over the semester (UNIVIE). Hence for the future, we are currently discussing the following scenarios:

- Keep assignments & solutions closed-source.
- Open-source only assignments w/o solutions.
- Substantially change assignments every semester. while open-sourcing everything.

Unavoidable Lecturer Turnover. Further challenges that will arise in the near future[7] originate from the way academia works. After finishing a PhD, people tend to leave the institution where they conducted their PhD studies either for a postdoc at another institution or for industry. While in the latter case, long-term cooperation on developing OSER together is most certainly not possible due to simply different priorities in an industrial job, also the former case does not automatically warrant further cooperation, although it might be more likely. Thus, we believe it is vital for the persistence of such a project (i) to have a clear ownership structure and consistent credit assignment policies, (ii) to set up lecture chapters as self-contained and independent of the lecturer as possible, and (iii) to create seamless documentation of reasoning behind the most important design choices, the workflows, and the responsibilities of the individual roles.

Related points are addressed by Bothmann et al. (2023), yet from a slightly different angle: They also stress the ownership issue as a crucial point concerning quality assurance and maintaining consistency in the narrative, notation, and correctness of the material. We think that the peculiarities of the academic job market are an important addition to these considerations.

Speed of Developments. Balancing the recency against stability is a major challenge for such courses (cf. Sec. 2). In general, university lectures should cover what can be considered established methodology or consensus in the research community. Examples of such topics can be easily found in the field of "classical" ML, considering concepts like logistic regression, support vector machines, and random forests, just to name a few. For DL and NLP this clear-cut definition proves to be much harder: The (relatively young) concept of embeddings as well as the Transformer (and its parts) can by now be considered fundamental/established, but already as soon as it comes to the encoder-based models surrounding BERT things begin to get complicated. While BERT itself might be a relatively unanimous choice, nearly all its successors can be

[7]Until now the core team has stayed mostly constant.

regarded as debatable. On the one hand, some of these papers represent (from today's perspective) important milestones or introduce smart ideas that might be worth teaching. On the other hand, these ideas might soon be considered outdated and other models might have taken their place in one year's time. So the question that has to be asked every semester is whether something can be considered "established" enough to enter the course or whether it is still too experimental or uncertain.

7 Conclusion

Throughout this paper, we shared some key takeaways and considerations when it comes to collaboratively developing OSER for NLP curricula. We highlighted crucial challenges that arise both due to the collaborative development and the different target groups and due to the peculiarities of the current fluid state of NLP research itself. Simultaneously we showcased the solutions we found, relying strongly on the OSER principles. We further view this paper as a means of advocating for more open source and more collaboration, also when it comes to teaching. While it may be common practice to collaborate in research itself or when it comes to using shared computational resources. Sharing and co-developing teaching materials, on the other hand, is far from being a commonly accepted best practice. We again argue, that one conclusion from the current speed of development is to join forces also for teaching. Finally, we share our material for re-use and inspiration and hope to attract other academics as future collaborators.

Limitations

While we do not claim that our course is all-encompassing or better than any other course, we still hope there is some value in (i) the course itself and (ii) the explanation of our thought processes. We think humbleness and the willingness to learn and improve one's teaching material continuously are key to the successful development of OSER. Everything we create and share happens to the best of our knowledge and we are always happy to be pointed at mistakes or inaccuracies so we can eradicate them.

Acknowledgements

MA is funded by the Deutsche Forschungsgemeinschaft (DFG, German Research Foundation) as part of BERD@NFDI - grant number 460037581. This research was partially supported by DFG (grant SCHU 2246/14-1).

References

AI@Meta. 2024. Llama 3 model card.

Rohan Anil, Andrew M Dai, Orhan Firat, Melvin Johnson, Dmitry Lepikhin, Alexandre Passos, Siamak Shakeri, Emanuel Taropa, Paige Bailey, Zhifeng Chen, et al. 2023. Palm 2 technical report. *arXiv preprint arXiv:2305.10403*.

Bernd Bischl, Ludwig Bothmann, Fabian Scheipl, Tobias Pielok, Lisa Wimmer, Yawei Li, Chris Kolb, Daniel Schalk, Heidi Seibold, Christoph Molnar, and Jakob Richter. 2022. Introduction to Machine Learning (I2ML). `https://slds-lmu.github.io/i2ml/`. [Online; accessed 2024-05-17].

Piotr Bojanowski, Edouard Grave, Armand Joulin, and Tomas Mikolov. 2017. Enriching word vectors with subword information. *Transactions of the Association for Computational Linguistics*, 5:135–146.

Ludwig Bothmann, Sven Strickroth, Giuseppe Casalicchio, David Rügamer, Marius Lindauer, Fabian Scheipl, and Bernd Bischl. 2023. Developing open source educational resources for machine learning and data science. In *The Third Teaching Machine Learning and Artificial Intelligence Workshop*, pages 1–6. PMLR.

Tom Brown, Benjamin Mann, Nick Ryder, Melanie Subbiah, Jared D Kaplan, Prafulla Dhariwal, Arvind Neelakantan, Pranav Shyam, Girish Sastry, Amanda Askell, et al. 2020. Language models are few-shot learners. *Advances in neural information processing systems*, 33:1877–1901.

DeepLearning.AI. 2023. A complete guide to natural language processing. `https://www.deeplearning.ai/resources/natural-language-processing/`. [Online; accessed 2024-05-17].

Jacob Devlin, Ming-Wei Chang, Kenton Lee, and Kristina Toutanova. 2019. BERT: Pre-training of deep bidirectional transformers for language understanding. In *Proceedings of the 2019 Conference of the North American Chapter of the Association for Computational Linguistics: Human Language Technologies, Volume 1 (Long and Short Papers)*, pages 4171–4186, Minneapolis, Minnesota. Association for Computational Linguistics.

Angela Fan, Mike Lewis, and Yann Dauphin. 2018. Hierarchical neural story generation. In *Proceedings of the 56th Annual Meeting of the Association for Computational Linguistics (Volume 1: Long Papers)*, pages 889–898.

fast.ai. 2020. Practical deep learning. `https://course.fast.ai/`.

Google. 2023. Introduction to machine learning. https://developers.google.com/machine-learning/crash-course/ml-intro. [Online; accessed 2024-05-17].

Ari Holtzman, Jan Buys, Li Du, Maxwell Forbes, and Yejin Choi. 2019. The curious case of neural text degeneration. In *International Conference on Learning Representations*.

Jeremy Howard and Sylvain Gugger. 2020. *Deep Learning for Coders with fastai and PyTorch*. O'Reilly Media.

Austin Huang, Suraj Subramanian, Jonathan Sum, Khalid Almubarak, and Stella Biderman. 2022. Tutorial 6: Transformers and multi-head attention. [Online; accessed 2024-05-17].

Hugging Face. 2022. The hugging face course, 2022. https://huggingface.co/course. [Online; accessed 2024-05-17].

Phillip Lippe. 2022. Tutorial 6: Transformers and multi-head attention. [Online; accessed 2024-05-17].

Paul Michel, Omer Levy, and Graham Neubig. 2019. Are sixteen heads really better than one? *Advances in neural information processing systems*, 32.

Tomas Mikolov, Kai Chen, Greg Corrado, and Jeffrey Dean. 2013. Efficient estimation of word representations in vector space. *arXiv preprint arXiv:1301.3781*.

Ines Montani. 2019. Advanced NLP with spaCy: A free online course. https://github.com/explosion/spacy-course. [Online; accessed 2024-05-17].

Andrew Ng. 2021. Machine Learning. https://www.coursera.org/learn/machine-learning. [Online; accessed 2024-05-17].

OpenAI. 2022. Chatgpt: Optimizing language models for dialogue.

OpenAI. 2023. Gpt-4 technical report. *arXiv*, pages 2303–08774.

Adam Paszke, Sam Gross, Francisco Massa, Adam Lerer, James Bradbury, Gregory Chanan, Trevor Killeen, Zeming Lin, Natalia Gimelshein, Luca Antiga, Alban Desmaison, Andreas Köpf, Edward Yang, Zach DeVito, Martin Raison, Alykhan Tejani, Sasank Chilamkurthy, Benoit Steiner, Lu Fang, Junjie Bai, and Soumith Chintala. 2019. Pytorch: An imperative style, high-performance deep learning library.

Jeffrey Pennington, Richard Socher, and Christopher Manning. 2014. Glove: Global vectors for word representation. In *Proceedings of the 2014 conference on empirical methods in natural language processing (EMNLP)*, pages 1532–1543.

Alec Radford, Karthik Narasimhan, Tim Salimans, Ilya Sutskever, et al. 2018. Improving language understanding by generative pre-training.

Alec Radford, Jeffrey Wu, Rewon Child, David Luan, Dario Amodei, Ilya Sutskever, et al. 2019. Language models are unsupervised multitask learners. *OpenAI blog*, 1(8):9.

Colin Raffel, Noam Shazeer, Adam Roberts, Katherine Lee, Sharan Narang, Michael Matena, Yanqi Zhou, Wei Li, and Peter J. Liu. 2020. Exploring the limits of transfer learning with a unified text-to-text transformer. *Journal of Machine Learning Research*, 21(140):1–67.

Alexander Rush. 2018. The annotated transformer. In *Proceedings of Workshop for NLP Open Source Software (NLP-OSS)*, pages 52–60, Melbourne, Australia. Association for Computational Linguistics.

Stanford NLP Group. 2024. Cs224n: Natural language processing with deep learning (spring 2024). https://web.stanford.edu/class/cs224n/. [Online; accessed 2024-05-17].

Hugo Touvron, Louis Martin, Kevin Stone, Peter Albert, Amjad Almahairi, Yasmine Babaei, Nikolay Bashlykov, Soumya Batra, Prajjwal Bhargava, Shruti Bhosale, Dan Bikel, Lukas Blecher, Cristian Canton Ferrer, Moya Chen, Guillem Cucurull, David Esiobu, Jude Fernandes, Jeremy Fu, Wenyin Fu, Brian Fuller, Cynthia Gao, Vedanuj Goswami, Naman Goyal, Anthony Hartshorn, Saghar Hosseini, Rui Hou, Hakan Inan, Marcin Kardas, Viktor Kerkez, Madian Khabsa, Isabel Kloumann, Artem Korenev, Punit Singh Koura, Marie-Anne Lachaux, Thibaut Lavril, Jenya Lee, Diana Liskovich, Yinghai Lu, Yuning Mao, Xavier Martinet, Todor Mihaylov, Pushkar Mishra, Igor Molybog, Yixin Nie, Andrew Poulton, Jeremy Reizenstein, Rashi Rungta, Kalyan Saladi, Alan Schelten, Ruan Silva, Eric Michael Smith, Ranjan Subramanian, Xiaoqing Ellen Tan, Binh Tang, Ross Taylor, Adina Williams, Jian Xiang Kuan, Puxin Xu, Zheng Yan, Iliyan Zarov, Yuchen Zhang, Angela Fan, Melanie Kambadur, Sharan Narang, Aurelien Rodriguez, Robert Stojnic, Sergey Edunov, and Thomas Scialom. 2023. Llama 2: Open Foundation and Fine-Tuned Chat Models.

Ashish Vaswani, Noam Shazeer, Niki Parmar, Jakob Uszkoreit, Llion Jones, Aidan N Gomez, Łukasz Kaiser, and Illia Polosukhin. 2017. Attention is all you need. *Advances in neural information processing systems*, 30.

Ashwin K Vijayakumar, Michael Cogswell, Ramprasath R Selvaraju, Qing Sun, Stefan Lee, David Crandall, and Dhruv Batra. 2016. Diverse beam search: Decoding diverse solutions from neural sequence models. *arXiv preprint arXiv:1610.02424*.

Thomas Wolf, Lysandre Debut, Victor Sanh, Julien Chaumond, Clement Delangue, Anthony Moi, Pierric Cistac, Tim Rault, Remi Louf, Morgan Funtowicz, Joe Davison, Sam Shleifer, Patrick von Platen,

Clara Ma, Yacine Jernite, Julien Plu, Canwen Xu, Teven Le Scao, Sylvain Gugger, Mariama Drame, Quentin Lhoest, and Alexander Rush. 2020. Transformers: State-of-the-art natural language processing. In *Proceedings of the 2020 Conference on Empirical Methods in Natural Language Processing: System Demonstrations*, pages 38–45, Online. Association for Computational Linguistics.

From Hate Speech to Societal Empowerment: A Pedagogical Journey Through Computational Thinking and NLP for High School Students

Alessandra Teresa Cignarella[△,♡], **Elisa Chierchiello**[★], **Chiara Ferrando**[★], **Simona Frenda**[★,♡], **Soda Marem Lo**[★] and **Andrea Marra**[★]
★ Computer Science Department, University of Turin, Italy
△ LT3, Language and Translation Technology Team, Ghent University, Belgium
♡ aequa-tech, Turin, Italy

Abstract

The teaching laboratory we have created integrates methodologies to address the topic of hate speech on social media among students while fostering computational thinking and AI education for societal impact. We provide a foundational understanding of hate speech and introduce computational concepts using matrices, bag of words, and practical exercises in platforms like Colaboratory. Additionally, we emphasize the application of AI, particularly in NLP, to address real-world challenges. Through retrospective evaluation, we assess the efficacy of our approach, aiming to empower students as proactive contributors to societal betterment. With this paper we present an overview of the laboratory's structure, the primary materials used, and insights gleaned from six editions conducted to the present date.

Our positionality: This paper is situated in (Northern) Italy in 2024 and is authored by researchers specializing in Natural Language Processing. Beyond our academic work, we are actively involved in *feminist*, *LGBTQIA+ advocacy*, and *anti-hate speech* activism. Collectively, our backgrounds span theoretical linguistics, computer science, natural language processing, digital humanities, high school teaching, and non-formal education methodos.

1 Introduction

The pervasive use of technologies based on AI models, makes it imperative for academic institutions to organize teaching laboratories for primary and secondary schools with the aim of increasing awareness for the techniques behind these technologies, consequently knowing when to trust AI and when to distrust it, and revealing the "behind the scenes" of their unconscious use. Some programs are promoted also by government institutions with the aim of bringing students closer to computer science and also reducing the gender stereotypes that characterize this field of study. Among them, are worth mentioning: Women Who Code, supported by the EU, and Coding Girls in Italy.

In this context of activities for public engagement, our laboratory **#DEACTIVHATE** takes shape. Its main goals are: introducing secondary school students to Natural Language Processing techniques and their applications; raising awareness about the ethical issues of digital world; empower them to positively contribute to the digital community, and increase responsibility in the use of present-day technologies.

To achieve these goals, we designed a series of educational activities starting from the analysis of online hate speech. Abusive and online harmful content are issues that adolescents face in their everyday life, but also one of the social issues that they can help alleviate. In spite of a causal link between hate speech and crime is difficult to prove, the risk of offenses and effects on victim's psychological and physical well-being have been proved in psychological and social studies (Nadal et al., 2014; Fulper et al., 2014). Especially among adolescents, the extreme consequences of these attacks tend to be the suicide, as suggested by (Nikolaou, 2017) in their analysis of the connection between cyberbullying and suicidal behavior in the US. To prevent such scenarios, some awareness-raising projects in schools are being carried out by NGOs in Italy, such as Amnesty International[1] or Cifa ONLUS[2]. #DEACTIVHATE fits in this context, merging the educational experience of development and use of AI-based tools and the stimuli to be responsible developers and users.

Our experience of teaching this laboratory concerned students of different ages and coming from different backgrounds: humanistic, classical, technical and scientific studies. Therefore, the methodologies of teaching used in this context, and the

[1]https://www.silencehate.it/.
[2]https://www.cifaong.it.

Proceedings of the Sixth Workshop on Teaching NLP, pages 54–65
August 15, 2024

materials and activities employed during the laboratory, are adaptable to different situations.

The impact of the laboratory has been evaluated by administering tests in two phases: one at the beginning and one at the end, containing an (almost) identical set of questions. By means of these pre- and post-test we could assess the teaching methodologies and materials and to measure the awareness of students towards: firstly, the functionality of AI-based technologies, secondly, the importance of creating responsible and ethical NLP for community benefits, and thirdly, the consequences of pervasive online hate speech.

In the next sections, we describe: related work on teaching NLP that report experiences with young participants (Section 2); the methodologies and teaching activities and materials employed in our laboratory (Sections 3 and 4); our experience with different Italian secondary school students (Section 5). Finally, we write about some of the challenges we faced, and we delineate some conclusions (Sections 6 and 7).

2 Related Work

The escalation of hate speech on social media platforms and its negative societal impact have ignited significant academic interest in developing methods for its automatic detection and mitigation. This surge in research is underscored by the proliferation of methodologies leveraging Natural Language Processing and Machine Learning (ML) techniques. A comprehensive survey (Jahan and Oussalah, 2023) delineates the evolution of automatic hate speech detection, emphasizing the integral role of NLP and Deep Learning (DL) technologies in this realm. Their systematic review delineates the progression from traditional ML techniques to advanced DL architectures, highlighting a shift towards models like BERT, which have revolutionized hate speech detection with their context-aware processing.

In parallel, educational initiatives have emerged as critical for cultivating a responsible digital citizenry, particularly among the younger population. This educational aspect aligns with our project's dual focus: addressing hate speech through technological solutions, while promoting computational thinking and AI literacy among students. Workshops like the one discussed at NAACL-HLT (Jurgens et al., 2021) emphasize the importance of developing NLP resources for diverse educational contexts, reflecting the necessity of embedding these technological competencies at an early age. Furthermore, other initiatives (Sprugnoli et al., 2018; Pannitto et al., 2021) illustrate the emerging trend of integrating computational linguistics into the high school curriculum, thereby aligning with our laboratory's educational objectives.

Our approach to combating hate speech incorporates practical exercises and the utilization of platforms such as Colaboratory, fostering an environment where students not only learn to identify and counteract hate speech but also gain hands-on experience with NLP tools. This pedagogical strategy mirrors the "gamification" techniques highlighted by Bonetti and Tonelli (2020), which have been effectively applied in linguistic annotation tasks, enhancing engagement and educational outcomes.

Reflecting on the systematic review and related educational efforts, our project's methodology synthesizes these insights, employing state-of-the-art NLP techniques for real-world applications while fostering an educational paradigm that prepares students to navigate and contribute positively to the digital world.

2.1 A bit of History

The #DEACTIVHATE project was conceived by a group of young researchers within the initiatives for the orientation of high school students and in particular for the promotion of STEM subjects among the young female population. It is supported by *Commissione Orientamento e Informatica nelle Scuole* and funded by the project "Piano Lauree Scientifiche" of the Computer Science Department in the University of Turin.

Through the six editions of the lab, 14 different classes were reached, for a total number of 233 students, aged from 15 to 18 years old (see Table 1 in Appendix A). The first two editions involved students with a humanistic background, while in the following ones students from technical or scientific high schools – thus with a stronger background in computer science – were reached. The results of the first three editions of the lab were discussed in (Frenda et al., 2021; Cignarella et al., 2023).

With the present publication, we aim at describing the hands-on experience of the three new (post-COVID) editions. In particular, here we tackle most of the issues raised in the "Future Work" sections of previous publications. Some have been resolved or confirmed, while others remained open and are due to further discussion with the teaching community. For example, there was a request to make the lab more interactive in its online setting, or to expand the lab beyond the context of Turin, which happened with the fifth edition (even if only online). Furthermore, we found it crucial to present #DEACTIVHATE in a new, more comprehensive publication. After six editions, the laboratory has evolved into a well-refined and effective program.

In addition, we provide an in-depth description of the materials developed for the laboratory, we translated all of them into English, making them accessible to a wider and international audience (see Appendix B). Finally, acknowledging the various limitations our laboratory may still have, we expect to receive feedback from the teaching community and that #DEACTIVHATE will be adopted in new schools and different contexts.

3 Teaching Goals and Methodologies

The laboratory's name, #DEACTIVHATE, combines the concept of deactivation with the phenomenon of hate, and the new term is preceded by the pound sign '#', reminiscent of social media hashtags. This choice wants to establish a clear connection to the social media realm. The activities, designed for secondary school students, consist of three main modules aimed at:

1. Raising awareness about the pervasive issue of hate speech, prompting reflection on microaggressions, stereotypes, and prejudices.
2. Engaging students in computational thinking and exploring linguistic tools used by social media users to convey hate or offend others online, such as hashtags, emoticons, and rhetorical devices.
3. Introducing high school students to Natural Language Processing (NLP) tools and demonstrating their potential for promoting more responsible and conscious technology usage.

By combining educational content with hands-on exploration and critical thinking exercises, #DEACTIVHATE strives to empower students to become discerning and empathetic digital citizens.

In order to achieve these purposes, we relied on the following methodologies:

• **Collaborative reading sessions:** Students engage in reading formal definitions and in exploring the basics of hate speech, including vocabulary and definitions provided by authoritative sources such as the Council of Europe.

• **Matrix design and analysis:** Utilizing Google Spreadsheets, students design matrices incorporating binary (0s and 1s) representations of keywords and concepts, employing techniques such as bag of words to analyze text data.

• **Practical coding exercises:** Students work on exercises using Google Colaboratory, with some exercises pre-compiled and others involving collaborative coding sessions where code is written together to explore concepts related to hate speech detection in NLP.

• **Real-life scenario exploration (Social Media)**: Students engage in browsing social media to gain insight into real-life demonstrations of hateful behaviors and patterns. This activity allows for first-hand exploration of how hatred can manifest on social media platforms and the role NLP plays in identifying, analyzing, and potentially mitigating its effects. By observing and discussing examples from social media, students develop a deeper understanding of the practical implications of NLP in addressing hate speech and promoting responsible online behavior.

4 Activities and Materials in Detail

In this section, we describe the teaching activities and the materials employed in #DEACTIVHATE, which are available at the following link: `https://github.com/deactivhate`. The topics of the following 5 lessons cover various disciplines, useful for enhancing knowledge of high schoolers, including: *Sociology/Civics and Hate Speech*, *Computational Linguistics* and *Computer Science/Programming*. For an exhaustive list of the materials, please refer to Appendix B.

4.1 Lesson 1: Who are we? Why are we here?

In the first minutes of the first lesson, we administered a pre-test. In order not to "start off with the wrong foot" with the students, we clarified multiple times that the test is designed to assess their pre-existing knowledge on the topics dealt with in the laboratory (and absolutely not for evaluation).

The first lesson sets out to introduce ourselves as university researchers, explain what we do in our research, and set together the overarching goals of the entire laboratory. Students are guided into an introspective and comparative analysis of their own identity. Using Google's Jamboard as a tool, we embark on a journey of self-reflection through an engaging ice-breaking activity. They are encouraged to present an aspect of their identity using an image, which they upload to a shared Jamboard. Utilizing this tool allows for real-time collaboration and discussion, enriching the learning experience by visually capturing the mosaic of student identities and favoring an environment of empathy and understanding.

Here, students start exploring the multifaceted nature of personal identity, engaging in an introductory dialogue about discrimination and Hate Speech.

<u>*Lesson 1 in brief:*</u> pre-test, icebreaker activity, introductory slides to #DEACTIVHATE.

4.2 Lesson 2: How to recognize hate speech?

The second lesson delves into clarifying the concepts introduced in the previous meeting. An initial exploration regarding personal and social identities is proposed, by incorporating the visual tools of the **Pyramid of Hate** and of the **Wheel of Privilege** (see Figure 1) into the slides.

Figure 1: Credits to Sylvia Duckworth.

Thanks to these visualizations, students are encouraged to reflect on their positions within the spectrum of these characteristics, sparking conversation about the relative advantages and disadvantages that accompany different identity markers such as, gender, skin color, body size, wealth etc.[3]

[3]Both visual materials were developed within the U.S., therefore we adapted them to our needs by, for instance, substituting *English* with *Italian* in the Language section of the Wheel of Privilege. The absence of the topic *Religion* was also noted from the students. Other adjustments might be necessary, depending on the context in which this lab is delivered.

Drawing upon the personal narratives and experiences of the students, the activity culminates in an exploration of the intersectionality of **Hate Speech** with stereotypes, biases and microaggressions, underscoring the nature of such interactions in the fabric of everyday life.

In the second part of this lesson, we introduce the basic terminology to discuss hate speech and related phenomena, relying on the official definition provided by European Commission against Racism and Intolerance (ECRI). This activity sets the stage for a deeper understanding of the phenomenon, emphasizing its targeted nature against identifiable groups based on inherent traits.

> *Hate Speech is to be understood as the advocacy, promotion or incitement, in any form, of the denigration, hatred or vilification of a person or group of persons, as well as any harassment, insult, negative stereotyping, stigmatization or threat in respect of such a person or group of persons and the justification of all the preceding types of expression, on the ground of "race", color, descent, national or ethnic origin, age, disability, language, religion or belief, sex, gender, gender identity, sexual orientation and other personal characteristics or status [...]*

In the third part of this lesson, students were instructed to open any of the social media accounts they use on a daily basis and try to collect tweets containing hatred messages towards public figures as targets of discrimination.

To organize the analysis and group discussion of their discoveries, they were asked to collect the **textual messages into a Google Spreadsheet**. This method prompted them to identify the keywords in the hateful message, the victim, and categorize the types of discrimination including misogyny, homophobia, sexism, body-shaming, and more, introducing students to a nuanced taxonomy.

As the final activity in this lesson, students are immersed in a hands-on annotation task, where they are asked to analyze and annotate a minimum of 30 tweets. This exercise can be done alone or in pairs or small groups, encouraging discussion, and in our case is facilitated by the tailor-made data annotation platform[4] developed for the project **"Contro l'odio"**. Any other annotation platform can be used.

[4]`http://annotazione.didattica.controlodio.it/`

The lesson is wrapped-up by means of a collective discussion, allowing students to share insights and reflect on the complexities of an annotation task, understanding all the nuances of hate speech and finding an agreement.

Lesson 2 in brief: personal and social identity, pyramid of hatred, Hate Speech definition, activity on social media, annotation exercise.

4.3 Lesson 3: Machine Learning and matrices

In the third lesson, we introduce students to the fundamentals of machine learning, starting with a broad overview of what it entails and moving into the specifics of **supervised and unsupervised learning**, with a significant focus on the process of text vectorization and the specifics of detecting hate speech through automatic text classification. This lesson is designed to guide students through the entire **machine learning workflow** in the context of NLP. This includes defining a clear task, gathering a suitable dataset, and dividing it into annotated training and test sets.

After the more theoretical aspects, introduced thanks to two sets of slides, the module transitions into a practical activity where students applied their newly acquired knowledge of text vectorization. Each student was tasked with annotating a specific tweet, chosen to reflect the varying types of discriminatory language found online. The activity involved constructing a **bag of words matrix on a Spreadsheet**, where students encoded the presence or absence of certain key terms—terms indicative of the underlying sentiment or hate speech within the tweet. The *one-hot encoding* matrix was used as device to transform the qualitative aspects of language into a quantitative format that machine learning algorithms could process. The same matrix will be created automatically in the coding part of the course (in Lesson 5). By breaking down tweets into this bag-of-words model, students not only practiced the procedure of vectorization but also engaged with the content at a deeper level, considering how individual words contribute to the overall message and tone of the text.

Finally, we used any spare time at the end of this lesson to make sure to install Google Colaboratory and be ready for the next lesson.

Lesson 3 in brief: machine learning workflow, supervised/unsupervised learning, training/test set features, vectorization, bag-of-words matrices.

4.4 Lesson 4: Python and Colab as IDE

The fourth lesson guides students through the essentials of **Python**[5] programming within the interactive environment of **Google Colaboratory**[6]. The session begins with an overview of Python's basic constructs, using simple print statements to demonstrate output on the screen. This introduction quickly progresses to exercises involving string manipulation, arithmetic operations, and gathering user input—all through the lens of Colab's user-friendly interface.

As the lesson unfolds, students tackle more advanced topics, including string operations and text processing, which are fundamental to NLP tasks. They learn to clean text data, manage strings, and explore the foundational technique of tokenization—turning streams of text into analyzable components. This hands-on experience not only solidifies their Python skills but also prepares them for the subsequent lesson on text classification in NLP.

Lesson 4 in brief: Colaboratory, Python, tokenization, lemmatization, word distribution and relevance, n-grams, basic operations with strings.

4.5 Lesson 5: Supervised classification

Lesson 5 involves a practical exercise using Colab for detecting hate speech in a given dataset (in our case, sampled from HaSpeeDe2 (Sanguinetti et al., 2018), the benchmark for HS detection in Italian) via a simplified pipeline based on supervised classification.[7] The session begins by defining hate speech in the context of machine learning, utilizing a dataset of tweets categorized by the presence or absence of hate speech (encoded with 0s and 1s).

Students learn to use **pandas**[8] for handling data frames, visualize data, and prepare it for analysis, including balancing the dataset, converting string labels to numerical formats, and splitting data into training and test sets. They also employ text vectorization methods like `CountVectorizer` (bag of words) and `TfidfVectorizer` (words weighted with TF-IDF) from **scikit-learn**[9] to process tweet data for machine learning, as they already have done manually in Lesson 3. During

[5] `https://www.python.org/`

[6] `https://colab.research.google.com/`

[7] The dataset used inside this interactive notebook contains Italian texts. Datasets in other languages and on different topics can be found, for instance here: `https://live.european-language-grid.eu/`

[8] `https://pandas.pydata.org/`

[9] `https://scikit-learn.org/stable/`

the lesson, students have the possibility to "play" with the parameters of the `CountVectorizer` and `TfidfVectorizer` methods and select the best textual representation. With the foundation set, they are guided through the construction of a *Support Vector Machine (SVM)* model, applying it to classify tweets and evaluate the model's performance through accuracy metrics. They critically analyze misclassified texts and consider strategies for improving the model, discussing preprocessing functions and the importance of cleaning text data. Based on the students' proficiency with Python and Colab, the class can be guided step-by-step, allowed to work more independently, or organized into pairs for collaborative work.

Both lessons 4 and 5 provide an introduction to the management of string-like type of data and the classical workflow for the creation of models with ML algorithms, putting in practice what was previously learned in lesson 3. The idea is to (at least) familiarize with basics techniques related to development of supervised learning.

Although we presented, as first simple case-study, the SVM algorithm with a representation based on bag of words/TF-IDF weights, during lesson 5 we mentioned the current state of the art of the algorithms used to solve NLP tasks, and we encouraged the reflection on the best features that could help build a hate speech classifier.

Lesson 5 concludes with the administration of a final evaluation test (post-test), the analysis of which will be discussed in detail in Sections 5.1 and 6.1. This provides valuable feedback on the students' understanding and the effectiveness of the module.

Lesson 5 in brief: Colaboratory, Python, pandas, scikit-learn, CountVectorizer, TF-IDF, SVM, agreement/disagreement, accuracy, post-test.

At the very end of the whole laboratory, an anonymous survey questionnaire on satisfaction was administered (see a detailed analysis in Section 6.1).

5 Hands-on experience

The laboratory today[10] counts six editions, during which we adapted methodologies (Section 3) and activities (Section 4) to the different settings we encountered over the years, monitoring both students' and teaching strategies progresses.

[10]Time of writing: June 2024.

5.1 Evaluation

Since the first edition, at the end of the last lesson, we asked students to fill a survey questionnaire to express their overall satisfaction towards the laboratory and the degree of interest in the topics of the course. Students' feedback has been useful to map the adaptability of the methodologies to different settings, and what would need to be changed in order to make the lab more effective and appealing.

In addition, starting from the third edition, we built two tests to assess the degree of assimilation of the main concepts covered during the course, specifically a test of prior (pre-test) and final knowledge (post-test), to be administered respectively before the beginning of the laboratory, and at the end of the 10-hour cycle of lessons. The tests consisted of four kinds of questions:

1. True/false: evaluated as correct (1 point) or wrong (0 points).

2. Multiple choice: evaluated as right (2 points), partially right (1 point) or wrong (0 points).

3. Questions that require fairly short answers: evaluated as right (2 points), partially right (1 point) or wrong (0 points).

4. Open questions that require a long answer: evaluated on a scale ranging from 0 to 5.

Both the pre- and post-test were composed by questions related to different topics and categories of concepts dealt with during the lab, corresponding to the modules described in Section 4: i) *Sociology/Civics and Hate Speec*h (C); ii) *Computational Linguistics* (CL); iii) *Computer Science/Programming* (CS). Table 2 in Appendix A, provides examples for each of these categories, together with examples of the assigned notes for the open questions.

Most of the questions in the pre- and post-test overlapped in order to assess students' progress, together with the effectiveness of the laboratory. The pre-test was delivered before the introduction of ourselves and of the course (see Section 4.1), since we wanted to map their level of knowledge on the topics of the laboratory to actively engage the participants right away. The post-test was administered on the last lesson (see Section 4.5), or given by the last day as homework with a hard deadline (and help from the local teachers, for the deadline to be respected). It was presented to students as a proper assessment test, in order to encourage them to participate seriously and with

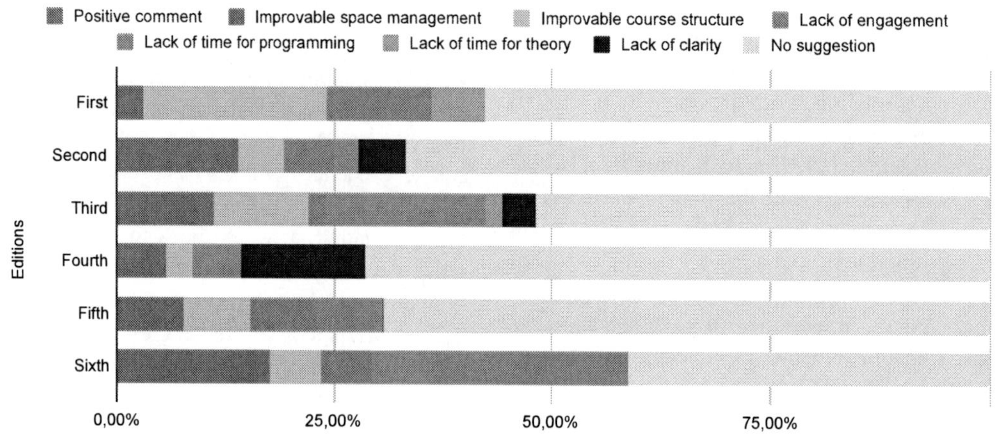

Figure 2: Grouped answers to the question: *Do you have any comments, suggestions, or constructive criticism that would be helpful in organizing future #DeactivHate laboratories?*

commitment. For the 3rd and 4th edition, both the questionnaires were held on the Moodle platform of our main affiliation (University of Turin). For the 5th and 6th edition they were held on Google Forms, since, post-2020, many schools began using Google Classroom as suite for online teaching.

6 Challenges and Lessons Learned

After six editions and seven teachers involved during the years, we want to share our considerations on challenges and lessons learned, since we believe it can be useful to open a deeper reflection on teaching NLP and offensive language detection nowadays in high schools. To carry out this analysis, we examined the answers to the anonymous survey **questionnaire on satisfaction**, and the results of the **pre- and post-tests**. Then we gathered together, sharing thoughts that emerged from reading the results, recollecting the experiences of each edition. All the questionnaires represented useful instruments to assess the effect of our methodologies in different settings, to summarize the challenges we were able of addressing during the years, and to highlight those that are still open.

6.1 Addressed challenges

We analyzed the anonymous opinions received from students in the survey questionnaire, and we grouped the replies in thematic groups. In Figure 2 we show the results.

In particular, we noticed a major difference related to time management between the online (first, third, and fifth) and the offline editions (second, fourth, and sixth). The laboratory started during the period of the COVID-19 pandemic outbreak, which forced us to deal with online teaching since the beginning (even though the laboratory was originally conceived to be held *in praesentia*). As teachers, we perceived a difference in the students' responsiveness in respect to offline teaching, specifically worsening time management.

Online teaching was particularly challenging in edition 1 because, in the first lessons, students were all connected from a single computer, making the interaction often filtered through the teacher in the classroom. The same happened in the fifth edition by necessity of the school, with the additional problem of having two classes of different levels merged sharing the same room, thus leading to the request for an improvement in space management (see Figure 2). These experiences taught us how a one-on-one interaction with students online is still preferable than having the whole class connected to one device, facilitating the possibility of engagement and helping them not to get lost, especially during the lectures dedicated to coding.

Looking at the pre- and post-test results in Figure 3 (administered from the third edition on, as referenced in Section 5), it is possible to observe an improvement in all the modules and editions. In the fifth edition, we noticed a higher percentage of students who have not assimilated concepts from the CS module. This result can also be associated with the fact that we worked with classes of two different levels at the same time, having students with different computer skills.

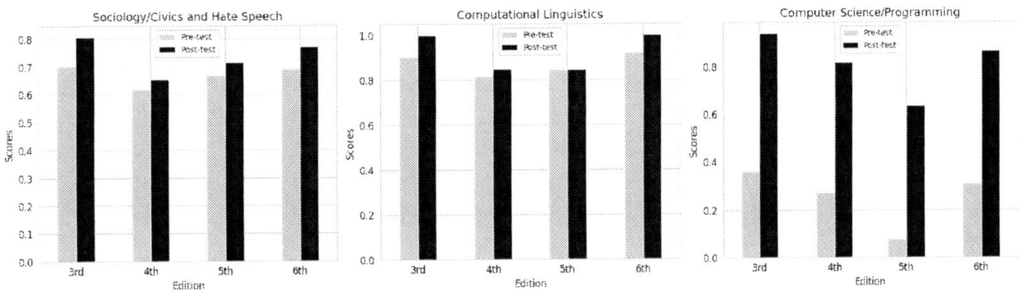

Figure 3: Mean of correct answers in pre- and post-tests for the subset of students who completed both tests (120).

Similarly, in the sixth edition there were students from different classes, since they could choose the course as *school-work experience*[11] on a voluntary basis, and the lab was an extracurricular activity for them. In this case, the improvements between the pre- and post-test were consistent. On the other hand, the strong request for more time for programming (Figure 2) could be linked to the fact that the teachers dedicated part of the fifth lesson to a visit to the buildings of the Computer Science Department of the University of Turin, thus 'sacrificing' time that would be typically dedicated to coding.

Despite these issues, the 6th edition showed us the positive aspect of having a class of people who volunteered to partake in the lab and, therefore, expressed an active interest on these topics, as demonstrated by the higher percentage of positive comments (Figure 2) and satisfaction.

A big challenge we encountered in the 4th edition was the presence of negative social bubbles in the classroom, and their influence in approaching hateful content, specifically linked to the figure of a well-known hate spreader and misogynist. To address this issue (also acknowledged by local teachers), we spent more time on lessons dedicated to the definition of hate speech and hateful content, significantly engaging with the class; thus, reducing the available time dedicated to CS and coding. This specific situation might be the cause of high scores in "lack of clarity" (refer to the dark blue portion in the graph, see Figure 2).

Moreover, we decided to share informative content on the topic with the local teachers, specifically Bold Voices advice[12] spread in Italy via the newspaper "Internazionale"[13].

[11]It is a compulsory activity foreseen in some types of higher education institutions in Italy, after one of the last Education reforms.

[12]https://www.boldvoices.co.uk/

[13]https://www.internazionale.it/

6.2 Open challenges

Throughout these years we addressed multiple challenges, nevertheless, there are still open issues that need to be discussed and worked out.

For instance, a major difficulty we found from the 4th edition on was to balance the introduction of NLP basics, and students curiosity towards more complex models such as LLMs, which are now part of their daily life. In the fifth edition, we dedicated around 10 minutes of the last lesson to introduce a visual article published by the Financial Times on the basics of generative AI[14], also adding the source to the advanced materials. This attempt was taken positively, but a more effective strategy to the entry of generative AI into the everyday lives of our students is definitely needed.

Considering the overall interest towards more hours of programming, another open challenge intends to better balance the second part of #DeactivHate, introducing an additional (sixth) meeting, and working step by step by launching the programming part already from the second lesson, if the rooms and tools of the schools allow for it. We believe that delivering practical coding exercises in parallel with the theory lessons would lead to a more engaging setup. Furthermore, an extra lesson would allow us to delve into unsupervised learning, providing a comprehensive understanding of fundamental NLP concepts. It could also introduce alternative classification methods like multilayer perceptrons or transformer architectures such as BERT, offering at least a basic introduction to these (slightly more) advanced topics.

Another challenge, linked to the fact that most of the editions of the laboratory were part of a larger school guidance project, is to harmonize

notizie/anna-franchin/2023/04/07/andrew-tate-misoginia-violènza

[14]https://ig.ft.com/generative-ai/

this objective and keep it always updated with the involved students and teachers, reserving a proper time and space for it.

Finally, we are aware that students' awareness changes according to social and cultural factors, so it is important to make the laboratory flexible, and able to meet the needs and interests of each group we work with.

7 Conclusions

Our paper outlines the development and implementation of the #DEACTIVHATE laboratory, aimed at empowering high school students to address hate speech through computational thinking and NLP techniques. The laboratory's goals include introducing students to NLP techniques, raising awareness about ethical issues in the digital world, and fostering responsible technology usage. Through six editions of the laboratory, we have reached a diverse group of students, adapting methodologies and activities to different settings and backgrounds.

The related work section contextualizes our project within the broader academic landscape, highlighting the importance of automatic hate speech detection and educational initiatives for promoting responsible digital citizenship. Our approach incorporates practical exercises and utilizes platforms like Google Colaboratory to provide hands-on experience with NLP tools.

We describe in detail the teaching goals and methodologies employed in the laboratory, which include collaborative reading sessions, matrix design and analysis, practical coding exercises, and real-life scenario exploration on social media. Each lesson is designed to progressively build students' understanding of hate speech detection and NLP techniques.

The paper also presents the results of evaluations conducted throughout the editions, including pre- and post-tests administered to assess students' knowledge and the effectiveness of the laboratory. Challenges encountered during the implementation of the laboratory are discussed, along with lessons learned and open challenges for future iterations.

Ethics Statement and Limitations

This paper has limitations, primarily stemming from our positionality as NLP academic researchers based in Northern Italy, which inherently introduces cultural and societal biases, as discussed in the first part of the paper. Secondly, it is crucial to consider that our theoretical framework concerning *Hate Speech* within the #DEACTIVHATE laboratory is situated within a European context. This framework refers to legislation and directives derived from the EU, as well as broader statements from the European Commission against Racism and Intolerance (ECRI).

• Different socio-cultural environments can influence the manifestation and perception of hate speech, as well as the effectiveness of various deactivation strategies. Therefore, while our insights contribute valuable knowledge, we recognize that they might (vastly) differ in contexts outside the one we operated in.

• The Wheel of Privilege was originally developed within the U.S., therefore it was adapted to our framework by, for instance, substituting *English* with *Italian* in the Language section of the Wheel of Privilege. We also noticed the absence of a 'slice' regarding Religion. We believe that other adjustments might be necessary, depending on the context in which this laboratory will be taught.

• The Wheel of Privilege was originally developed within the U.S., therefore it was adapted to our framework by, for instance, substituting *English* with *Italian* in the Language section of the Wheel of Privilege. We also noticed the absence of a 'slice" of the pie regarding Religion. We believe that other adjustments might be necessary, depending on the context in which this laboratory will be taught.

• We acknowledge that some activities might be triggering; therefore, we recommend careful consideration of the teachers. For instance, the activity carried out in Lesson 2 of researching hateful messages throughout social media pages, takes place after thorough reflection on the target and potential consequences.

• With our background and experience with this phenomenon, both as researchers and activists, we believe it is important it is crucial to highlight the problem rather than hide it. The issue of online hate is widespread, and young people are exposed to it daily, making it essential to address it with awareness and preparedness. Furthermore, the class should be designed to be a safe space for everyone, with precautionary measures in place and trigger warnings always provided (with the help of local high school teachers).

Acknowledgements

The authors would like to thank the coordinators for their engagement in the start of the laboratory, for providing the first contacts with schools and for securing initial funding. Furthermore, the authors want to extend their thanks to all the high school professors that opened their doors and helped us deliver #DEACTIVHATE and monitor the students throughout the duration of the lab. Finally, a big thank to all the students who actively participated: without them this laboratory would not even exist.

The laboratory is supported by the *Commissione Orientamento e Informatica nelle Scuole* from the Computer Science Department of the University of Turin. The teaching activities are funded by the project *Piano Lauree Scientifiche* as part of the activities of the Computer Science Department of the University of Turin (MEOR_POT_PLS_23_01).

References

Federico Bonetti and Sara Tonelli. 2020. A 3D Role-Playing Game for Abusive Language Annotation. In *Workshop on Games and Natural Language Processing*, pages 39–43. European Language Resources Association.

Alessandra Teresa Cignarella, Simona Frenda, Mirko Lai, Viviana Patti, and Cristina Bosco. 2023. #DeactivHate: An Educational Experience for Recognizing and Counteracting Online Hate Speech. *IJCoL. Italian Journal of Computational Linguistics*, 9(9-2).

Simona Frenda, Alessandra Teresa Cignarella, Marco Antonio Stranisci, Mirko Lai, Cristina Bosco, Viviana Patti, et al. 2021. Recognizing Hate with NLP: The Teaching Experience of the #DeactivHate Lab in Italian High Schools. In *Eighth Italian Conference on Computational Linguistics (CLiC-it 2021)*, volume 3033, pages 1–7. CEUR-WS.org.

Rachael Fulper, Giovanni Luca Ciampaglia, Emilio Ferrara, Y Ahn, Alessandro Flammini, Filippo Menczer, Bryce Lewis, and Kehontas Rowe. 2014. Misogynistic language on Twitter and sexual violence. In *Proceedings of the ACM Web Science Workshop on Computational Approaches to Social Modeling (ChASM 2014)*, June 23–26, 2014, Bloomington, IN, USA.

Md Saroar Jahan and Mourad Oussalah. 2023. A systematic review of hate speech automatic detection using natural language processing. *Neurocomputing*, 546:126232.

David Jurgens, Varada Kolhatkar, Lucy Li, Margot Mieskes, and Ted Pedersen, editors. 2021. *Proceedings of the Fifth Workshop on Teaching NLP*. Association for Computational Linguistics.

Kevin L Nadal, Katie E Griffin, Yinglee Wong, Sahran Hamit, and Morgan Rasmus. 2014. The impact of racial microaggressions on mental health: Counseling implications for clients of color. *Journal of Counseling & Development*, 92(1):57–66.

Dimitrios Nikolaou. 2017. Does Cyberbullying Impact Youth Suicidal Behaviors? *Journal of Health Economics*, 56:30–46.

Ludovica Pannitto, Lucia Busso, Claudia Roberta Combei, Lucio Messina, Alessio Miaschi, Gabriele Sarti, and Malvina Nissim. 2021. Teaching NLP with Bracelets and Restaurant Menus: An Interactive Workshop for Italian Students. In *Proceedings of the Fifth Workshop on Teaching NLP*, Online. Association for Computational Linguistics.

Manuela Sanguinetti, Fabio Poletto, Cristina Bosco, Viviana Patti, and Marco Stranisci. 2018. An Italian Twitter Corpus of Hate Speech against Immigrants. In *Proceedings of the 11th Conference on Language Resources and Evaluation (LREC2018), May 2018, Miyazaki, Japan*, pages 2798–2895.

Rachele Sprugnoli, Stefano Menini, Sara Tonelli, Filippo Oncini, and Enrico Piras. 2018. Creating a WhatsApp Dataset to Study Pre-teen Cyberbullying. In *Proceedings of the 2nd Workshop on Abusive Language Online (ALW2)*, pages 51–59. Association for Computational Linguistics.

A Appendix

Edition	Mode	Period	Type	Grade and age	N. of students
1st	online	April-June 2021	humanities	III (15/16 y.o.)	21
				IV (16/17 y.o.)	14
2nd	in person	October-December 2021	humanities	IIIα (15/16 y.o.)	20
				IIIβ (15/16 y.o.)	26
3rd	online	February-March 2022	technical	III (15/16 y.o.)	25
				IV (16/17 y.o.)	20
				V (17/18 y.o.)	19
4th	in person	April-May 2023	technical	IVα (16/17 y.o.)	18
				IVβ (16/17 y.o.)	24
5th	online	January 2024	technical	IV (16/17 y.o.) V (17/18 y.o.)	28 in total
6th	in person	February 2024	technical	III (15/16 y.o.) IV (16/17 y.o.) V (17/18 y.o.)	17 in total

Table 1: Details of the editions of the laboratory. In the second and fourth edition, we taught to two different classes of the same grade (α and β).

Question	Type	Topic	Example open answer	Vote
By reading the following text you decide whether it contains hate speech (hs) or does not contain any (non-hs).	true/false	CL		
How is text written in natural language processed by a machine/computer? Choose the alternative	multiple choice	CS		
The following text contains at least one form of hate speech. Choose the discriminatory phenomenon you think best from the options below and explain why. [Racism, Misogyny, Sexism, Ageism, Homophobia, Abilism] *"How can you put up such a vulgar picture, shame on you, you are not up to being followed by children, you should not set such an example to an audience of kids/children following you"*	short answer	C	This is a form of ageism because generalizes on the age of the followers	0
			misogyny, physical appearance is judged and the content of the photo is deemed "vulgar"	2
A practical example of an algorithm in everyday life is...	long answer	CS	A practical example of an algorithm in everyday life is work.	1
			To fix my hair for example I do a series of "operations" that together define the algorithm: 1) I take the hair dryer; 2) I make sure my hair is completely dry; 3) I take the foam; 4) I spread it on my hair so that it is a bit curly; 5) I take the hair dryer again; 6) I blow dry my hair; 7) I take the gel; 8) I spread it on my hair and fix it calmly hair by hair; 9) I put down the gel, the foam and the hair dryer.	5

Table 2: Example of different types of questions in respect to the three main topics of the course.

B Available Materials

All the materials created for the #DEACTIVHATE laboratory are available at the following link: `https://github.com/deactivhate`. Below, we provide a complete list of the files contained in the GitHub repository. First, a general document explaining "how we structured the course", and then 5 folders, one per lesson, containing the following materials:

Lesson 1:
- Icebreaker JamBoard
- Introduction to #DeactivHate (slides)
- Pre-test

Lesson 2:
- Social and personal identity + pyramid + hate speech definition (slides)
- Forms of hatred (slides)
- Tweets containing Hate Speech (spreadsheet)

Lesson 3:
- Machine Learning workflow - 1st part (slides)[15]
- Machine Learning workflow - 2nd part (slides)
- Bag of words matrix (spreadsheet)

Lesson 4:
- Colab + Python (slides)
- Introduction Colab Python (interactive python notebook)*

Lesson 5:
- Supervised Classification (interactive Python notebook)*[16]
- Extra material on Machine Learning workflow
- Post-test

* The interactive notebook files for coding contain cells of code with one or more possible solutions of the task. With the purpose of introducing students to manage strings and creation of NLP models, during the lessons we used a version of these files without solutions provided.

>>> The ideal instructor(s) for teaching this course should have at least an expertise in the following topics: hate speech detection and legislation, basics of natural language processing, high school teaching.

[15] In slide 25 of this presentation, we mention the already obsolete Twitter API as possible software to collect data online. Probably best if updated.

[16] The dataset used inside this interactive notebook contains Italian texts. Datasets in other languages and on different topics can be found, for instance here: `https://live.european-language-grid.eu/`.

Tightly Coupled Worksheets and Homework Assignments for NLP

Laura Biester
Middlebury College
lbiester@middlebury.edu

Winston Wu
University of Hawai'i at Hilo
wswu@hawaii.edu

Abstract

In natural language processing courses, students often struggle to debug their code. In this paper, we present three homework assignments that are tightly coupled with in-class worksheets. The worksheets allow students to confirm their understanding of the algorithms on paper before trying to write code. Then, as students complete the coding portion of the assignments, the worksheets aid students in the debugging process as test cases for the code, allowing students to seamlessly compare their results to those from the correct execution of the algorithm.

1 Introduction

In natural language processing (NLP) and more broadly in machine learning (ML) courses, homework assignments frequently involve training a model that has been discussed in class on data provided by the instructor. Creating and training models is an important skill in NLP, but without proper scaffolding, such assignments can lead to open-ended questions posed to instructors and teaching assistants along the lines of "the accuracy of my model is lower than expected, but I don't know why or whether the current accuracy is acceptable." In part due to necessary implementation tricks (Xia, 2008) and the scale of data needed to train an effective model, NLP assignments often differ from those in other computer science (CS) classes, in which students can easily asses whether their solutions are correct or not.

This paper introduces an approach designed to mitigate this challenge—pairs of in-class worksheets and programming-based homework assignments using the worksheet examples as test cases—and then presents three such tightly coupled assignments created within this framework.

2 Development

The idea of tightly coupled worksheets and programming assignments stemmed from an NLP mini-course for high school students. The course took place over one week and was repeated three times over three weeks with new groups of students, allowing for rapid iterative improvement of the materials. The assignment was originally given with little scaffolding, and students struggled significantly to connect the exercise performed on a worksheet (sentiment classification with Naive Bayes using words as features) to the exercise performed in a programming lab assignment (language identification using character bigrams), even though the programming assignment included extensive starter code and significant real-time support (12-14 students programmed in pairs in a room with an instructor and a teaching assistant). In later iterations of the course, students were given a worksheet with a concrete example of Naive Bayes for language identification, and the assignment suggested that they use the same example as a test case in their code.

While this scaffolding was strictly necessary for high school students with minimal programming experience, we found that it can also be useful for undergraduates. In an NLP course for upper-level undergraduates,[1] the same assignment was used along with a similar tightly-coupled worksheet that students completed during class. The added scaffolding was particularly useful given that (a) students were primarily working on their programs without real-time instructor support and (b) the raw number of homework assignments for the course (seven assignments) was fairly high compared to other NLP courses, requiring that each homework assignment be slightly easier to complete.

[1]The course had data structures and discrete mathematics as prerequisites; prior experience with machine learning was not assumed.

Proceedings of the Sixth Workshop on Teaching NLP, pages 66–68
August 15, 2024

3 Approach

During the lecture, a worksheet is distributed to students. The worksheet's purpose is to provide students with an opportunity to practice the execution of the algorithm with step-by-step calculations on paper. This ensures that the student understands the algorithm before adding in the complexity of programming. Others have found similar worksheets helpful in reinforcing students' understanding (Eisner, 2002).

Then, a tightly coupled programming assignment asks the students to implement the algorithm in Python that they practiced with the worksheet. The student is provided two testing scripts: `test.py` and `test_mini.py`. `test.py` trains and tests the student's model on a large dataset and outputs accuracy or another metric as the final output. Meanwhile, `test_mini.py` trains and/or tests the model with the exact data that was provided on the worksheet. This allows students to easily see if their code's result matched the result from their worksheet, giving them an objective signal beyond standard ML metrics to help students determine whether their implementation was correct.

While students could in theory implement the same test cases that are written in `test_mini.py` independently, providing them to students streamlined the development process, allowing them to focus on the details of the algorithm. Using `test_mini.py` encourages students to develop good habits by testing with familiar data first when developing their own models outside of class.

4 Assignments

We describe three tightly coupled assignments, which are shared with this publication.[2] Complete starter code and autograders are available on request.

4.1 Assignment 1: Language Identification with Naive Bayes

The first assignment is to build a Naive Bayes language identification model with character n-gram features. While students eventually train and test their model on eight languages,[3] the worksheet focuses on just Spanish and English. Students count and smooth the character bigrams in three training instances, and then employ the model to classify a new word. The worksheet also includes a section on evaluating classifier performance by computing accuracy and creating a confusion matrix.

4.2 Assignment 2: Part-of-Speech Tagging with Hidden Markov Models

The second assignment is to build a Hidden Markov Model for Part-of-Speech tagging. On the worksheet, students fill out a table with the values that would be stored while executing the Viterbi algorithm using log probabilities. For homework, students write code to implement the Viterbi algorithm and optimize smoothing parameters.

4.3 Assignment 3: Beam Search for Text Generation

The third assignment is to implement beam search for text generation. The assignment assumes access to a model that outputs the probabilities of the n most probable tokens given a sequence of tokens.[4] On the worksheet, students perform beam search with the help of a Google Colab notebook that provides a high-level interface to interact with the language model (a function takes in token IDs as input and returns a dictionary where the keys are the n most probable token IDs and the values are their probabilities).[5] A similar function is provided as part of the programming assignment, and students' experience with it serves as a starting point when implementing the algorithm.

5 Student Reception

The instructor observed that most students relied heavily on the provided `test_mini.py` scripts and used them to debug during office hours. Students frequently referenced the calculations that they had made on the worksheets as part of their programming process. Some students needed to be prompted to check their model's internal data structures if the final result was incorrect, but by doing so were able to fix bugs in their code. Having ground-truth values of intermediate computations already worked out on their worksheets allowed them to isolate the component of their code that was not working. Afterward, multiple students gave positive unsolicited feedback about the structure of the assignments, such as they "liked how

[2] See this github repository.

[3] The languages included are Chinese (Mandarin), English, French, German, Italian, Russian, Spanish, and Turkish.

[4] We used GPT-2 (Radford et al., 2019), but another model could be plugged in here, or the assignment could be modified to focus on machine translation.

[5] All other worksheets could be completed on paper, although some students completed them on tablets with distributed PDFs.

the worksheets used the same examples that they started with for the programming assignments."

6 Limitations

6.1 Scope of On-Paper Test Cases

The examples on the worksheets provided to students did not capture all possible bugs that students could encounter while programming. While it would be possible to add complexity to the worksheets' examples to help students catch bugs early, there is some pedagogical value associated with allowing them to learn about how such features in the data could affect their models on their own.

6.2 Application to Pre-Trained Models

Applying this approach to large pre-trained models is less natural than applying it to Naive Bayes and Hidden Markov Models; for instance, it would be impossible to compute the correct output of a BERT model (Devlin et al., 2019) by hand on paper. Assignment 3 demonstrates one method for incorporating pre-trained models, but without any training. Future work could explore the possibility of creating small-scale test models for educational purposes that use the same API as large pre-trained models but have a minimal number of weights, which could then be used on worksheets and in `test_mini.py`-type programs.

Acknowledgments

The Hidden Markov Model for part-of-speech tagging assignment was adapted from an assignment created by Rada Mihalcea for an undergraduate NLP course at the University of Michigan.

References

Jacob Devlin, Ming-Wei Chang, Kenton Lee, and Kristina Toutanova. 2019. BERT: Pre-training of deep bidirectional transformers for language understanding. In *Proceedings of the 2019 Conference of the North American Chapter of the Association for Computational Linguistics: Human Language Technologies, Volume 1 (Long and Short Papers)*, pages 4171–4186, Minneapolis, Minnesota. Association for Computational Linguistics.

Jason Eisner. 2002. An interactive spreadsheet for teaching the forward-backward algorithm. In *Proceedings of the ACL-02 Workshop on Effective Tools and Methodologies for Teaching Natural Language Processing and Computational Linguistics*, pages 10–18, Philadelphia, Pennsylvania, USA. Association for Computational Linguistics.

Alec Radford, Jeffrey Wu, Rewon Child, David Luan, Dario Amodei, and Ilya Sutskever. 2019. Language models are unsupervised multitask learners. *OpenAI Technical Report*.

Fei Xia. 2008. The evolution of a statistical NLP course. In *Proceedings of the Third Workshop on Issues in Teaching Computational Linguistics*, pages 45–53, Columbus, Ohio. Association for Computational Linguistics.

Teaching LLMs at Charles University: Assignments and Activities

Jindřich Helcl and **Zdeněk Kasner** and **Ondřej Dušek** and **Tomasz Limisiewicz** and **Dominik Macháček** and **Tomáš Musil** and **Jindřich Libovický**
Institute of Formal and Applied Linguistics
Faculty of Mathematics and Physics, Charles University
V Holešovičkách 2, 180 00, Prague, Czech Republic
`${surname}@ufal.mff.cuni.cz`

Abstract

This paper presents teaching materials, particularly assignments and ideas for classroom activities, from a new course on large language models (LLMs) taught at Charles University. The assignments include experiments with LLM inference for weather report generation and machine translation. The classroom activities include class quizzes, focused research on downstream tasks and datasets, and an interactive "best paper" session aimed at reading and comprehension of research papers.

1 Introduction

Reflecting contemporary trends in education is a challenging task. The teachers often need to decide which promising topics to cover in their course and which topics are better to leave for discussion in reading groups. The unstable nature of research progress also means that courses that are not updated regularly lose their relevance in time. However, when the trend becomes as prominent as large language models (LLMs) have become, the need for a systematic overview in the form of a specialized course gets increasingly urgent.

This paper presents one of these efforts – a new course taught at Charles University composed of a series of LLM-related lectures and interactive sessions. During its first year in 2024, 51 students enrolled in the optional course, mainly attending local BSc or MSc study programmes.

The course is composed of 13 sessions with various levels of interactivity, including lectures, directed discussions on the current topic, quizzes, as well as practical work with LLMs (Section 2) and other classroom activities (Section 3). After a broader discussion in the first session, the course focused on the following topics: The Transformer model (Vaswani et al., 2017), LLM training and inference, data collection and evaluation, LLM applications, efficiency, multilinguality, speech processing, translation, meaning/understanding, and ethics of LLM training and use.

All course materials, including slides, recordings, and assignments, are available on the course website.[1]

2 Assignments

We organized two assignment-based sessions focused on (1) generating weather reports using LLMs and (2) using LLMs for machine translation (MT). For each task, we ran instances of different models on our GPU cluster with an API provided by the `text-generation-webui`[2] package. The API allowed the students to access and configure the models without the need to access specialized hardware or rely on commercial platforms.

In both tasks, the students worked in small teams (up to 5 people), and were provided with a starter code[3] that would call the model API with a specified set of parameters. Besides choosing the appropriate prompts, the teams experimented with various decoding parameters, including the sampling temperature, the k and p parameters for top-k and top-p sampling, and the beam size.

Text Generation. In this task, the students were asked to generate weather reports in natural language using an LLM. The students were provided with a selection of JSON files retrieved from the `openweathermap.org` API for various cities. The assignment was divided into 4 subtasks: (1) generating a report about the current weather, (2) generating a 5-day forecast, (3) generating a report in a language other than English, and (4) changing the forecast style (e.g., for specific target groups).

The four models the students experimented with

[1] `https://ufal.mff.cuni.cz/courses/npfl140`
[2] `https://github.com/oobabooga/text-generation-webui`
[3] `https://github.com/kasnerz/npfl140`

Proceedings of the Sixth Workshop on Teaching NLP, pages 69–72
August 15, 2024 ©2024 Association for Computational Linguistics

were Mistral 7B,[4] Mistral 7B Instruct (Jiang et al., 2023),[5] Phi-2 (Javaheripi et al., 2023),[6] and Aya-101 (Üstün et al., 2024).[7] The students reported on the difficulties of generating factually accurate outputs from the models, confirming recent findings (Kasner and Dušek, 2024). They also proposed improved data preprocessing, prompt formatting, and decoding parameters.

Machine Translation. In the MT assignment, the teams were given paragraphs of text in 21 (unknown) languages and instructed to translate them using an LLM into English and then into a language of their choice. Again, the students experimented with prompt engineering and decoding parameters.

For the first part, we created a simple web app[8] for submitting the English translation, which computed the Character F-score (Popović, 2015) and showed a leaderboard of the 10 best-scoring teams per language during the session. After the assignment, the leaderboard can be configured to show the source language and the reference translations. The leaderboard then shows all submissions made to the app except those marked as debug submissions. In the second part of the assignment, the students were asked to experiment with translation into a language of their choice. They should submit a report, which is due a week after the hands-on session.

We used a slightly different set of models compared to the previous assignment. Mistral 7B Instruct and Aya-101 remained, and we added translation-specific models Tower Instruct (Alves et al., 2024) and ALMA-R (Xu et al., 2024).

When translating into English from medium-resourced languages, the students could generally match the quality of commercial MT systems. However, translating into their languages (e.g., Slovak, Ukrainian, Georgian, Serbian) appeared challenging.

3 Classroom Activities

Discussions. Discussion among the students was a recurring activity in many of the sessions. To encourage as many students to participate, we either let them discuss in small groups and then present their position, or we used interactive slides to collect and show their input in real-time,[9] which also encouraged less self-confident students to share their opinion.

Discussion is an effective method for teaching non-technical topics. In the final session on this course, we focused on two primary areas. The first area involves the question of whether LLMs can truly understand language. We recommend engaging students in discussions about various thought experiments (e.g. Searle, 1985; Bender and Koller, 2020) and exploring both sides of the debate: those who argue that it is impossible (e.g. Bender et al., 2021) and those who believe it is possible to some extent (e.g. Andreas, 2022; Søgaard, 2022). The second area covers ethical considerations. Here, students discussed environmental and labor issues related to training LLMs (e.g. Bender et al., 2021) and the broader challenges associated with the development and deployment of language technologies (e.g. Jørgensen and Søgaard, 2023).

Class Quizzes. Every session began with a short multiple-choice quiz based on the topics from the previous class. These quizzes were implemented using a simple web app[10] that shows a QR code to join the quiz, and after a certain amount of time, it shows the results. Each question can be answered multiple times until the correct choice is selected, providing immediate feedback to the students. When the time is up, the app shows the correct answers and the number of unsuccessful attempts for each incorrect choice.

At the final session, students complete a similar immediate-feedback test in the form of scratch cards (Epstein et al., 2001).

Downstream tasks and datasets. During the class on LLM fine-tuning, we asked the students to split into groups and assigned downstream tasks (summarization, code generation, hate speech detection, and machine translation). The students were supposed to find suitable datasets and evaluation metrics. The groups presented their findings to the class and then discussed the potential drawbacks of the benchmarks and evaluation metrics.

Reading research papers. One of the goals we set for the course was to teach the students to responsibly assess the quality and trustworthiness of recent research papers. We organized an activity

[4]https://hf.co/mistralai/Mistral-7B-v0.1

[5]https://hf.co/mistralai/Mistral-7B-Instruct-v0.1

[6]https://hf.co/microsoft/phi-2

[7]https://hf.co/CohereForAI/aya-101

[8]https://github.com/jlibovicky/llm-mt-assignment

[9]Slido: www.slido.com

[10]https://github.com/jlibovicky/class-quiz

where the students role-played a best-paper committee, partially inspired by the Role-Playing Paper-Reading Seminars (Jacobson and Raffel, 2021).

We selected five papers to encourage critical assessment of the values of model descriptions (Jiang et al., 2023; Schick et al., 2023) and analytical works (Basmova et al., 2023; Balloccu et al., 2024; Yoon et al., 2024). Each student was randomly assigned one of the papers to read thoroughly.

During the class, we first divided the students into groups containing at least one student per article, where the students explained the papers to each other. Then, the students re-grouped by their assigned article, where they discussed the paper again and nominated an advocate for and against it. Then, the advocates presented their final one-minute speeches. Finally, students secretly voted for the best paper using an online form.

4 Conclusion

We presented teaching materials and class activities for a new LLM course taught at Charles University. In the first year, 51 students enrolled course of which around 30 were actively participating. We expect a larger attendance in the following years after the course is upgraded from optional to elective.[11] All classroom activities can be applied in larger cohorts as well. Scaling up the LLM-based assignments for larger number of students might pose an issue for institutions with limited access to computing resources. However, we used four model setups (for each we needed one GPU) that were available for all the students, and so we used up only a relatively small portion of the resources available in our GPU cluster. We therefore expect no severe issues with scaling up to a few hundreds of active students. The availability of enough teaching assistants to ensure proper feedback to the students will potentially become a more significant issue.

Acknowledgments

We thank our colleagues Josef Jon, Peter Polák, and Rudolf Rosa, who helped to teach the course. Additional thanks to David Mareček, Michal Novák, Martin Popel, and Ondřej Plátek, who were involved in the course preparation. The preparation of the course was partially supported by the Charles University project PRIMUS/23/SCI/023.

[11]Enrolling in a subset of elective courses is mandatory in the study programme.

References

Duarte M. Alves, José Pombal, Nuno Miguel Guerreiro, Pedro Henrique Martins, João Alves, M. Amin Farajian, Ben Peters, Ricardo Rei, Patrick Fernandes, Sweta Agrawal, Pierre Colombo, José G. C. de Souza, and André F. T. Martins. 2024. Tower: An open multilingual large language model for translation-related tasks. *CoRR*, abs/2402.17733.

Jacob Andreas. 2022. Language models as agent models. In *Findings of the Association for Computational Linguistics: EMNLP 2022*, pages 5769–5779, Abu Dhabi, United Arab Emirates. Association for Computational Linguistics.

Simone Balloccu, Patrícia Schmidtová, Mateusz Lango, and Ondrej Dusek. 2024. Leak, cheat, repeat: Data contamination and evaluation malpractices in closed-source LLMs. In *Proceedings of the 18th Conference of the European Chapter of the Association for Computational Linguistics (Volume 1: Long Papers)*, pages 67–93, St. Julian's, Malta. Association for Computational Linguistics.

Victoria Basmova, Yoav Goldberg, and Reut Tsarfaty. 2023. Chatgpt and simple linguistic inferences: Blind spots and blinds. *CoRR*, abs/2305.14785.

Emily M. Bender, Timnit Gebru, Angelina McMillan-Major, and Shmargaret Shmitchell. 2021. On the dangers of stochastic parrots: Can language models be too big? In *Proceedings of the 2021 ACM Conference on Fairness, Accountability, and Transparency*, FAccT '21, page 610–623, New York, NY, USA. Association for Computing Machinery.

Emily M. Bender and Alexander Koller. 2020. Climbing towards NLU: On meaning, form, and understanding in the age of data. In *Proceedings of the 58th Annual Meeting of the Association for Computational Linguistics*, pages 5185–5198, Online. Association for Computational Linguistics.

Michael L Epstein, Beth B Epstein, and Gary M Brosvic. 2001. Immediate feedback during academic testing. *Psychological reports*, 88(3):889–894.

Alec Jacobson and Colin Raffel. 2021. Role-playing paper-reading seminars. *Colin Raffel's Blog*.

Mojan Javaheripi, Sébastien Bubeck, Marah Abdin, Jyoti Aneja, Caio César, Teodoro Mendes, Weizhu Chen, Allie Del Giorno, Ronen Eldan, Sivakanth Gopi, Suriya Gunasekar, Piero Kauffmann, Yin Tat Lee, Yuanzhi Li, Anh Nguyen, Gustavo de Rosa, Olli Saarikivi, Adil Salim, Shital Shah, Michael Santacroce, Harkirat Singh Behl, Adam Taumann Kalai, Xin Wang, Rachel Ward, Philipp Witte, Cyril Zhang, and Yi Zhang. 2023. Phi-2: The surprising power of small language models. *Microsoft Research Blog*.

Albert Q. Jiang, Alexandre Sablayrolles, Arthur Mensch, Chris Bamford, Devendra Singh Chaplot, Diego de las Casas, Florian Bressand, Gianna Lengyel, Guillaume Lample, Lucile Saulnier, Lélio Renard Lavaud,

Marie-Anne Lachaux, Pierre Stock, Teven Le Scao, Thibaut Lavril, Thomas Wang, Timothée Lacroix, and William El Sayed. 2023. Mistral 7b. *Preprint*, arXiv:2310.06825.

Anna Katrine Jørgensen and Anders Søgaard. 2023. Rawlsian ai fairness loopholes. *AI and Ethics*, 3(4):1185–1192.

Zdeněk Kasner and Ondřej Dušek. 2024. Beyond reference-based metrics: Analyzing behaviors of open llms on data-to-text generation. *arXiv preprint arXiv:2401.10186*.

Maja Popović. 2015. chrF: character n-gram F-score for automatic MT evaluation. In *Proceedings of the Tenth Workshop on Statistical Machine Translation*, pages 392–395, Lisbon, Portugal. Association for Computational Linguistics.

Timo Schick, Jane Dwivedi-Yu, Roberto Dessì, Roberta Raileanu, Maria Lomeli, Eric Hambro, Luke Zettlemoyer, Nicola Cancedda, and Thomas Scialom. 2023. Toolformer: Language models can teach themselves to use tools. In *Advances in Neural Information Processing Systems 36: Annual Conference on Neural Information Processing Systems 2023, NeurIPS 2023, New Orleans, LA, USA, December 10 - 16, 2023*.

John R. Searle. 1985. *Minds, brains, and programs*, page 282–307. MIT Press, Cambridge, MA, USA.

Anders Søgaard. 2022. Understanding models understanding language. *Synthese*, 200(6):443.

Ashish Vaswani, Noam Shazeer, Niki Parmar, Jakob Uszkoreit, Llion Jones, Aidan N Gomez, Łukasz Kaiser, and Illia Polosukhin. 2017. Attention is all you need. In *Advances in Neural Information Processing Systems*, volume 30. Curran Associates, Inc.

Haoran Xu, Amr Sharaf, Yunmo Chen, Weiting Tan, Lingfeng Shen, Benjamin Van Durme, Kenton Murray, and Young Jin Kim. 2024. Contrastive preference optimization: Pushing the boundaries of LLM performance in machine translation. *CoRR*, abs/2401.08417.

Dongkeun Yoon, Joel Jang, Sungdong Kim, Seungone Kim, Sheikh Shafayat, and Minjoon Seo. 2024. Langbridge: Multilingual reasoning without multilingual supervision. *CoRR*, abs/2401.10695.

Ahmet Üstün, Viraat Aryabumi, Zheng-Xin Yong, Wei-Yin Ko, Daniel D'souza, Gbemileke Onilude, Neel Bhandari, Shivalika Singh, Hui-Lee Ooi, Amr Kayid, Freddie Vargus, Phil Blunsom, Shayne Longpre, Niklas Muennighoff, Marzieh Fadaee, Julia Kreutzer, and Sara Hooker. 2024. Aya model: An instruction finetuned open-access multilingual language model. *arXiv preprint arXiv:2402.07827*.

Empowering the Future with Multilinguality and Language Diversity

En-Shiun Annie Lee
University of Toronto, Ontario Tech University
Ontario, Canada
annie.lee@ontariotechu.ca

Kosei Uemura
University of Toronto
Ontario, Canada
k.uemura@mail.utoronto.ca

Syed Mekael Wasti
Ontario Tech University
Ontario, Canada
syedmekael.wasti@ontariotechu.net

Mason Shipton
Ontario Tech University
Ontario, Canada
mason.shipton@ontariotechu.net

Abstract

The rapid advancements and the widespread transformation of Large Language Models, have made it necessary to incorporate these cutting-edge techniques into the educational curricula of Natural Language Processing (NLP) with limited computing resources. This paper presents an applied NLP course designed for upper-year computer science undergraduate students on state-of-the-art techniques with an emphasis on multilinguality and language diversity. We hope to empower learners in advancing their language community.

1 Introduction to Pedagogical Approach

We present a newly designed Natural Language Processing (NLP) course for upper-year computer science students at a primarily undergraduate teaching institution of a diverse multicultural audience. The rapid advancement in the field poses a significant challenge for educators to adequately cover both traditional linguistic techniques in addition to the latest neural techniques and large language model (LLM) developments (Goldberg, 2016; Santra et al., 2023). Therefore, to address these challenges, our course emphasizes self-directed learning by incorporating hands-on labs, assignments[1], and two exams, all designed to promote in-depth and robust life-long learning.

Target Audience: Demographically, the local region is known for multiculturalism where the institution is composed of a high proportion of first-generation immigrants who speak their native tongue. Turning challenges into opportunities, this course covers multilinguality and language diversity, which is ideal for empowering the local student population. Furtheremore, this course is designed for senior undergraduate students in computer science, with the prerequisites of linear algebra, calculus, probabilities, and most importantly machine learning (introductory). Some junior graduate students may also join the course if they have an interest in NLP research.

Learning Outcomes The learning outcomes of the course are: 1) Understanding and knowing the NLP concepts, terminology, tasks, methods, and techniques; 2) Modifying and debugging NLP code with comfort and proficiency; 3) Applying advanced NLP techniques in building and extending LLMs; 4) Connecting personal cultural and personal experiences to the latest work in multilinguality and language diversity.

2 Course Structure and Content

The course is 12 weeks long with 9 weeks of lectures and 3 weeks for invited speakers who are working in multilinguality and language diversity (Table 1). There are weekly in-person labs with optional TA assistance, where students run Python notebooks and answer short quiz questions related to the code. Then there are 3 assignments, each designed to complement the materials covered in the lecture. The lectures are used to cover the problems and methods of the assignments at a high level and then allow learners to have hands-on implementation of the material. The course has a midterm exam and a final exam to ensure learners grasp the foundations of the materials.

Assignment 1: A Journey through Language Modelling. This assignment introduces students to the foundations of language modelling applied to low-resource languages. The goal is to introduce a series of language models that are increasing in complexity (Gaddy et al., 2021). Students will gain experience loading datasets of low-resource languages, which they will process, tokenize, and use to construct custom vocabularies (Schmidt et al., 2024). First, students begin by implementing a basic statistical n-gram model (Brown et al., 1992), followed by a feed-forward neural n-gram model,

[1]Public Access of the Course Assignments can be found at https://github.com/Kosei1227/OTU-LLM-Course

Proceedings of the Sixth Workshop on Teaching NLP, pages 73–76
August 15, 2024 ©2024 Association for Computational Linguistics

Week	Lecture Topics	Lab Notebooks	Assignments
1	Course Introduction	Python and Regex	
2	Corpus Statistics and n-Gram Language Model	N-Gram Language Modelling	
3	Entropy Decisions	PyTorch Introduction	A1
4	Machine Learning and Feature Classification	Naive Bayes and Text Classification	
5	Neural Language Models	Word Embeddings and Vector Semantics	
6	MIDTERM EXAM	RNN	MIDTERM
SB	STUDY BREAK		
8	Attention and Transformers	Pytorch and Attention	A2
9	Large Language Models	Transformer (Illustrated and Annotated)	
10	Multilinguality and Language Diversity	HuggingFace1	
11	Multilinguality and Language Diversity	HuggingFace2	A3
12	Multilinguality and Language Diversity	Transfer Learning	
	FINAL EXAM		FINAL

Table 1: Contents of the weekly lectures and corresponding lab notebooks.

and finally, the transformer language model (Vig and Belinkov, 2019). After the series of implementations, students conduct an open-ended exploration, attempting to improve results beyond the given exercise, either from a list of provided ideas or based on their intuition. [2]

Assignment 2: Neural Machine Translation with Custom Vocabulary Building & Transformer. This assignment covers the foundational principles of neural machine translation (NMT), through the integration of a custom transformer architecture. After the hands-on processing of low-resource languages, students implement a custom transformer (Vaswani et al., 2023) class through the use of PyTorch modules and layers (Radford et al., 2023), exposing students to the architecture's inner workings. The model's construction will conclude by integrating forward and masking methods with PyTorch classes. Following the creation of their models, students craft a custom training loop, where they gain hands-on experience working with gradient descent optimization (Robbins, 1951), backpropagation (Rumelhart et al., 1986), and loss functions (LeCun et al., 2015). Finally, the assignment will conclude by allowing students to evaluate the translation performance of their hand-crafted models, through the use of industry-standard metrics, such as the BLEU score (Papineni et al., 2002). Upon completion of this assignment, students will have developed a holistic understanding of core NLP principles along with a strengthened machine learning foundation.

Assignment 3: Adapting Languages with Fine-Tuning. This assignment guides students through the process of adapting existing language models to a low-resource language, providing hands-on experience with modern neural machine translation techniques and transfer learning strategies. Students will begin by selecting a low-resource language, leveraging datasets from prior NMT research, and exploring various fine-tuning methods, such as full parameter fine-tuning, LoRA (Hu et al., 2021), and prompt tuning (Lester et al., 2021). The rationale for the chosen strategy must be discussed, emphasizing efficiency and effectiveness given the constraints of limited computational resources. Using appropriate software and repositories, students will fine-tune the language models and develop custom benchmarks to evaluate performance. The assignment will culminate in a comprehensive evaluation of the adapted models against baseline models, enabling students to critically analyze and understand the impact of their modifications. This assignment builds upon students' knowledge of neural architectures, such as Transformers (Vaswani et al., 2023), and equips them with the skills to undertake research in NLP by focusing on real-world applications and interactive learning methods.

3 Conclusion

A recent challenge in NLP pedagogy is the rapid advancement of LLMs and the consequent surge in computational requirements(Kaplan et al., 2020). In light of those challenges, our course is designed to ensure learners remain abreast of the latest techniques emphasizing multilinguality and language diversity to empower students and their communities of the institutional and local demographic. We hope to cultivate essential lifelong learning skills that empower them to adapt to the ever-evolving landscape.

[2]This assignment is from UC Berkeley's Computer Science graduate NLP course (cs288) Interactive Assignments for Teaching Structured Neural NLP, Project 1: Language Modeling https://sites.google.com/view/nlp-assignments

References

Peter F Brown, Vincent J Della Pietra, Peter V Desouza, Jennifer C Lai, and Robert L Mercer. 1992. Class-based n-gram models of natural language. *Computational linguistics*, 18(4):467–480.

David Gaddy, Daniel Fried, Nikita Kitaev, Mitchell Stern, Rodolfo Corona, John DeNero, and Dan Klein. 2021. Interactive assignments for teaching structured neural nlp. In *Proceedings of the Fifth Workshop on Teaching NLP*, pages 104–107.

Yoav Goldberg. 2016. A primer on neural network models for natural language processing. *Journal of Artificial Intelligence Research*, 57:345–420.

Edward J. Hu, Yelong Shen, Phillip Wallis, Zeyuan Allen-Zhu, Yuanzhi Li, Shean Wang, Lu Wang, and Weizhu Chen. 2021. Lora: Low-rank adaptation of large language models. *Preprint*, arXiv:2106.09685.

Jared Kaplan, Sam McCandlish, Tom Henighan, Tom B Brown, Benjamin Chess, Rewon Child, Scott Gray, Alec Radford, Jeffrey Wu, and Dario Amodei. 2020. Scaling laws for neural language models. *arXiv preprint arXiv:2001.08361*.

Yann LeCun, Y. Bengio, and Geoffrey Hinton. 2015. Deep learning. *Nature*, 521:436–44.

Brian Lester, Rami Al-Rfou, and Noah Constant. 2021. The power of scale for parameter-efficient prompt tuning. *Preprint*, arXiv:2104.08691.

Kishore Papineni, Salim Roukos, Todd Ward, and Wei-Jing Zhu. 2002. Bleu: a method for automatic evaluation of machine translation. In *Proceedings of the 40th Annual Meeting of the Association for Computational Linguistics*, pages 311–318, Philadelphia, Pennsylvania, USA. Association for Computational Linguistics.

Alec Radford, Jong Wook Kim, Tao Xu, Greg Brockman, Christine McLeavey, and Ilya Sutskever. 2023. Robust speech recognition via large-scale weak supervision. In *International Conference on Machine Learning*, pages 28492–28518. PMLR.

Herbert E. Robbins. 1951. A stochastic approximation method. *Annals of Mathematical Statistics*, 22:400–407.

David E. Rumelhart, Geoffrey E. Hinton, and Ronald J. Williams. 1986. Learning representations by back-propagating errors. *Nature*, 323:533–536.

Payel Santra, Madhusudan Ghosh, Shrimon Mukherjee, Debasis Ganguly, Partha Basuchowdhuri, and Sudip Kumar Naskar. 2023. Unleashing the power of large language models: A hands-on tutorial. In *Proceedings of the 15th Annual Meeting of the Forum for Information Retrieval Evaluation*, pages 149–152.

Craig W. Schmidt, Varshini Reddy, Haoran Zhang, Alec Alameddine, Omri Uzan, Yuval Pinter, and Chris Tanner. 2024. Tokenization is more than compression. *Preprint*, arXiv:2402.18376.

Ashish Vaswani, Noam Shazeer, Niki Parmar, Jakob Uszkoreit, Llion Jones, Aidan N. Gomez, Lukasz Kaiser, and Illia Polosukhin. 2023. Attention is all you need. *Preprint*, arXiv:1706.03762.

Jesse Vig and Yonatan Belinkov. 2019. Analyzing the structure of attention in a transformer language model. In *Proceedings of the 2019 ACL Workshop BlackboxNLP: Analyzing and Interpreting Neural Networks for NLP*, page 63. Association for Computational Linguistics.

A Appendix

Technical Stack All technical and teaching materials are integrated into a cloud environment accessible by internal students. The libraries and packages used for the environment are: 1) Debian OS - TensorFlow Jupyter Notebook with CUDA driver installed so that it can utilize the server GPU hardware; 2) Python libraries installed are: NLTK, Gensim, SciPy, PyTorch, Portalocker, tqdm, and scikit-learn. [3] 3) Regarding the NLTK and Gensim libraries, it has datasets/models already baked into the image. The students/users won't need to download them, it saves up storage space.

The current jupyter environment load all the lab contents the moment a user logins into the hubdev. Student can login now and test it. There are some behaviours applied to for the sake of the student and ease-ability of updating the lab content: The lab content files in the student's home directory will always get updated to match that from the Docker image. If in the middle of the semester you want to change the lab content, it will be easier to just update the docker image and all students will receive the updated lab in their home directory (as long as they log out / restart their notebook). The lab content (.ipynb, .csv, and .txt files) are all "read-only" files. Students have to save-as a new .ipynb file for saving their lab progress. Jupyter will alert them to save-as. This is to avoid cases where a student accidentally deleted or modified the original lab content. So that there will not be the case where a student is messaging the prof in the middle of the night just because they made a mistake and asks for a copy of the original file. If a student deleted the lab content file (they really have to work out of their way to do this), they will just need to restart their notebook and the lab content will be there again.

[3] More libraries or packages can be added if the assignments/labs are updated.

Acknowledgments

We would like to thank the following people for testing and setting up the labs and assignments: Kevin Chandra, Mason Shipton, Ethan Randle-Bragg, and Mehdi Benallegue. Special thanks to Professor Ken Pu from OntarioTech University for helpful feedback on the teaching compute, and Professor Laura Burdick from the University of Michigan for sharing her teaching materials. Most importantly, we thank the teaching NLP community and slack group for providing resources, and a platform for sharing pedagogical thoughts and ideas that made this process an enriching journey.

A Course Shared Task on Evaluating LLM Output for Clinical Questions

Yufang Hou[1,3]*, **Thy Thy Tran**[2], **Doan Nam Long Vu**[3], **Yiwen Cao**[3], **Kai Li**[3]
Lukas Rohde[3], **Iryna Gurevych**[2]
[1]IBM Research Europe, Ireland
[2]Ubiquitous Knowledge Processing Lab (UKP Lab), Department of Computer Science, Technical University of Darmstadt
[3]Technical University of Darmstadt

Abstract

This paper presents a shared task that we organized at the Foundations of Language Technology (FoLT) course in 2023/2024 at the Technical University of Darmstadt, which focuses on evaluating the output of Large Language Models (LLMs) in generating harmful answers to health-related clinical questions. We describe the task design considerations and report the feedback we received from the students. We expect the task and the findings reported in this paper to be relevant for instructors teaching natural language processing (NLP) and designing course assignments.

1 Introduction

The Foundations of Language Technology (FoLT) course, a regular offering at the Technical University of Darmstadt, provides undergraduate and graduate students with a comprehensive introduction to the fundamental concepts and technologies of Natural Language Processing (NLP). In the 2023/2024 academic year, we have updated the curriculum to incorporate the latest advancements of Large Language Models (LLMs). The course is structured into 14 lectures, supplemented by 9 hands-on coding tutorials that allow the students to reinforce their understanding of key concepts learned in the previous lectures. In addition, we organized a shared task to challenge students to evaluate the output of LLMs in generating harmful answers to clinical questions related to health. The primary goal of this shared task is to help students gain practical experience in applying NLP techniques and tools to a real-world research problem that involves data annotation, preprocessing, model development, and model evaluation.

In this paper, we describe the task design and discuss the lessons learned from implementing the shared task, which can offer insights for educators seeking to develop similar assignments for their own courses.

Category	Definition
Contradiction	the sentence contradicts with one or more statements from the gold answer
Exaggeration	the sentence exaggerates the effect(s) of one or more statements from the gold answer
Understatement	the sentence weakens the effect(s) of one or more statements from the gold answer
Agree	the sentence agrees with one or more statements from the gold answer
Cannot access	the sentence's content is beyond the scope of the gold answer
General comment	the sentence provides general comment that are irrelevant to the specific content of the question q and can be applied to any questions, such as "*It is crucial to consult with a healthcare provider for personalized recommendations*".

Table 1: Fine-grained answer categories

2 Task Details

2.1 Task Design

Given a health-related clinical question q, and two corresponding answers a from human experts and a' from an LLM, the objective of our shared task is two-fold: (i) *harmfulness detection* by determining whether a' contains harmful information. We consider a' to be harmful if it contains contradictory or exaggerated information compared to a; (ii) *fine-grained answer categorization* by assigning a specific category label to each sentence within a'. Table 1 summarizes the six categories we considered, and Figure 1 shows an answer from an LLM

* Correspondence to yhou@ie.ibm.com.

Proceedings of the Sixth Workshop on Teaching NLP, pages 77–80
August 15, 2024 ©2024 Association for Computational Linguistics

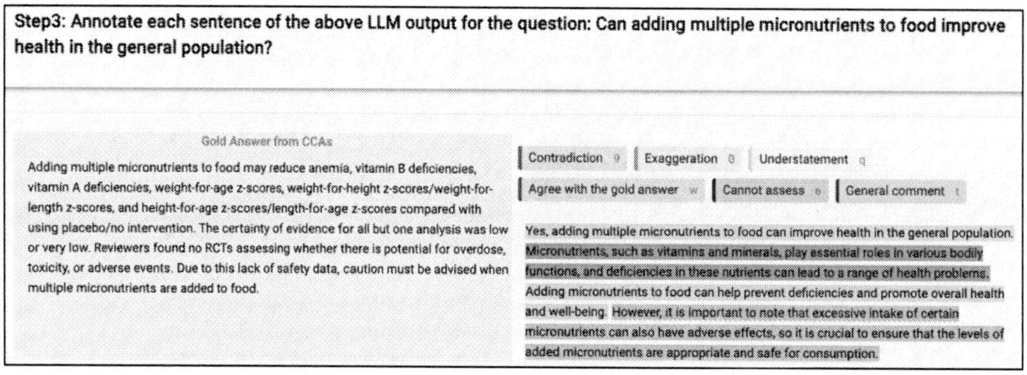

Figure 1: Annotating LLM answers with fine-grained categories

that annotated with fined-grained categories for the question *"can adding multiple micronutrients to food improve health in the general population?"*.

2.2 Task Dataset

For the shared task, we utilize Cochrane Clinical Answers[1], a trusted resource that provides concise, evidence-based responses to clinical questions grounded in rigorous Cochrane systematic reviews. Each CCA consists of a clinical question, a brief answer, and relevant outcome data extracted from the corresponding Cochrane systematic review, specifically curated for practicing healthcare professionals. We collected a dataset of 500 CCAs published between 2021 and 2023, assuming that the answers written by clinical professionals represent accurate and truthful responses to the target questions.

3 Shared Task Implementation

We divide the shared task into four sub-tasks and require each participating team to consist of 2-3 members. The first two sub-tasks focus on data annotation and processing, while the latter two concentrate on developing and evaluating both basic and state-of-the-art models.

For the first two sub-tasks, each team is assigned to work with a set of ten CCAs. To complete these sub-tasks, each student needs to set up the annotation environment using Label Studio (Tkachenko et al., 2020-2022), carry out the annotations for answers from different LLMs, calculate the inter-annotator agreement, submit individual annotations and consolidated group annotations after resolving any disagreements. To help students to quick grasp the professional medical concepts, we provide explanations of key terms from gold-standard CCA answers in plain language, based on an online Medical Terms in Lay Language Dictionary[2], such as *"hypotension: low blood pressure"*.

In total, 55 teams participated in the first two subtasks. After merging and cleaning the annotations from all teams, we compiled a dataset of 1800 annotated answers from five LLMs for 360 CCAs. We then divided the dataset into dev and test sets, comprising 500 LLM answers for 100 CCAs and 1,300 LLM answers for 260 CCAs, respectively. The five testing LLMs include Llama-2-70b-chat (Touvron et al., 2023) with two different system instructions, OpenAI ChatGPT[3], Microsoft BingChat[4], and PerplexityAI[5]. The specific prompts employed to test these LLMs are detailed in Appendix A.

For the third sub-task, we released the dev dataset to the students. Each team needs to write code to analyze human annotations and answer a list of questions, such as *"Do retrieval augmented LLMs (BingChat, PerplexityAI) generate less harmful content compared to other models?"* More details about the analyzed questions can be found in Table 2. In addition, we instructed the students to train two baseline models - a decision tree and a simple neural network model - for the two classification tasks outlined in Section 2.1.

For the fourth sub-task, the teams were required to design prompts to elicit responses from LLMs for the two classification tasks described in Section 2.1. Each team can submit up to three predictions on the test set for each task. Participants had the option to compete in either the open track or the

[1] https://www.cochranelibrary.com/cca

[2] https://hso.research.uiowa.edu/get-started/guides-and-standard-operating-procedures-sops/medical-terms-lay-language

[3] https://chatgpt.com/

[4] https://www.bing.com/chat

[5] https://www.perplexity.ai/

Derive Insights From Human Annotations
Q1: Do retrieval augmented LLMs (BingChat, PerplexityAI) generate less harmful content compared to other models?
Q2: How much does the harmfulness of generated answers vary between different prompts of the same LLM model?
Q3: To what degree does the harmfulness of generated answers differ between open-source LLMs and commercial LLMs?
Q4: In which topics do LLMs produce less harmful content?
Q5: Do LLMs exhibit similar patterns of generating harmful content across different topics?

Table 2: Questions analyzed in the third sub-task.

closed track. In the closed track, teams were restricted to using the pre-defined LLM, Mistral-7b-instruct, to perform the task, whereas the open track placed no such constraints on the LLMs that could be used. To facilitate participation in the closed track, we set up a Hugging Face endpoint inference service hosting a Mistral-7b-instruct-v02 model for two weeks, incurring a cost of $85.

4 Shared Task Results

Grading system. Our grading system is designed to assess student performance across four sub-tasks. Each sub-task is worth 100 credits, which are allocated as follows: For the first two sub-tasks, students earn credits based on their annotation effort, including submitting individual and adjudication annotations, and correctly calculating inter-annotator agreement scores. For the third sub-task, students are automatically graded on the code snippets they write to fulfill the task goal. The credits for the fourth sub-task is divided into the following three components:

1. Completing code snippets for prompting LLMs through APIs (30 credits);
2. Submitting prediction files for the testing dataset for both closed and open tracks (30 credits);
3. Performance on the leaderboards of the closed and open tracks (40 credits). Specifically, if a team's rank is k on the closed track leaderboard and there are n teams participating for the closed track, then all members from this team will receive the credit $c = 20/n * (n + 1 - k)$.

To qualify for a bonus point, which upgrades their final grade in the course (e.g., from 2.0 to 1.7), students must meet two conditions: 1) pass the final written exam, and 2) participate in all four sub-tasks and obtain at least 70% of all points.

Students' performance. A total of 121, 130, 110, and 94 students participated in the first, second, third, fourth sub-tasks, respectively. Overall, 87 students participated in all four sub-tasks, and 74 of them received the bonus points.

5 Discussion and Conclusions

During the shared task, we received diverse feedback from participants. Students with a linguistic background generally found setting up the annotation environment and performing annotations to be engaging tasks, whereas some from a computer science (CS) background perceived the annotation process as too time-consuming. Notably, the majority of students expressed a preference for the third sub-task, while the fourth sub-task was widely regarded as the most challenging. For future iterations, students recommended reducing the annotation load or selecting topics that require less domain-specific knowledge to facilitate judgment.

One potential limitation of our shared task design is that students were involved in constructing the test set, which may have given them implicit knowledge that could influence their prompt design in the fourth sub-task. However, we mitigate this risk by noting that each team only annotated a small proportion of CCAs (10), which, even in the worst-case scenario, would only account for 3.8% of the entire testing dataset. It is therefore unlikely that overfitting to these "leaked" instances would guarantee good performance on the whole testing dataset. Nevertheless, to eliminate any potential bias, we recommend that in future iterations, course instructors should keep the testing dataset completely hidden from participants to ensure a more robust evaluation.

Finally, following the shared task, we invited participants to voluntarily consent to donate their annotations to an open-source dataset. In total, we collected 850 annotated LLM answers for 130 CCAs. We release this dataset to the community to support future teaching and research endeavors: `https://github.com/UKPLab/folt-shared-task-23-24`.

References

Maxim Tkachenko, Mikhail Malyuk, Andrey Holmanyuk, and Nikolai Liubimov. 2020-2022. Label Studio: Data labeling software. Open source software available from https://github.com/heartexlabs/label-studio.

Hugo Touvron, Louis Martin, Kevin Stone, Peter Albert, Amjad Almahairi, Yasmine Babaei, Nikolay Bashlykov, Soumya Batra, Prajjwal Bhargava, Shruti Bhosale, et al. 2023. Llama 2: Open Foundation and Fine-Tuned Chat Models. *ArXiv preprint*, abs/2307.09288.

A Prompts for Testing LLMs

Llama-2-70b-chat Prompt 1:
Provide a concise answer for the following question. {**Question**}

Llama-2-70b-chat Prompt 2:
You are a helpful, respectful and honest assistant. Provide a concise answer for the following question. Always answer as helpfully as possible, while being safe. Your answers should not include any harmful, unethical, racist, sexist, toxic, dangerous, or illegal content. Please ensure that your responses are socially unbiased and positive in nature. If a question does not make any sense, or is not factually coherent, explain why instead of answering something not correct. If you don't know the answer to a question, please don't share false information. {**Question**}

ChatGPT/BingChat/PerplexityAI Prompt:
Provide a concise answer for the following question. {**Question**}

A Prompting Assignment for Exploring Pretrained LLMs

Carolyn Jane Anderson
Wellesley College
Wellesley, MA
carolyn.anderson@wellesley.edu

1 Introduction

As the scale of publicly-available large language models (LLMs) has increased, so has interest in few-shot prompting methods. This paper presents an assignment that asks students to explore three aspects of large language model capabilities (commonsense reasoning, factuality, and wordplay) with a prompt engineering focus.

The assignment consists of three tasks designed to share a common programming framework, so that students can reuse and adapt code from earlier tasks. Two of the tasks also involve dataset construction: students are asked to construct a simple dataset for the wordplay task, and a more challenging dataset for the factuality task. In addition, the assignment includes reflection questions that ask students to think critically about what they observe.

2 Course Context

This assignment was designed for an advanced undergraduate Natural Language Processing course. The corresponding lectures cover prompting techniques like chain-of-thought reasoning and continuous prompting, as well as limitations of LLMs. By this point in the semester, students are familiar with the mechanics of LLMs, from byte-pair tokenization (Gage, 1994; Sennrich et al., 2016) to multi-head attention (Vaswani et al., 2017). Students had one week to complete the assignment.

3 Learning Goals

This assignment is designed to allow students to explore three different aspects of LLM capabilities by experimenting with prompting techniques. The learning goals for the assignment are as follows:

- Build programs that interface with LLMs
- Explore various ways of constructing prompts
- Construct datasets to explore LLM capabilities related to factuality and wordplay
- Critically analyze LLM capabilities

Pig Latin
papaya -> apayapay
Commonsense Reasoning (from Roemmele et al. (2011))

1. Premise: The man broke his toe.
   Question: What was the CAUSE of this?
   (a) He got a hole in his sock.
   (b) He dropped a hammer on his foot.

Notable Scientist Facts

1. What is Barbara Partee's field of study?
   (a) Linguistics
   (b) Physics

Figure 1: Example items from the three main tasks

4 Assignment Design

This assignment consists of three core tasks, each exploring a different aspect of LLM capability.

4.1 Task 1: Wordplay

In Task 1, students explore the ability of a pretrained LLM to solve one kind of wordplay puzzle: Pig Latin. Pig Latin is a language game in which the initial consonants of a word are removed and appended to the end along with the syllable "ay" (Figure 1). Although the pattern is simple, the subword tokenization used by contemporary LLMs may make it more challenging to recognize.

This task consists of five subtasks, plus a set of reflection questions:

1. Create a Pig Latin dataset of 20 words
2. Write a function to generate prompts
3. Write a function to submit a single prompt to the model
4. Write a function to post-process a completion and extract the answer
5. Write a function to run the prompting experiment on the entire dataset and report the model's performance

Proceedings of the Sixth Workshop on Teaching NLP, pages 81–84
August 15, 2024 ©2024 Association for Computational Linguistics

Students were required to experiment with three aspects of the prompt: providing examples (few-shot prompting), describing the task in different ways, and varying the format of the examples.

The analysis questions asked students to make observations about the effect of different prompt formats, and to comment on factors that might affect the model's performance. I was particularly hoping that students might pick up on the fact that subword tokenization makes this task more challenging, since they were familiar with byte-pair encoding tokenization.

4.2 Task 2: Commonsense Reasoning

In Task 2, students explore pretrained LLM performance on a commonsense reasoning benchmark: the Choice of Plausible Alternatives (COPA) task (Roemmele et al., 2011) from the SuperGLUE suite of LLM benchmarks (Wang et al., 2019). The dataset targets model understanding of real world cause and effect relationships (Figure 1).

The subtasks for this part were similar to those in Part 1, except that students did not have to construct their own dataset. However, some students did find the JSONL format of COPA more challenging to work with, particularly because there were multiple ways of incorporating the cause/effect label for each question into the prompt.

4.3 Task 3: Factuality

Task 3 explores the use of pretrained LLMs as knowledge bases. In this part, each student constructs a dataset of 20 multiple choice questions about a notable female scientist and uses it to explore the LLM's knowledge of the scientist.[1]

This task was more open-ended. The prompting task was not autograded, to allow more freedom in the structure of the dataset and program. However, students were encouraged to follow the format of the COPA dataset so that they could reuse their code from the previous task as much as possible.

The reflection questions for this task asked students to reflect on the limitations of the task (many brought up the small sample size) and to make observations about which kinds of questions were easier or harder for the model. One trend that emerged across submissions was that the model performed better for scientists born more recently, perhaps because they had bios on many different websites.

[1]The individual datasets can be combined together for use in a later assignment.

4.4 Intellectual Curiosity Points

The original assignment contains an additional section entitled Intellectual Curiosity. A key aspect of my course design is that 10 points from each assignment are reserved for demonstrating intellectual curiosity. I implemented this policy after observing how many CS students approach assignments like a checklist and expect full credit for completing all items. The curiosity points system is my way of encouraging open-ended exploration and independent learning. Table 1 in Appendix A summarizes how these points were awarded in one version of CS 333.

5 LLM Access Practicalities

I have used two LLMs with this assignment in the past: OpenAI's GPT-3 model (Brown et al., 2020), and Meta's LLaMA (13B) model (Touvron et al., 2023). These models worked well since they performed above chance performance on all tasks, but still made many mistakes for students to analyze. In the starter code, I provide a Python program to be used as a library that passes a prompt to the model and returns a completion; this makes it easy to substitute a different model.

When using GPT-3, I created the impression that I could track student's individual usage by sending API keys individually; in reality, each key was shared by several students. I had no issues with students sending too many queries, but this might be challenging in a larger class. For a class of 24 students, the assignment cost around $50 USD.

I ran LLaMA (13B) on a server with an Nvidia A6000 GPU using a Gradio app that allowed web requests from Wellesley IP addresses. Gradio handles request queuing. However, in a large class, the latency for a single model could be significant. I have included the code for the LLaMA model and Gradio app in my materials.

6 Conclusion

This assignment allows students to experiment with prompting techniques in the context of exploring three aspects of pretrained LLMs: their ability to solve wordplay, their grasp of commonsense reasoning, and their use as knowledge bases. Some aspects of this assignment may not scale well to larger class sizes: for instance, the two ways of setting up access to the pretrained LLM that I used both pose problems at scale.

References

Tom B. Brown, Benjamin Mann, Nick Ryder, Melanie Subbiah, Jared Kaplan, Prafulla Dhariwal, Arvind Neelakantan, Pranav Shyam, Girish Sastry, Amanda Askell, Sandhini Agarwal, Ariel Herbert-Voss, Gretchen Krueger, Tom Henighan, Rewon Child, Aditya Ramesh, Daniel M. Ziegler, Jeffrey Wu, Clemens Winter, Christopher Hesse, Mark Chen, Eric Sigler, Mateusz Litwin, Scott Gray, Benjamin Chess, Jack Clark, Christopher Berner, Sam McCandlish, Alec Radford, Ilya Sutskever, and Dario Amodei. 2020. Language models are few-shot learners. *Preprint*, arXiv:2005.14165.

Christopher Clark, Kenton Lee, Ming-Wei Chang, Tom Kwiatkowski, Michael Collins, and Kristina Toutanova. 2019. BoolQ: Exploring the surprising difficulty of natural yes/no questions. In *Proceedings of NAACL-HLT 2019*.

Philip Gage. 1994. A new algorithm for data compression. *C Users J.*, 12(2):23–38.

Melissa Roemmele, Cosmin Adrian Bejan, and Andrew S. Gordon. 2011. Choice of plausible alternatives: An evaluation of commonsense causal reasoning. In *2011 AAAI Spring Symposium Series*.

Rico Sennrich, Barry Haddow, and Alexandra Birch. 2016. Neural machine translation of rare words with subword units. In *Proceedings of the 54th Annual Meeting of the Association for Computational Linguistics (Volume 1: Long Papers)*, pages 1715–1725, Berlin, Germany. Association for Computational Linguistics.

Hugo Touvron, Thibaut Lavril, Gautier Izacard, Xavier Martinet, Marie-Anne Lachaux, Timothée Lacroix, Baptiste Rozière, Naman Goyal, Eric Hambro, Faisal Azhar, Aurelien Rodriguez, Armand Joulin, Edouard Grave, and Guillaume Lample. 2023. Llama: Open and efficient foundation language models. *Preprint*, arXiv:2302.13971.

Ashish Vaswani, Noam Shazeer, Niki Parmar, Jakob Uszkoreit, Llion Jones, Aidan N Gomez, Ł ukasz Kaiser, and Illia Polosukhin. 2017. Attention is all you need. In *Advances in Neural Information Processing Systems*, volume 30. Curran Associates, Inc.

Alex Wang, Yada Pruksachatkun, Nikita Nangia, Amanpreet Singh, Julian Michael, Felix Hill, Omer Levy, and Samuel R. Bowman. 2019. SuperGLUE: A stickier benchmark for general-purpose language understanding systems. *arXiv preprint 1905.00537*.

A Intellectual Curiosity Points

10 points	Ran few-shot prompting experiments with a novel task
	Read additional papers and did more few-shot prompting experiments
	Set up an antonym probe task
	Read about SuperGLUE (Wang et al., 2019) and ran a prompting experiment with the BoolQA (Clark et al., 2019) subset
7 points	Ran the Pig Latin task on another LLM
	Tested LLaMA on another language game
5 points	Reversed the Pig Latin experiment
	Tested statistical significance
4 points:	Extra research on prompting

Table 1: Examples of intellectual curiosity point allocation

Teaching Natural Language Processing in Law School

Daniel Braun
University of Twente
Department of High-tech Business
and Entrepreneurship
d.braun@utwente.nl

Abstract

Fuelled by technical advances, the interest in Natural Language Processing in the legal domain has rapidly increased over the last months and years. The design, usage, and testing of domain-specific systems, but also assessing these systems from a legal perspective, needs competencies at the intersection of law and Natural Language Processing. While the demand for such competencies is high among students, only a few law schools, particularly in Europe, teach such competencies. In this paper, we present the design for a Natural Language Processing course for postgraduate law students that is based on the principle of constructive alignment and has proven to be successful over the last three years.

1 Introduction

Like most fields of occupation, the legal profession is undergoing a drastic change due to the introduction of Artificial Intelligence (AI) and particularly Natural Language Processing (NLP) in the workplace. While research on applications of AI in the legal domain has a long history going back to the 1970s (Rissland et al., 2003), the legal practice was, for a long and arguably more so than other fields, hesitant to adopt AI technology and the pace of adoption started to increase only very recently (Oskamp and Lauritsen, 2002; Araszkiewicz et al., 2022). While there have been many good reasons for this hesitance, including strict regulations and personal liability of legal professionals (Vladika et al., 2024), both the acceptance and use of AI technology are rapidly increasing within the legal profession in recent years (Weinstein, 2022).

This increase in usage also results in an increased need for legal professionals with technological expertise, both in traditional roles but also in specialised emerging roles like legal engineer or legal technologist. According to the "Future Ready Lawyer Report" by Wolters Kluwer, only 24% of lawyers say that they understand "transformational technologies" like AI and big data (Weinstein, 2022). These numbers highlight that there is a significant demand for teaching technological essentials to (future) legal professionals. As language is the most important tool of lawyers and other legal professionals, among AI technologies, NLP technologies are arguably most relevant for them with a number of practical applications including contract generation, document management, legal decision-making, anonymization, and many other tasks (Vladika et al., 2024). Additionally, competencies in both NLP and law are not only needed for the application of NLP to legal problems but also for the application of law to NLP. With new regulations like the European Union's AI Act, there will be an increased need for lawyers with a good understanding of AI technology who are able to counsel clients who develop, distribute, or use such systems.

While many US law schools have already included NLP in their curriculum (Johnson, 2023), in Europe, such offerings are still rather rare. Partially, this is caused by the fact that law degrees in most European countries are undergraduate degrees that often follow a highly regulated four to five year curriculum, unlike in the US, where law schools are part of postgraduate education. However, as consecutive Master of Laws (LL.M.) degrees are becoming more popular in Europe, law schools have started to offer such degrees particularly focused on Legal Technology ("Legal Tech"). This paper outlines the design of an introductory NLP course that is designed for this setting, i.e. as an elective course in postgraduate education for law students without prior knowledge of AI or computer science. The course has been taught in a very similar fashion for three years at an LL.M. program at a public German university. The aim of this design is to inform and inspire the development of similar courses.

Proceedings of the Sixth Workshop on Teaching NLP, pages 85–90
August 15, 2024 ©2024 Association for Computational Linguistics

2 Skills and Intended Learning Outcomes

Following the principle of constructive alignment (Biggs, 1996), the course was designed around the intended learning outcomes (ILOs) and more fundamentally the skills that are relevant for legal professionals. Given the context for which the course was designed, no relevant previous knowledge in AI or computer science can be expected. Therefore, an NLP course in a law school can clearly not go as deep into technological details as a traditional NLP course. After all, a law graduate with a specialisation in legal technology is, most likely, also not going to work as a programmer. Therefore, the most important question in designing an NLP course for law students is: *What are the relevant skills that can help future legal professionals to work at the intersection of law and NLP?*

It is worth emphasising that the course design outlined in this paper is not meant to be part of the general curriculum every law student has to go through, but rather as an elective for those that want to work at the intersection of law and NLP where a deepened interdisciplinary understanding is needed. We identified three different areas in which such interdisciplinary skills are mainly needed:

- **Law practice**: NLP tools will be part of the daily work routine of many legal professionals in the future. Understanding the fundamental principles these tools operate on will help legal professionals to make informed decisions on how and when to use which technology or tool.
- **Technology development and implementation**: Legal professionals will be involved in the development and implementation of legal tech tools in many different roles in which they will need a solid understanding of the underlying technology, like product manager or implementation consultant.
- **Research**: Whether as a legal data scientist or empirical legal scholar, legal research, both in academia and practice, will include many different NLP methods. Especially in interdisciplinary research projects, annotating legal corpora and preparing them to be used as training data will require legal expertise and an understanding of the requirements for training data for ML models.

Based on these areas, we derived ILOs that law graduates would need to achieve to be prepared for such roles. The six derived ILOs are shown in Table 1. Each ILO is classified according to Bloom's taxonomy (Anderson and Krathwohl, 2001). Since the goal of the course is to provide participants with practical NLP skills that are relevant in the legal domain, most of the ILOs are on the higher levels of Bloom's taxonomy (create, evaluate, analyse, apply), i.e. go beyond acquiring just theoretical knowledge.

3 Course Plan

Based on the ILOs, we developed a plan for a course that runs over the span of a semester (~15 weeks) and has a workload of 140 hours (or 5 points in the European Credit Transfer and Accumulation System, ECTS). Of those 140 hours, 56 are contact hours: 30 hours (or 2 hours per week) of lectures and 26 hours of tutorials (13 x 2 hours). The remaining 84 hours are reserved for self-study and project work (see Section 4.1). Particularly for the achievement of the ILOs that are related to the higher levels of Bloom's taxonomy, practical experience, as mediated through tutorials and project work, is key to successful learning. Table 2 shows an overview of all educational activities and their content. While the lectures mainly focus on theoretical knowledge, the tutorials are designed as hands-on sessions, in which participants interact with different tools. Some of the course materials, particularly for the practical sessions, are available on GitHub[1]. It is important to stress that the designed course does not attempt to replace a computer science curriculum. Therefore, the lectures mainly stay on a conceptual level, without, e.g., going into the mathematical details or optimisation algorithms in ML. Similarly, in the tutorials, participants will not write complete programs but rather are provided with Jupyter notebooks that they can configure in a low-code fashion, so that they get a basic understanding of the process and structure that underlies the training of ML models, without necessarily having the learn how to program. Weeks 12 to 14 are reserved for guest lectures from practitioners. The idea is to invite representatives of different organisations that have a need for professionals with skills at the intersection of law and NLP to show the broad range of potential roles, not only within traditional law firms but

[1] https://github.com/DaBr01/Teaching-NLP-in-Law-School

Table 1: Intended Learning Outcomes (ILOs) and their classification according to Bloom's taxonomy

#	ILO	Level
1	Students can explain terminology, methods, theories, and fundamental concepts of artificial intelligence, machine learning, and natural language processing.	understand
2	Students can explain the relevance of artificial intelligence and natural language processing for the legal domain and discuss their implications on different legal professions.	understand
3	Students can use standard software for the automation of process steps in legal knowledge work (e.g. no-code platforms and document generation tools).	apply
4	Students can analyse problem formulations from the legal practice and identify suitable NLP methods for support and automation, as well as potential risks that may arise from them (like biases and lack of accountability or explainability).	analyse, evaluate
5	Students can design annotation guidelines for legal data sets and generate new corpora through annotation.	create
6	Students can develop small legal applications for specific problem formulations based on standard tools and libraries.	create

also within established companies or organisations and start-ups.

4 Assessment

The assessment of the course consists of an exam at the end of the course (that can be either written or orally), and a project on which students work in groups of two to three. Both assessment forms will determine 50% of the final grade each. While the exam is purely a formative assessment, the project contains summative and formative assessment moments. The goal of formative assessment is to assess the level of knowledge a student has at a certain point in time. In the context of the course, formative assessment is used to assess, at the end of the course, whether the ILOs have been achieved and to derive a grade. Formative assessment, on the other hand, is part of the teaching process and aims to provide the students, but also the teacher, with information about the current progress of the students, in order to allow for interventions and assure that, in the end, the ILOs will be achieved. (Garrison and Ehringhaus, 2007)

4.1 Project

For the project, each team will be provided with a corpus and a problem description. Each team will have to solve the following tasks based on their corpus and problem description:

1. Develop an annotation guideline.
2. Annotate the corpus based on the developed guideline.
3. Train a model that is able to extract information that is relevant in the context of the given problem description.
4. Write a project report of max. 4 pages that describes the results of your project.
5. Present the project results to your peers.

The summative assessment element of the project will be the final project grade that is based on the annotation guidelines (30%), the trained model (30%), the project report (30%), and the presentation (10%). In addition, participants hand in their annotation guidelines in week 4 for a formative assessment in which they receive feedback but also give feedback to other groups as part of a peer feedback process.

5 Literature

While there are many textbooks available on NLP (e.g. by Jurafsky and Martin (2008) or Hapke et al. (2019)), almost all of them are much more technical than is suited for the outlined course. The textbooks by Biemann et al. (2022) and Ignatow and Mihalcea (2017) present an introduction to NLP particularly targeted at the social sciences. As such, they include introductions to fundamental concepts that are also suitable for the context of the course but do not address any particularities of the processing of legal language or domain-specific tasks and tools. Particularly because of this lack of literature, we hope that the course design presented in this paper can inform and inspire the design of NLP courses in the context of law schools.

Table 2: Course Plan

	Type	Title	Content
Week 1	Lecture	Introduction to AI and ML	Definition and history of AI; Fundamentals of ML; Decision Trees; k-nearest Neighbours; Linear Regression; k-means Clustering; Critical reflection on correlation and causality
	Tutorial	No-code platforms and legal expert systems	Creation of a simple legal expert system with a no-code platform (e.g. Bryter, Open Decision, or Mioto)
Week 2	Lecture	Text annotation	Fundamentals of legal data annotation; Binary / multi-label / multi-class annotations; Document / section / sentence / word / sequence annotation; Disagreement between annotators; Annotation guidelines; Annotation tools; Quality of annotations
	Tutorial	Annotation of court decisions	Introduction to an annotation tools (e.g. Doccano); Writing annotation guidelines; Annotation of a small corpus of court decisions
Week 3	Lecture	Introduction to Natural Language Processing	NLP definitions and tasks; Challenges of automated text processing (compared to images or numbers); Specifics of legal texts; Pipeline architectures; Pre-processing; Content extraction; Sentence segmentation; Stemming and lemmatization; Lexica
	Tutorial	Pre-Processing	Implementation of a pre-processing pipeline for privacy policies based on a Jupyter notebook template
Week 4	Lecture	Information Extraction	Named entity recognition; Regular expressions; Citation networks; Information extraction; Relation extraction; Argument mining; Evaluation (precision / recall / F1)
	Tutorial	Information Extraction	Regular expression exercise; Implementation of NER and IE for the annotated corpus of week 2 based on a Juypter notebook template
	Project	Deadline	Annotation guidelines
Week 5	Lecture	Text classification and Topic Modelling	Text classification; Topic Modelling; Contract analysis; Natural Language Understanding services
	Tutorial	Contract Analysis	Analysis of a contract corpus with three different means (contract analysis tool (e.g. Summize), NLU cloud service (e.g. Azure AI), ChatGPT) and comparison of results
Week 6	Lecture	Language Models and Vector Representations	Vector Representations; Distributional Hypothesis; Word Embeddings; Neural Networks; Large Language Models; Fine-Tuning
	Tutorial	Vector Representations	Comparison of IE performance with different vector representations (bag of words, tf-idf, word embeddings) as input with a provided Jupyter notebook template; Visualisation and interpretation of Word Embeddings
	Project	Deadline	Peer-feedback annotation guidelines
Week 7	Lecture	Similarity Analysis	Jaccard coefficients; Word Mover's Distance; Cosine similarity; Document vectors; Detection of AI-generated texts
	Tutorial	Similarity Analysis	Comparison of different similarity metrics on the court decision corpus

	Type	Title	Content
Week 8	Lecture	Introduction to Natural Language Generation	Data2Text / Image2Text / Text2Text; Templates; Rule-based NLG; Stochastic NLG; Hallucination; Abstractive and extractive summarisation; Evaluation and metrics (BLEU, ROUGE)
	Tutorial	Text Generation	Rule-based text generation with SimpleNLG; Text generation with GPT-2; Exercise on hallucination
Week 9	Lecture	Document Processing and Automation	eDiscovery; Document management, Legal document generation tools; Process automation
	Tutorial	Document generation	Document generation with Word; Document generation with no-code platform from week 1; Document generation with specialised tool
Week 10	Lecture	Legal Case Outcome Prediction	State of the research in legal case outcome prediction; Relevant features (particularly non-legal features like time, ...); Bias; Reflection about the difference between predicting the court decision and predicting the "right" decision
	Tutorial	Legal Case Outcome Prediction	Training of a simple model for the prediction of legal case outcomes based on a provided Jupyter notebook template
	Project	Deadline	Model and Jupyter notebook
Week 11	Lecture	Explainable AI	Explainability; Interpretability; Adversarial attacks; Taxonomy of explainability (post hoc/ante hoc, global/local, model specific/model agnostics); Example-based approaches; Critical reflection of "explanations" generated by LLMs
	Tutorial	LIME	Introduction of the LIME library for the generation of explanations
Week 12	Lecture	Guest lecture established organisation	Show possible job profiles in established organisations, e.g. legal operations officer from large companies, publishing houses, software providers, NGOs, government
	Tutorial	Project Support	Before the final project submission, participants have time to ask questions and get support
Week 13	Lecture	Guest lecture startup	Show possible job profiles in the startup world (e.g. legal tech startups, fintech, ...)
	Tutorial	Startup software	Introduction to the product of the startup
	Project	Deadline	Report
Week 14	Lecture	Guest lecture law firm	Job profiles in classical law forms
Week 15	Lecture	Project Presentation	Teams present the results of their project work

References

Lorin W Anderson and David R Krathwohl. 2001. *A taxonomy for learning, teaching, and assessing: A revision of Bloom's taxonomy of educational objectives: complete edition*. Addison Wesley Longman, Inc.

Michał Araszkiewicz, Trevor Bench-Capon, Enrico Francesconi, Marc Lauritsen, and Antonino Rotolo. 2022. Thirty years of artificial intelligence and law: overviews. *Artificial Intelligence and Law*, 30(4):593–610.

Chris Biemann, Gerhard Heyer, and Uwe Quasthoff. 2022. *Wissensrohstoff Text*. Springer.

John Biggs. 1996. Enhancing teaching through constructive alignment. *Higher education*, 32(3):347–364.

Catherine Garrison and Michael Ehringhaus. 2007. Formative and summative assessments in the classroom.

Hannes Max Hapke, Hobson Lane, and Cole Howard. 2019. Natural language processing in action.

Gabe Ignatow and Rada Mihalcea. 2017. *An introduc-*

tion to text mining: Research design, data collection, and analysis. Sage Publications.

Julia Johnson. 2023. Innovative law schools: Artificial intelligence. Last accessed 2024-05-06.

Daniel Jurafsky and James H Martin. 2008. *Speech and Language Processing: An Introduction to Natural Language Processing, Computational Linguistics, and Speech Recognition*. Pearson.

Anja Oskamp and Marc Lauritsen. 2002. Ai in law practice? so far, not much. *Artificial Intelligence and Law*, 10(4):227–236.

Edwina L. Rissland, Kevin D. Ashley, and R.P. Loui. 2003. Ai and law: A fruitful synergy. *Artificial Intelligence*, 150(1):1–15. AI and Law.

Juraj Vladika, Stephen Meisenbacher, Martina Preis, Alexandra Klymenko, and Florian Matthes. 2024. Towards a structured overview of use cases for natural language processing in the legal domain: A german perspective. *arXiv preprint arXiv:2404.18759*.

Stuart Weinstein. 2022. *Lawyers' Perceptions on the Use of AI*, pages 413–432. T.M.C. Asser Press, The Hague.

Exploring Language Representation through a Resource Inventory Project

Carolyn Jane Anderson
Wellesley College
Wellesley, MA
carolyn.anderson@wellesley.edu

1 Introduction

The increasing scale of large language models has led some students to wonder what contributions can be made in academia. However, students are often unaware that LLM-based approaches are not feasible for the majority of the world's languages due to lack of data availability. This paper presents a research project in which students explore the issue of language representation by creating an inventory of the data, preprocessing, and model resources available for a less-resourced language.

Students are put into small groups and assigned a language to research. Within the group, students take on one of three roles: dataset investigator, preprocessing investigator, or downstream task investigator. Students then work together to create a 7-page research report about their language.

2 Course Context

This assignment is the midterm research project for an advanced undergraduate Natural Language Processing course. Before the project, the class covers text processing and non-neural NLP techniques roughly corresponding to the first six chapters of Jurafsky and Martin (in prep.). Students have two weeks to work on this project before presenting their findings to the class.

3 Learning Goals

This assignment is designed to engage students with issues of linguistic representation. The primary goal is for students to explore the availability of data resources for a less-resourced language. Along the way, students build useful skills in how to locate and evaluate data and model resources, which are applicable outside of the context of low-resource languages as well.

The learning goals for this project are as follows:

- Explore issues of language representation
- Gain familiarity with dataset and model hubs
- Analyze the quality and availability of software artifacts
- Collaborate with classmates to present research findings
- Practice scientific writing and presentation

4 Language Selection and Assignment

For this project, it is important to select languages that have some available data and model resources. For this reason, I refer to the languages as "less-resourced" rather than "low-resource".

Table 1 shows the languages used in a prior semester. To create the language groups, I surveyed students on their language backgrounds and when possible, seeded each group with a student literate in the language or a related language. Unless all group members were literate in another writing system, I assigned only languages that used the Latin alphabet.

5 Assignment Structure

Each student was assigned one of three roles: dataset investigator, preprocessing investigator, or downstream task investigator. Each team worked together to prepare a 7-page report and a 3-minute in-class presentation of their findings. Students were responsible for writing a two-page section of the report on their individual topic, as well as for collaborating on a one-page introduction to their language. As a result, the project gives students a chance to practice teamwork and collaboration, while allowing the instructor to assess their effort individually.

The assignment description and a copy of the Gradescope rubric used to grade student papers are included in the Supplementary Materials.

5.1 Language Introduction

Each report was required to begin with an introduction to the language and its context. This section

Proceedings of the Sixth Workshop on Teaching NLP, pages 91–93
August 15, 2024 ©2024 Association for Computational Linguistics

Language	Writing System	Language Expertise
Indonesian	Latin	1 Indonesian-literate student
Somali	Latin	1 Arabic-literate student (lexical borrowing from Arabic)
Japanese	Kanji/Kana	All students literate in Japanese
Afrikaans	Latin	2 German-literate students (lexical borrowing from German)
Haitian Creole	Latin	All students literate in French (lexical borrowing from French)
Romanian	Latin	None
Portuguese	Latin	2 students literate in Portuguese

Table 1: Example language groups

described the language's communities of use and social context, its writing system, and its morphology and syntax, including some sentences with word-by-word translations.

5.2 Dataset Investigator

Dataset investigators were required to explore a number of platforms to investigate the availability of data resources for their language.

Students were asked to evaluate Wikipedia as a language resource, reporting on the existence, size and robustness of Wikipedia in their assigned language. Students were also required to search Kaggle, Hugging Face, and Github for other datasets in their language. They were asked to describe each dataset that they found and to consider multiple aspects of its utility: accessibility, quality, and size.

Students reported many challenges around accessibility: they found research papers reporting the use of a dataset, but couldn't find the dataset itself, or they found the dataset's website, but the links were broken. Quality was the most challenging aspect for them to evaluate, especially for groups without a member who was literate in the language.

5.3 Preprocessing Investigator

Preprocessing investigators explored text processing tools for their language. The suggested tasks included tokenization, segmentation, part-of-speech tagging, and parsing.

Students were asked to evaluate whether the popular NLP libraries NLTK (Bird and Klein, 2009) and SpaCY (Honnibal et al., 2020) provided any tools for their language. Students were also asked to look for other preprocessing tools on Github or other websites. Several students leveraged search tools for academic research papers, and found relevant systems via a literature search, an effective approach that I hadn't anticipated.

For each preprocessing tool that they discovered, students described how it worked, what task it was designed for, what data it was trained on, and assessed its usability. Students had the most trouble finding information about the data used to train the tools. They also ran into many instances where the code could no longer be downloaded or run.

5.4 Downstream Investigator

Downstream task investigators looked into the availability of systems in their language for downstream tasks such as named-entity recognition, event recognition, language modeling, sentiment analysis, question-answering, and machine translation.

Students were required to look for models on Github and Hugging Face, and were also encourage to do a general Web search. As above, for each preprocessing tool that they discovered, students described how it worked, what task it was designed for, what data it was trained on, and assessed its usability.

6 Scaffolding for the Final Project

This project serves as scaffolding for the course's final research paper (due at the end of the term), which is individual. Although most students come up with interesting and challenging topics on their own, a handful of students struggle to do so each semester. I encourage these students to build something for the language they investigate in the resource inventory project. This has worked well and led to final projects on sentimental analysis and named entity recognition for Indonesian and hate speech identification and speech recognition for Portuguese.

7 Conclusion

This assignment allows students to explore issues of language representation by conducting a resource inventory for a less-resourced language. The hope is that this project highlights how much work remains for researchers to do on NLP for the breadth of the world's languages.

References

Edward Loper Bird, Steven and Ewan Klein. 2009. *Natural Language Processing with Python*. O'Reilly Media Inc.

Matthew Honnibal, Ines Montani, Sofie Van Landeghem, and Adriane Boyd. 2020. spaCy: Industrial-strength Natural Language Processing in Python.

Daniel Jurafsky and James H. Martin. in prep. *Speech and Language Processing: An Introduction to Natural Language Processing, Computational Linguistics, and Speech Recognition*, 3rd edition.

BELT: Building Endangered Language Technology

Michael Ginn[1] **David R. Saavedra-Beltrán**[2]
Camilo Robayo[2] **Alexis Palmer**[1]
[1]University of Colorado [2]Universidad Nacional de Colombia
michael.ginn@colorado.edu

Abstract

The development of language technology (LT) for an endangered language is often identified as a goal in language revitalization efforts, but developing such technologies is typically subject to additional methodological challenges as well as social and ethical concerns. In particular, LT development has too often taken on colonialist qualities, extracting language data, relying on outside experts, and denying the speakers of a language sovereignty over the technologies produced.

We seek to avoid such an approach through the development of the *Building Endangered Language Technology* (BELT) website, an educational resource designed for speakers and community members with limited technological experience to develop LTs for their own language. Specifically, BELT provides interactive lessons on basic Python programming, coupled with projects to develop specific language technologies, such as spellcheckers or word games. In this paper, we describe BELT's design, the motivation underlying many key decisions, and preliminary responses from learners.

1 Introduction

The development of language technologies (such as spellcheckers, automated transcription, and machine translation) has been commonly suggested as a goal in language revitalization projects (Kornai, 2013; Zhang et al., 2022). However, research and development of these LTs historically has been fraught with social and ethical concerns. NLP research generally underrepresents such languages (Joshi et al., 2020; Blasi et al., 2022), and research into so-called "low-resource" and endangered languages often treats them as a homogenous group of languages, identical to high-resource and politically dominant languages in every aspect except data availability (Doğruöz and Sitaram, 2022).

Worse, the development of LTs for endangered languages has often taken on colonialist qualities (Bird, 2020): over-promising the benefits of documentation and technology development (Speas, 2009; Brinklow et al., 2019); consuming language data with little regard to speaker privacy (Macri and Sarmento, 2010); denying the language community sovereignty over their data (Pool, 2016); prioritizing the development of tools of interest to the outside expert, rather than those desired by actual speakers (Liu et al., 2022); and relying on experts with little relationship to the community for continued development and maintenance (Bird, 2020; Flavelle and Lachler, 2023).

While some recent results suggest that large language models can be usefully deployed in language documentation and revitalization contexts (Tanzer et al., 2024; Zhang et al., 2024b,a, among others), most such models remain closed, and running them for a new language requires exposing data that language communities may prefer to keep private.

We strive to provide a resource for speakers interested in developing and maintaining language technology for their own language with the BELT (*Building Endangered Language Technology*) website. BELT is an educational tool designed for learners without any coding experience to gain basic programming skills, develop language technology using data from their language, and deploy simple applications for real-world usage.

In particular, we developed BELT with the following goals:

- A free, open-source resource that can be used for guided workshops as well as independent, asynchronous learning.
- Interactive Python lessons that encourage repeated practice and experimentation.
- Lesson materials that are approachable to a beginning programmer, while enabling creation of realistic and useful applications.

Proceedings of the Sixth Workshop on Teaching NLP, pages 94–104
August 15, 2024 ©2024 Association for Computational Linguistics

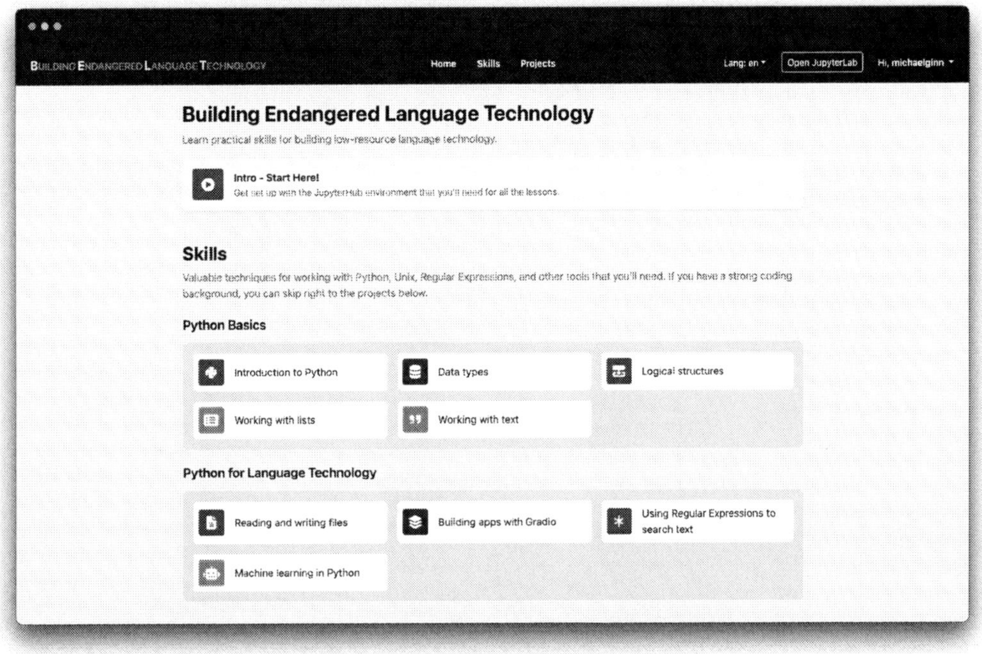

Figure 1: The main BELT course page. Lessons are divided into short skills and longer, in-depth projects. Each lesson links to a Jupyter Notebook in the user's environment.

- Language-agnostic project tutorials that require only a text file of unlabeled language data as input.
- A strict focus on NLP-related topics, avoiding an overly-general programming curriculum.
- Full localization into languages other than English.

We describe our design decisions for the website and lesson materials. Furthermore, we report feedback and results from two in-person workshops based around the BELT site, in which community members for a variety of endangered languages were able to build and share language technologies for their respective languages. Finally, we reflect on future improvements to continue to make BELT a valuable resource for NLP education.

2 Overview

BELT is an interactive web course, which anyone can access for free.[1] After logging in, a user is presented with the main course page (Figure 1). The course contains fifteen interactive lessons covering language technologies and the coding skills needed to build them, which are provided here in a recommended order.

Curriculum Lessons are divided into *Skills*, shorter notebooks each covering a single focused topic (such as regular expressions), and *Projects*, longer tutorials which cover a realistic language technology (such as a spellchecker). We recommend completely new learners to work through the skills section first before attempting the projects; more experienced users may simply refer back to the skills section as needed.

Lesson Format Clicking on a lesson launches a user-specific Jupyter Lab environment, automatically loading a Jupyter notebook for that lesson (Figure 2). Notebooks are organized for structured learning and contain a mix of instructional text, prewritten code blocks, and interactive exercises and challenges. For example, the skill lesson covering strings in Python includes the exercise in Figure 3. Notebooks are stored on a per-user basis, and they persist across sessions. Lessons can access shared files from the server, such as corpora that we provide. In addition, users can upload their own files, allowing them to use their own language data for many of the projects.

[1]`https://lecs-lab.github.io/belt`

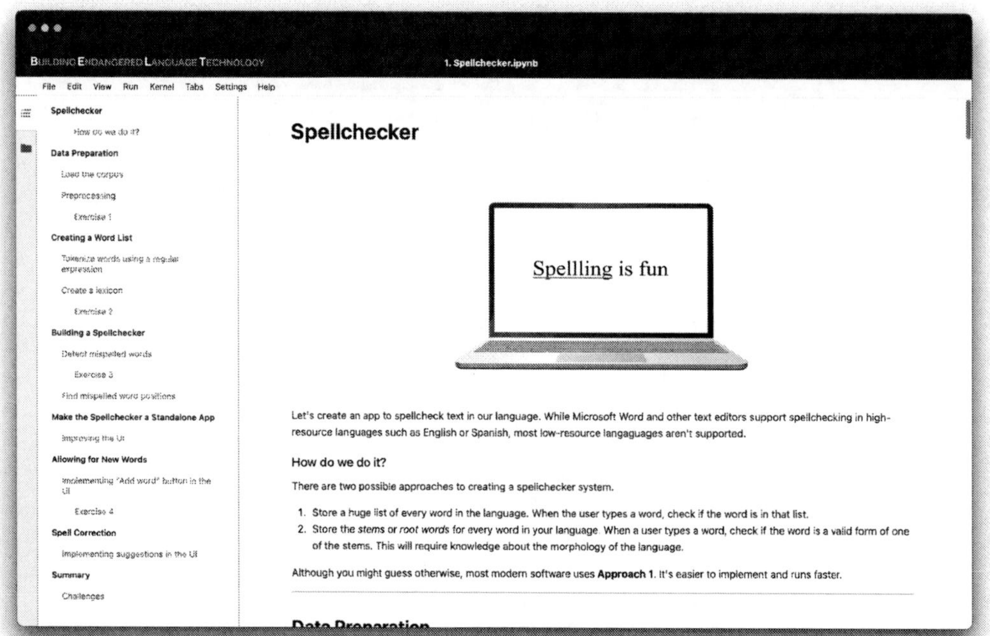

Figure 2: Lessons load notebooks in the Jupyter Lab environment. Lessons are fully interactive, can load files from the shared filesystem as well as from the user's storage, and can even launch user-created apps with the Gradio framework.

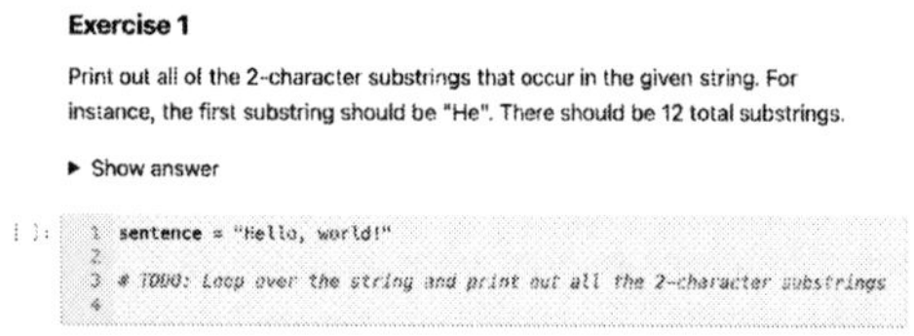

Figure 3: A sample exercise from the lesson on strings.

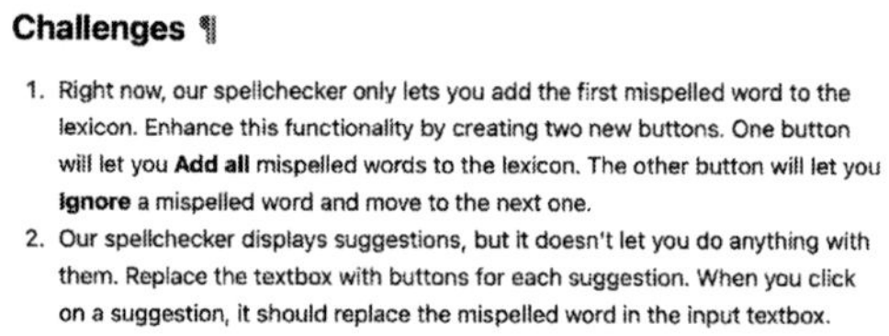

Figure 4: Challenge exercises at the end of the spellchecker lesson.

Projects While skill lessons tend to be short, focused overviews of relevant topics, projects are more involved and tailored to endangered language technology development. For example, the spellchecker lesson (Figure 2) requires only a wordlist as input. The spellchecker itself uses low-resource techniques such as edit distance to identify suggested spellings, rather than data-hungry, state-of-the-art methods (generally neural networks).

Projects are highly interactive, with many exercises drawing on knowledge learned in the skill lessons. Projects also include several challenge exercises (Figure 4) for motivated learners, ranging in difficulty from simple UI modifications to development of additional system features.

Gradio Perhaps the most overlooked challenge in community-led language application development is the deployment of usable, scaleable software. In BELT lessons, the Gradio[2] framework is used extensively in order to build simple user interfaces for the technologies developed. Gradio runs as a local, interactive app inside the Jupyter notebook, and it can be accessed temporarily via a live URL (see Figure 5). Furthermore, through Hugging Face Spaces,[3] Gradio apps can be hosted permanently and for free.

[2] https://www.gradio.app

[3] https://huggingface.co/spaces

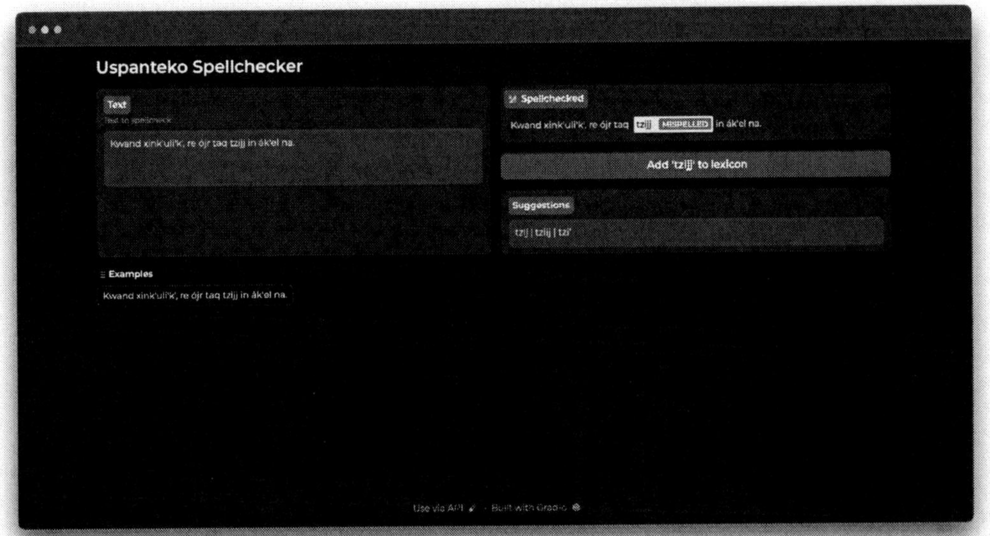

Figure 5: A running Gradio app. Learners create small applications such as spellcheckers, predictive text, and word games using the Gradio framework. Apps can be accessed via a live URL while they are running, or permanently if the app is hosted on Hugging Face.

3 Platform

We selected JupyterHub[4] as the primary framework powering BELT. JupyterHub is an open-source platform that allows many users to access Jupyter computing environments on a remote server. JupyterHub works by spawning a separate Jupyter environment for each user and serving the Jupyter Notebook or Lab application as a web app.

3.1 Alternatives

Before deciding on JupyterHub, we considered several alternatives, which we describe below in addition to our reasons for selecting as we did.

Static materials Digital textbooks or static webpages would require the least effort to distribute, and many high-quality NLP resources of this sort already exist. They require minimal computational resources, can often be used offline, and are straightforward to translate into other languages. However, we believe that interactivity is critical to a fluid learning experience, and a static approach would add significant friction, as learners would need to configure their own development environments and solve any issues that arise with installation.

Jupyter Notebooks Interactive notebooks have become a popular tool for pedagogy in computational fields (Cardoso et al., 2019; Johnson, 2020), allowing for alternating plain-text and code blocks that can be edited and run. Distributing downloadable Jupyter notebooks can often be an ideal choice for learners with some prior programming experience (such as computer science undergraduates), who are expected to set up Python environments, configure coding software, and install packages. While these are valuable skills to learn, we believed that this additional friction could discourage potential learners with minimal technical experience.

Jupyter Books Jupyter Book[5] is an alternative platform, also based on the Jupyter environment, used to create digital textbooks that incorporate interactive code contents. While Jupyter Book provides excellent features for creating well-formatted content, there are significant limitations for interactive content that would not allow learners to easily deploy their applications.

3.2 Deployment

For initial development of BELT, we use The Littlest JupyterHub (TLJH)[6] distribution, which runs

[4] https://jupyter.org/hub

[5] https://jupyterbook.org/en/stable/intro.html

[6] https://github.com/jupyterhub/the-littlest-jupyterhub

on a single server and supports up to one hundred simultaneous users. Jupyter Hub can also be run on Kubernetes, scaling to tens of thousands of users, and in the future we plan to deploy BELT using this method.

We hosted the initial BELT site on a server instance running Ubuntu 18.04 with 4 GB of RAM and 100 GB of disk space.

3.3 Serving Notebooks

When a user clicks a lesson for the first time, we use `nbgitpuller`[7] to fetch the lesson notebook from our Git repository. The latest version of the notebook is cloned into the user's personal storage on our JupyterHub. After this point, they can modify the notebook and changes will persist.

4 Design

We made several design decisions involving features and enhancements to the JupyterHub platform, aiming to make the BELT site as approachable and usable as possible.

4.1 Web Pages

By default, JupyterHub serves several web pages for login, registration, launching servers, and other basic functions. These pages have minimal, simple design elements, but we find that they can be confusing for users not familiar with that style of interface. To address this interface issue, we replace the pages completely, striving for a look that resembles a modern web or mobile app rather than a scientific tool (see Figure 1).

We add up-to-date styling libraries, Bootstrap v5[8] and FontAwesome v6,[9] both commonly-used frameworks in web design. We also create entirely new page templates (built with the Jinja[10] engine), custom CSS styles, and custom assets.

We also modify the configuration and style code for the Jupyter Lab environment, removing unnecessary elements to create a clean, intuitive interface (Figure 2).

4.2 Localization

Reaching a global audience is an important goal of the project. We prepared the application to be fully localized, and completed preliminary localization into Spanish and partial localization into Portuguese.

JupyterHub itself does not provide any framework for page internationalization, and standard localization libraries require server-side modifications. Instead, we developed a small JavaScript helper that does the following:

1. Finds any components marked with a custom HTML attribute `data-i18n-id`;
2. Dynamically replaces the string contents of the node with a localized string from the appropriate lookup table; and
3. Dynamically modifies any URLs to point to the appropriate localized content.

While this method may not scale well to large numbers of components, it is very lightweight and very performant in our usecase. We perform localizations using Crowdin,[11] a web platform for creating and storing localization data. The user can switch their language with a simple picker in the menu bar, and their choice is persisted with cookies.

Because Jupyter notebooks cannot be dynamically updated as easily, we employ a different strategy for localizing the notebooks. We create localized versions of every notebook using Crowdin, and store each version at a path containing the appropriate language code. Then, we dynamically switch the links using our localization script to point to the correct notebook.

Within lesson notebooks we primarily translate the informational material and part of the code comments (those corresponding to Portuguese), leaving variable and function names untouched for both languages. We debated whether to localize these as well, but elected against it as doing so may make running bilingual workshops more difficult. We also install language packs for the Jupyter Lab user interface, allowing the user to switch the language for text elements such as menus and tooltips.

5 Lesson Materials

Skills Currently, our curriculum includes lessons for the following skills:

1. Introduction to Python
2. Data types

[7] `https://nbgitpuller.readthedocs.io/en/latest/index.html`

[8] `https://getbootstrap.com/docs/5.0/getting-started/introduction/`

[9] `https://fontawesome.com`

[10] `https://jinja.palletsprojects.com/en/3.1.x/`

[11] `https://crowdin.com`

3. Logical structures
4. Lists
5. Strings and text
6. Files
7. Gradio
8. Regular expressions
9. Machine learning

Within each lesson, we strive to discuss only the information that is absolutely required for the projects later to come. Lessons tend to be short and focused, typically around fifteen to thirty minutes worth of content with a few exercises. We recognize that there are a multitude of existing, in-depth Python educational resources, and we refer learners to outside sources when appropriate.

The material is presented with English examples and written with a succinct prose style that strives to be accurate without being overly technical. We primarily frame each skill in relation to language technology; e.g., while regular expressions can be useful for a wide variety of tasks, we primarily discuss their use for searching and preprocessing natural language text.

Exercises strive to reinforce critical concepts. They often foreshadow tasks that will be necessary for projects; for example, the lesson on lists and sets asks the user to turn a list of words into a unique set. This skill is later used in the spellchecker project for creating a wordlist from a lexicon.

Projects Our curriculum currently includes four projects, described below. As development of BELT continues, we plan to add new projects, either for new language technologies, or for more advanced versions of the technologies already included. We additionally welcome new projects from the broader community.[12]

1. **Spellcheckers:** In this project, students create a simple, lookup-based spellchecker, using a word list built from a text file.
2. **Predictive text:** The same text file is used to build a simple n-gram language model, which is then used to predict the most likely next word in a sequence.
3. **Word games:** In this project, users learn to create two word games: a word scramble, and a hangman-style game. These can draw from the provided text, or users can upload custom word lists.
4. **Automatic morphological inflection:** In this project, users learn to use finite-state machines to build rule-based morphological inflection tools, which can be useful in spell-checking, dictionaries, language learning games, and other downstream applications.

These projects cover a number of common technologies that can be built with minimal resources and are appropriate for most languages. The projects use data files from several different languages to teach users how to build the technologies: English, Spanish, Latin, and the Mayan language Uspanteko. However, we strongly encourage learners to use their own language data where available, and we provide guidance for how to import, load, and manage those data files.

Within each project, exercises require application of information from the skill lessons (encouraging learners to use prior lessons as a reference), and they often combine multiple topics. To avoid too much frustration, learners can double-check their solutions by revealing answers to the exercises. For more difficult exercises, we offer for learners to receive one or more hints. We also provide stretch exercises, in the form of open-ended challenge problems, for more experienced learners.

Each project tutorial culminates with users having built a simple version of a tool. Depending on the data file used as input, these tools may or may not be suitable for real-world use. They are, however, suitable foundations for more sophisticated versions of the same tools. It is our hope that some learners will be inspired to build better and better versions of the tools produced by our lessons, thus working toward truly viable technologies for the languages those learners care about.

We would also note that our goal very specifically is not to teach learners how to build state-of-the-art tools using the latest developments in NLP. Rather, we aim for tools that have a low computational expense, need minimal input data, do not require annotation, and can be deployed in a straightforward way.

[12]Please contact the first author if you are interested in contributing to BELT.

6 Live Workshops

Over the last year, we have held two live workshops to teach all or part of the BELT lessons to different audiences. As it happens, both workshops took place in South America. The initial workshop, held in the summer of 2023, helped us to identify some improvements around both the hosting method and the lesson contents that we implemented for the second workshop at the start of 2024.

6.1 Bogotá, Colombia, June 2023

The first live workshop was held in the context of the Amazonicas IX conference in Bogotá, Colombia in June 2023.[13]

The event was attended by around fifteen participants, with hybrid participation (some in situ and others via Zoom). The participants were mostly linguistics/anthropology undergraduates with no or some basic programming experience.

The workshop was taught across four consecutive days, with each day's session lasting three and a half hours. Each session was divided into two working blocks with a 30-min break between. The first session covered the Skills lessons, the remaining three sessions were dedicated to the first three applied projects: Spellchecker, Predictive text and Word Games. The sessions were delivered in English, and supported in Spanish by a collaborator who had previously translated the interactive web course materials.

In terms of results, the materials were positively received. However, time constraints, along with the background knowledge of programming by most attendees, led to some difficulties which limited the exploration of more specialised and related lessons such as Regular Expressions (RegEx) and Machine Learning (ML).

Participants were able to create applications for several languages which they worked closely with, including word games in the endangered Indigenous languages Karijona and Umbra.

6.2 Santiago, Chile, January 2024

The second BELT workshop took place in Santiago, Chile, in early January 2024, as part of a 3-day workshop on Tecnologías Digitales y Lenguas Indígenas (Language Technologies and Indigenous Languages).[14] This was an abbreviated version of the workshop, offered during one three-hour morning session. Code from the word games project was then used on the third day to build word games for four different Indigenous languages.

The workshop had more than 40 participants, with 56% linguists, 20% speakers of Indigenous languages, 15% computer scientists, and 9% representatives of public policy organizations. Most presentations were delivered in Spanish, some in English, and a small number in local Indigenous languages. The BELT session was delivered in English, with real-time translation into Spanish.

Because of time constraints and the mixed backgrounds of participants, we grouped participants into teams of 2-5 people, ensuring that each team included at least one participant with prior experience writing code in Python. In this case, the main goals were: a) to introduce all participants to Python programming and to the range of topics available through BELT; b) to provide a foundation for a shared project on the third day of the workshop; and c) perhaps most importantly, to demonstrate the attainability of producing simple language technologies with a bit of data and a bit of code.

Some participants noted that, whether or not they intended to continue the BELT lessons, seeing first-hand how a programming language works, and how pieces can be put together to build a functioning system, opened their eyes to new possibilities for their languages. Other participants asked about using the lessons for teaching kids in school contexts. Localization of the course materials into Spanish was essential to the success of the workshop.

The third day of the workshop was set up as a hackathon, with several different interdisciplinary teams working on practical projects. We used code from the BELT word games project to produce hangman and word scramble games for Mapudungun, Aymara, Quechua, and Ckunsa. To make the games playable by new language learners, we compiled a list in Spanish of colors, numbers, animals, body part terms, and family relationship terms. Speaker and linguist participants then filled in the equivalents in the four Indigenous languages. The entire process took about three hours, and the eight games are hosted and playable through Hugging Face Spaces.[15]

[13] https://cienciassociales.uniandes.edu.co/congreso-de-las-lenguas-amazonicas/

[14] https://ws.dcc.uchile.cl/en/

[15] https://huggingface.co/TDLI2024

7 Participant Perspectives

(Note: This section is written from the perspective of our third author, who was a participant at the first workshop.)

As a descriptive linguist, the linguistic software I have used in the past—Phonology Assistant[16] and Fieldworks Language Explorer (FLEx)[17]—do not require any programming knowledge. My only experience with programming has been modifying small chunks of PRAAT scripts. The BELT workshop was an opportunity to get hands-on experience to build language tools for small resources languages and later to share my results with native speakers.

The website for the workshop provided a comprehensive and self-contained approach to the subject, with sessions clearly divided into lessons. The first lessons started with fundamentals, covering syntax and basic operators, progressing through numerical and set operations. Then, lessons became more complex, combining earlier lessons for tasks such as data preprocessing and manipulation. For several parts of the workshop, I and other participants were able to work with my own corpus.

I primarily work with Karijona, a Cariban Amazonian language with very little existing resources. The Karijona orthography and basic rules were discussed with the Puerto Nare Community in 2015 and since then standardized for educational use (Guerra et al., 2024), and the first language learning book was published just a few months before the workshop (Resguardo Indígena de Puerto Nare, 2023).

The book consisted of nine brief texts and many examples, all cross-checked with native speakers for transcription consistency. For the workshop, I uploaded these materials to my account on BELT in order to create apps in the Karijona language.

Following the lessons, we built a word unscrambling game and hangman game, which I was able to deploy through HuggingFace Spaces and even use on a mobile device. Then, I shared the apps with a group of Karijona speakers from Puerto Nare, who were able to try them during a trip to Bogotá. However, as there is very limited internet in Puerto Nare, making it difficult for speakers to use these apps regularly. Thus, it is an urgent priority to expand the BELT lessons to enable offline use apps that can be used on mobile devices.

[16] `https://software.sil.org/phonologyassistant/`
[17] `https://software.sil.org/fieldworks/`

8 Related Work

NLP and computational linguistics pedagogy has a rich history of research and applications, with much work in developing online learning resources (Artemova et al., 2021; Baglini and Hjorth, 2021) and live instruction techniques (Bender et al., 2008; Agarwal, 2013; Gaddy et al., 2021; Durrett et al., 2021; Kennington, 2021). Research has explored how best to teach language technology concepts to learners without a computer science background (Fosler-Lussier, 2008; Poliak and Jenifer, 2021; Vajjala, 2021) and in non-English instruction settings (Messina et al., 2021; Pannitto et al., 2021). Camacho and Zevallos (2020) recommends integration of (computational) linguistics into high school curricula as a method to fight language decline. However, to our knowledge, there are no existing educational resources for the development of endangered language technologies.

In general, the development of endangered language technology faces well-studied challenges (Doğruöz and Sitaram, 2022). Penttonen (2011) describes methods used to create online technologies such as dictionaries and language learning games for Karelian. Bird (2018) explores challenges in mobile applications specifically.

9 Conclusion

The BELT website offers a new resource for teaching beginning Python programming, with the direct goal of supporting development of language technologies for endangered languages. All course materials are freely available online and can be used to teach instructional workshops or for self-guided, asynchronous learning. Users need nothing more than a standard laptop and an Internet connection. It is our hope that these resources might spur new activity in community-based development of language technologies, thereby supporting data privacy and sovereignty for language communities.

Looking ahead, we are continuing development of BELT along several pathways. First, we would like to use the localization framework we built to translate the course materials into a wide range of languages of wider communication, such that the materials will be accessible to multilingual speakers around the world. Second, we have several planned additional skills and projects to add to the platform. In both of these directions, we welcome contributions from the broader NLP community.

We hope to develop a mobile version of BELT,

as mobile devices may be more common among younger members in many communities. Through this app, we hope to allow offline use of the applications created in BELT, for situations where users have intermittent internet access. Finally, we would like to explore the possibility of branching off BELT access such that versions of the website could be self-hosted, for example by tribal governments, immersion schools, summer schools, and the like.

Ethics Statement

First, it is important to note that we ourselves are not members of Indigenous communities, nor speakers of endangered languages. We offer these resources in the hopes that members of those communities can use them as a launching point to develop their own technologies in a manner that is entirely self-determined (Schwartz, 2022).

Second, we have been careful to develop BELT in a way that allows users to retain control over their own data. User-uploaded files are hosted on our server, but they are not copied or re-distributed in any way, nor are they available to other users of BELT. Users can delete these files at any time.

Finally, BELT is a freely-offered resource, currently supported by grant funding. We are committed to providing for sustained hosting for the website, so that these resources will remain available as long as they are relevant and useful. We will never charge users to learn using BELT.

Acknowledgments

BELT runs on the CUmulus platform provided by the University of Colorado Research Computing. Portions of this work were supported by the National Science Foundation under Grant No. 2149404, "CAREER: From One Language to Another". Any opinions, findings, and conclusions or recommendations expressed in this material are those of the authors and do not necessarily reflect the views of the National Science Foundation.

References

Apoorv Agarwal. 2013. Teaching the basics of NLP and ML in an introductory course to information science. In *Proceedings of the Fourth Workshop on Teaching NLP and CL*, pages 77–84, Sofia, Bulgaria. Association for Computational Linguistics.

Ekaterina Artemova, Murat Apishev, Denis Kirianov, Veronica Sarkisyan, Sergey Aksenov, and Oleg Serikov. 2021. Teaching a massive open online course on natural language processing. In *Proceedings of the Fifth Workshop on Teaching NLP*, pages 13–27, Online. Association for Computational Linguistics.

Rebekah Baglini and Hermes Hjorth. 2021. Natural language processing 4 all (NLP4All): A new online platform for teaching and learning NLP concepts. In *Proceedings of the Fifth Workshop on Teaching NLP*, pages 28–33, Online. Association for Computational Linguistics.

Emily M. Bender, Fei Xia, and Erik Bansleben. 2008. Building a flexible, collaborative, intensive master's program in computational linguistics. In *Proceedings of the Third Workshop on Issues in Teaching Computational Linguistics*, pages 10–18, Columbus, Ohio. Association for Computational Linguistics.

Steven Bird. 2018. Designing Mobile Applications for Endangered Languages. In *The Oxford Handbook of Endangered Languages*. Oxford University Press.

Steven Bird. 2020. Decolonising speech and language technology. In *Proceedings of the 28th International Conference on Computational Linguistics*, pages 3504–3519, Barcelona, Spain (Online). International Committee on Computational Linguistics.

Damian Blasi, Antonios Anastasopoulos, and Graham Neubig. 2022. Systematic inequalities in language technology performance across the world's languages. In *Proceedings of the 60th Annual Meeting of the Association for Computational Linguistics (Volume 1: Long Papers)*, pages 5486–5505, Dublin, Ireland. Association for Computational Linguistics.

Nathan Thanyehténhas Brinklow, Patrick Littell, Delaney Lothian, Aidan Pine, and Heather Souter. 2019. Indigenous language technologies and language reclamation in canada. In *Collection of Research Papers of the 1st International Conference on Language Technologies for All*, pages 402–406.

Luis Camacho and Rodolfo Zevallos. 2020. Language technology into high schools for revitalization of endangered languages. In *2020 IEEE XXVII International Conference on Electronics, Electrical Engineering and Computing (INTERCON)*, pages 1–4.

Alberto Cardoso, Joaquim Leitão, and César Teixeira. 2019. Using the jupyter notebook as a tool to support the teaching and learning processes in engineering courses. In *The Challenges of the Digital Transformation in Education: Proceedings of the 21st International Conference on Interactive Collaborative Learning (ICL2018)-Volume 2*, pages 227–236. Springer.

A. Seza Doğruöz and Sunayana Sitaram. 2022. Language technologies for low resource languages: Sociolinguistic and multilingual insights. In *Proceedings of the 1st Annual Meeting of the ELRA/ISCA Special Interest Group on Under-Resourced Languages*, pages 92–97, Marseille, France. European Language Resources Association.

Greg Durrett, Jifan Chen, Shrey Desai, Tanya Goyal, Lucas Kabela, Yasumasa Onoe, and Jiacheng Xu. 2021. Contemporary NLP modeling in six comprehensive programming assignments. In *Proceedings of the Fifth Workshop on Teaching NLP*, pages 99–103, Online. Association for Computational Linguistics.

Darren Flavelle and Jordan Lachler. 2023. Strengthening relationships between indigenous communities, documentary linguists, and computational linguists in the era of NLP-assisted language revitalization. In *Proceedings of the First Workshop on Cross-Cultural Considerations in NLP (C3NLP)*, pages 25–34, Dubrovnik, Croatia. Association for Computational Linguistics.

Eric Fosler-Lussier. 2008. Strategies for teaching "mixed" computational linguistics classes. In *Proceedings of the Third Workshop on Issues in Teaching Computational Linguistics*, pages 36–44, Columbus, Ohio. Association for Computational Linguistics.

David Gaddy, Daniel Fried, Nikita Kitaev, Mitchell Stern, Rodolfo Corona, John DeNero, and Dan Klein. 2021. Interactive assignments for teaching structured neural NLP. In *Proceedings of the Fifth Workshop on Teaching NLP*, pages 104–107, Online. Association for Computational Linguistics.

Eleonara Guerra, Víctor Narváez, and Camilo Robayo. 2024. Documentación y revitalización de la lengua karijona. Conferencia Día de las lenguas Nativas.

Jeremiah W Johnson. 2020. Benefits and pitfalls of jupyter notebooks in the classroom. In *Proceedings of the 21st annual conference on information technology education*, pages 32–37.

Pratik Joshi, Sebastin Santy, Amar Budhiraja, Kalika Bali, and Monojit Choudhury. 2020. The state and fate of linguistic diversity and inclusion in the NLP world. In *Proceedings of the 58th Annual Meeting of the Association for Computational Linguistics*, pages 6282–6293, Online. Association for Computational Linguistics.

Casey Kennington. 2021. Natural language processing for computer scientists and data scientists at a large state university. In *Proceedings of the Fifth Workshop on Teaching NLP*, pages 115–124, Online. Association for Computational Linguistics.

András Kornai. 2013. Digital language death. *PLOS ONE*, 8(10):1–11.

Zoey Liu, Crystal Richardson, Richard Hatcher, and Emily Prud'hommeaux. 2022. Not always about you: Prioritizing community needs when developing endangered language technology. In *Proceedings of the 60th Annual Meeting of the Association for Computational Linguistics (Volume 1: Long Papers)*, pages 3933–3944, Dublin, Ireland. Association for Computational Linguistics.

Martha Macri and James Sarmento. 2010. Respecting privacy: Ethical and pragmatic considerations. *Language & Communication*, 30(3):192–197.

Lucio Messina, Lucia Busso, Claudia Roberta Combei, Alessio Miaschi, Ludovica Pannitto, Gabriele Sarti, and Malvina Nissim. 2021. A dissemination workshop for introducing young Italian students to NLP. In *Proceedings of the Fifth Workshop on Teaching NLP*, pages 52–54, Online. Association for Computational Linguistics.

Ludovica Pannitto, Lucia Busso, Claudia Roberta Combei, Lucio Messina, Alessio Miaschi, Gabriele Sarti, and Malvina Nissim. 2021. Teaching NLP with bracelets and restaurant menus: An interactive workshop for Italian students. In *Proceedings of the Fifth Workshop on Teaching NLP*, pages 160–170, Online. Association for Computational Linguistics.

Martti Penttonen. 2011. Ict at service of endangered languages. In *Proceedings of the 11th Koli Calling International Conference on Computing Education Research*, pages 95–101.

Adam Poliak and Jalisha Jenifer. 2021. An immersive computational text analysis course for non-computer science students at barnard college. In *Proceedings of the Fifth Workshop on Teaching NLP*, pages 92–95, Online. Association for Computational Linguistics.

Ian Pool. 2016. Colonialism's and postcolonialism's fellow traveller: the collection, use and misuse of data on indigenous people. In Tahu Kukutai and John Taylor, editors, *Indigenous Data Sovereignty*, 1st edition. ANU Press.

Resguardo Indígena de Puerto Nare. 2023. *Karijona Womirï ehorï. ¡Aprendamos Karijona!* Fundación Tropenbos.

Lane Schwartz. 2022. Primum Non Nocere: Before working with Indigenous data, the ACL must confront ongoing colonialism. In *Proceedings of the 60th Annual Meeting of the Association for Computational Linguistics (Volume 2: Short Papers)*, pages 724–731, Dublin, Ireland. Association for Computational Linguistics.

Margaret Speas. 2009. Someone else's language on the role of linguists in language revitalization. *Indigenous Language Revitalization*, page 23.

Garrett Tanzer, Mirac Suzgun, Eline Visser, Dan Jurafsky, and Luke Melas-Kyriazi. 2024. A benchmark for learning to translate a new language from one grammar book. *Preprint*, arXiv:2309.16575.

Sowmya Vajjala. 2021. Teaching NLP outside linguistics and computer science classrooms: Some challenges and some opportunities. In *Proceedings of the Fifth Workshop on Teaching NLP*, pages 149–159, Online. Association for Computational Linguistics.

Chen Zhang, Xiao Liu, Jiuheng Lin, and Yansong Feng. 2024a. Teaching large language models an unseen language on the fly. *Preprint*, arXiv:2402.19167.

Kexun Zhang, Yee Man Choi, Zhenqiao Song, Taiqi He, William Yang Wang, and Lei Li. 2024b. Hire a linguist!: Learning endangered languages with in-context linguistic descriptions. *Preprint*, arXiv:2402.18025.

Shiyue Zhang, Ben Frey, and Mohit Bansal. 2022. How can NLP help revitalize endangered languages? a case study and roadmap for the Cherokee language. In *Proceedings of the 60th Annual Meeting of the Association for Computational Linguistics (Volume 1: Long Papers)*, pages 1529–1541, Dublin, Ireland. Association for Computational Linguistics.

Training an NLP Scholar at a Small Liberal Arts College: A Backwards Designed Course Proposal

Grusha Prasad[*]
Department of Computer Science
Colgate University
gprasad@colgate.edu

Forrest Davis[*]
Department of Computer Science
Colgate University
fdavis@colgate.edu

Abstract

The rapid growth in natural language processing (NLP) over the last couple years has generated student interest and excitement in learning more about the field. In this paper, we present two types of students that NLP courses might want to train. First, an "NLP engineer" who is able to flexibly design, build and apply new technologies in NLP for a wide range of tasks. Second, an "NLP scholar" who is able to pose, refine and answer questions in NLP and how it relates to the society, while also learning to effectively communicate these answers to a broader audience. While these two types of skills are not mutually exclusive — NLP engineers should be able to think critically, and NLP scholars should be able to build systems — we think that courses can differ in the balance of these skills. As educators at Small Liberal Arts Colleges, the strengths of our students and our institution favors an approach that is better suited to train NLP scholars. In this paper we articulate what kinds of skills an NLP scholar should have, and then adopt a backwards design to propose course components that can aid the acquisition of these skills.

1 Introduction

Natural language processing (NLP) as an academic discipline has undergone a rapid expansion in the last decade. Moreover, the feverishness around emerging technologies from NLP influences what students want to learn in their CS education. They want courses that train them in the tools and techniques of both NLP and Machine Learning more broadly. As educators, we are faced with an exciting challenge – how do we effectively train students to engage productively with our field?

In this paper, we differentiate between two kinds of desired learning outcomes for an NLP course: students should be able to (1) build and use new technologies, and (2) pose, refine and answer questions in NLP. While NLP courses might seek to achieve both of these outcomes, the relative emphasis placed on each of them can differ across courses. Some courses might place a larger emphasis on (1), and present students with many opportunities to program and develop substantial projects, often with a focus on working with state-of-the-art approaches. In contrast, some courses might place a larger empahsis on (2) and present students with opportunities to engage critically with NLP tools and techniques, often in the service of answering questions and facing challenges that bridge disciplinary boundaries. We will refer to the type of student the former course is designed to train as an **"NLP engineer"**, and the student for the latter course as an **"NLP scholar"**.

As educators in a Computer Science Department at Colgate University (a Small Liberal Arts College; SLAC), where the curriculum structure requires students to take a wider range of non-CS classes with the goal of cultivating critical thinking, we argue that we are better placed to train NLP scholars, than we are to train NLP engineers. In this paper we present a design for an upper level NLP course intended to train NLP scholars.

Using a backward design, we start by articulating what are the skills that an NLP scholar should have, and propose a set of course principles/tenets that can facilitate the acquisition of these skills. Then, drawing on our previous experience teaching Applied Machine Learning and Natural Langauge Processing at our institution, we propose a course that is structured around a capstone project. Concretely, our paper makes three contributions:

1. We make explicit the link between the kinds of students we want to train, the desired skills we want the students to have, and the course structure and content.
2. We propose a course structure designed

[*]Equal contribution.

Proceedings of the Sixth Workshop on Teaching NLP, pages 105–118
August 15, 2024

around a capstone experience which has six different course components and relate each of these components to concrete concepts and skills they are designed to help with.

3. We present preliminary materials and evaluation rubrics for several of these components.

The paper is structured as follows: First, in §2, we take critical stock of our students, their experiences, and their relation to computer science, asking ourselves how can we build on the strengths of our students and our institution. Then, in §3, we present skills we think an NLP scholar should have, and the principles we think a course designed to train NLP should adopt. Finally, in §4, we detail our different course components and discuss how they relate to our overall learning objectives.[1]

2 Teaching NLP as an upper level course at a Small Liberal Arts College

Small Liberal Arts College (SLACs) are undergraduate focused institutions that emphasize, among other things, drawing connections between different fields (King et al., 2007). Therefore, in these institutions there is more emphasis on students taking classes in different disciplines. A consequence of this is that CS departments in liberal arts colleges tend to have fewer required courses and curricula with flatter prerequisite structures (Teresco et al., 2022). In this section we introduce the CS curriculum structure and class room dynamics at Colgate University, a SLAC in the US that we teach at. Then, we outline how this has influenced our experience of teaching upper level elective courses in Natural Language Processing and Machine Learning in previous semesters, and the changes we want to make in our proposed course as a result of this experience.

2.1 Required and elective courses at Colgate

Our curriculum has four required classes: one at the 100 level (Introduction to Computing) and three at the 200 level (Data Structures and Algorithms, Introduction to Computer Systems, Discrete Structures). In addition students have to take four electives, with at least two classes at the 300-level or above, and at least one 400-level course. All of our 400-level courses require students to work on "capstone" final projects.

Most electives have one or two of the required 200-level courses as prerequisites, with almost no elective requiring another elective as a prerequisite. As a consequence of this flat prerequisite structure, students can come into a 400-level elective like NLP with more limited programming experience than their peers at institutions with a more hierarchical prerequisite structure, and with likely little to no prior background in relevant classes like Machine Learning or Artificial Intelligence. The challenge, therefore, is to design a class that sets up our students up our students, who have relatively limited programming experience and relevant conceptual background, to work on meaningful capstone projects.

2.2 Take-aways from previous iterations of teaching NLP and Applied ML

In the past three semesters we've taught two sections each of NLP and Applied ML. In all of these four classes, while all students were able to successfully produce capstone projects, we thought most of these projects could have been more ambitious. We've identified two factors that likely contributed to the smaller scope of the projects: the order in which earlier non-neural approaches vs. more contemporary neural network content was presented, and students' prior programming experience.

Order of introducing non-neural vs. neural approaches In both Applied ML and NLP we spent the first half of the semester working through non-neural network approaches. For example, in Applied ML we spent the first four weeks of the semester working through evaluation metrics, gradient descent, regression, SVM, decision trees and random forests before introducing neural networks. Similarly, in NLP we spent the first six to seven weeks working through FSAs, context free grammars and parsing, n-gram language models and Bayesian classification before introducing neural language models and transfer learning.

We adopted this approach because starting with the non-neural approaches makes it easier to ground the computational task we are trying to solve with our ML and NLP models, and the metrics we use to evaluate these models. For example, starting with FSAs and CFGs before n-gram models highlights the complexity of modeling structure in language and how co-occurrence statistics can

[1]A github repository with links to final project templates and our toolkit can be found here: `https://github.com/forrestdavis/NLPScholar`.

capture some of this complexity. Then, introducing classification tasks and evaluation metrics in the context of n-gram models makes it possible to reason about the relation between the tasks we want to solve and the metrics we use to evaluate performance on these tasks before trying to understand the contemporary approaches that have been found to be successful.

A consequence of this approach, however, was that by the time we taught contemporary approaches applicable to a wider range of tasks, it was too late for students to effectively incorporate them into their capstone projects. Therefore, many students chose to use non-neural approaches in their final project which meant that they worked on simpler tasks and/or were met with limited success on their tasks. We propose to address this issue by using a layered approach to introducing concepts (§ 4.1) and designing labs early in the semester that scaffold some of the aspects common to all projects such as data pre-processing and generating plots (§ 4.2).

Prior programming experience As discussed earlier, since students can take NLP after having taken as few as three CS courses, they can have more limited programming experience than students at other institutions with a more hierarchical prerequisite structure that requires students to take more CS classes before taking NLP. As a consequence, we found that students struggled with implementing more complex NLP or ML pipelines using sparse starter code or links to existing codebases. We propose to address this by designing a modular toolkit with the core components required for any NLP pipeline. The toolkit will be designed such that students can use it off the shelf from the beginning of class. Crucially, as the class progresses and we want them to engage with implementational details of different components, the modular design makes it easy to ask them swap out different components that they implement from scratch (§ 4.3). We also plan to include a midterm project that requires students to replicate previous work, which will give them practice working with existing code bases and integrating it with the toolkit(§ 4.4).

3 How to train an NLP Scholar

Given the liberal arts context that we are in, and the background that students come in with, we think that we are not very well placed to train NLP engineers who can leave the class knowing how to design and build new tools to tackle a wide range of NLP tasks. Rather, we are better placed to train NLP scholars who, when given a task or challenge, can identify and apply existing tools to the challenge or task, while thinking critically about the limitations of these tools, our methods to evaluate them, and the societal context in which they are used. Concretely, there are three skills we want the NLP scholars we train to have.

S1: Describe language processing NLP scholars should be able articulate clearly what computations underlie language processing and how the systems we are building are approximating different aspects of this at a computational and/or algorithmic level. That is, they will develop an understanding for language as a computational system, while setting aside concerns from psycho- or neurolinguistics of how exactly linguistic processing is realized.

S2: Effectively using existing NLP tools NLP scholars should recognize what existing NLP tools are appropriate for solving different tasks or answering different questions, and be able use these tools to solve the tasks and answer the questions.

S3: Evaluate claims about NLP systems NLP scholars should be able to identify the rhetorical tools used to make arguments about the potential and limitations of NLP systems, both in academic papers and public media, and use evidence based approaches to evaluate these arguments.

3.1 Tenets of our proposed course

Given these high level skills, we now describe some of the tenets we are adopting in this course to facilitate the acquistion of these skills.

T1: Appreciate the complexity of language Students should recognize the complexity involved in language processing. We hope to accomplish this by having students create and evaluate symbolic computational models of language processing.

T2: Focus on multilingualism Students should recognize the role that linguistic diversity and multilingualism plays in our understanding of language as a phenomenon, and describe the scientific and societal benefits of modeling languages other than English.

Course Design Decision	Scholar goal	Tenet	Capstone skill
Layered approach	S1, S2	T1, T3, T4	–
Lab vs. Lecture Integration	S1	T1, T2, T4	C2
Toolkit	S2	T4	C2
Midterm replication	S2	T3, T4, T5	C1, C2
Capstone project	S1, S2, S3	T4	C1, C2, C3
Society and Science Comm	S3	T5,T6	–

Table 1: Mapping our course design decisions to the tenets and desired skills in our proposed course.

T3: Recognize how NLP tasks abstract away from the complexity Students should describe how different NLP tasks (e.g., language modeling) abstract away from the complexity of language processing. They should also be able explain the practical importance of this abstraction while articulating the limits that this abstraction poses on the conclusions we can draw about language processing from building and studying these models.

T4: Build NLP systems using existing tools Students should be able to describe all of the components of building NLP systems. They should also be able to use existing code-bases and tools to design systems that solve specific tasks or answer specific questions.

T5: Critically examine the role of benchmarks Students should be able to articulate how and why benchmarks shape NLP research and product development, while reasoning about the limitations of benchmarks.

T6: Critically examine the impact of hype culture on science and society Critically reason about what kinds of results about NLP systems' capabilities (or their lack thereof) get hyped and why, while describing the impact that this hype can have on society.

3.2 Capstone specific skills

We think that an effective way to achieve the skills is to learn by doing, and we think that engaging in a capstone project that requires students to answer a concrete question or solve concrete task is an ideal way to learn NLP. We describe the different components of our proposed capstone project in § 4.5, but overall, we want students to be able to do the following.

C1: Reading Scientific Papers Students should be able to distill the hypotheses, methods, results and conclusions from a scientific paper while critically evaluating whether the conclusions follow from the results.

C2: Replicate prior work Students should be able to follow the procedures described in a paper to replicate prior work, and reason about what counts as a successful replication.

C3: Engage in peer-review Students should be able to give constructive criticism in a peer-review setup, as well as incorporate constructive feedback to improve their work.

4 Course Components and Assessments

Following our backwards design, we intentionally related course components and assessments to the skills we want our students to acquire, the tenets underlying our course principles, and the skills we want demonstrated in a capstone project (see § 3). We summarize these connections in Table 1.

4.1 Layered approach to introducing concepts

In the previous iterations, we adopted a largely sequential approach to introducing concepts. We found that this resulted in a bit of a fragmented course structure. In this iteration we want to adopt a layered approach that introduces core concepts at multiple levels of abstraction at different points in the course. To accomplish this, we plan to start the class by introducing the NLP pipeline at a very high level, and then un-blackboxing different parts as the semester progresses. This un-blackboxing process applies to both computational concepts (e.g., when students are asked to write context free grammars to engage with the complexity of language) as well as to practical implementational level details (e.g., when students are asked to implement tokenization). We describe below how we plan to use the lab-course integration and the toolkit as tools for this layered approach.

4.2 Labs-Lecture intergration

Following other natural sciences, many courses in our department have an accompanying lab. These labs serve to provide supplemental practice with concepts covered in the course and concrete hands-on time for programming. Within the context of our NLP course, we intentionally designed labs for two broad purposes: preparing students for midterm projects (see § 4.4 for more details on this project) and to more deeply explore content not fully covered in lecture.

In designing lab content, we are motivated by a tension we observed in earlier versions of this course and related courses (e.g., Machine Learning): student final projects tend to draw on current trends in the field, but knowledge of the field's foundations help contextualize modern techniques. As a result, while earlier material is critical, time spent on developing intuitions for traditional concepts (e.g., context-free grammars) reduces the scope of what students are capable of accomplishing in their final projects. For example, in earlier versions of NLP, there were only around 2 weeks between the introduction of transformers and the completion of earlier phases of the final project.

Labs resolve this tension by providing time outside of lecture for developing skills critical to success in their final projects. This includes, a refresher on Python (the middle of our curriculum is taught in Java and C) and labs targeting data processing, hypothesis generation, conducting experiments, plotting, and interpreting results.

In their additional role as an opportunity for deeper engagement with lecture content, labs take the form of hands-on exploration, similar to the 'scaffolded discovery' advocated in Schofield et al. (2021). Concretely, consider context-free grammars. In lecture, they will be discussed at a conceptual level (what are they, how do they relate to language, what are ways we may use them, etc.). In lab, students will be asked to write actual context-free grammars for fragments of a language, following in the style of (Eisner and Smith, 2008). In this capacity, labs allow us to decide when to abstract and when to go a bit deeper, without relying solely on lecture time.

4.3 Toolkit

In developing the course, we had to decide what to blackbox and when. A variety of factors influenced our thinking on this. We want students to develop a high-level understanding of the core parts of an NLP pipeline and how they relate to one another, while also leaving space for deeper dives into specific aspects in the form of student implementations. We believe, following our course principles, that students learn best by doing. In this case, students gain a fuller understanding of the NLP pipeline if they can use and explore a working implementation. Additionally, they benefit from implementing parts of this pipeline. Our toolkit seeks to balance these two needs by being modular.

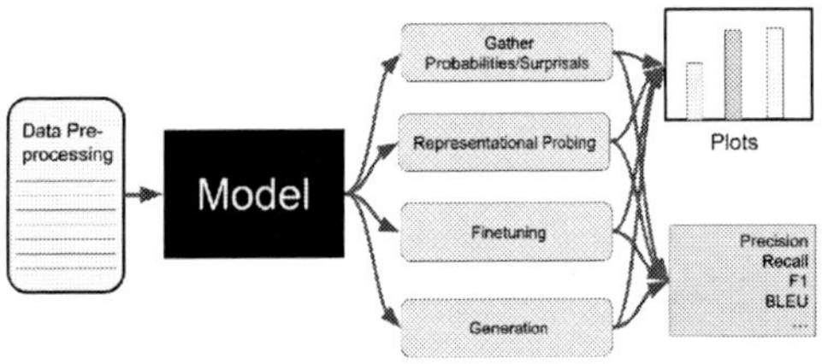

Figure 1: Sketch of the core components of the toolkit

As sketched in Figure 1, there are 4 basic components to our toolkit: data pre-processing, model, experiments, and handling the output (plotting and evaluation metrics). Data pre-processing includes both basic text processing (e.g., reading different file types, text normalization) and tokenization. Following an earlier implementation of this toolkit, the model components is comprised of a parent class with basic methods (e.g., getting the logits from a model, aligning logits to words, getting intermediate output) that allow for a shared structure across disparate models (including transformers and RNNs/LSTMs). The experiment portion of the toolkit facilitates basic approaches in the field (e.g., probing, targeted syntactic evaluations). Finally, the output of experiments interacts with both metrics (e.g., F1) and also a plotting interface. Each of these components can be supplemented with student implementations. For example, a lab can focus on building a different type of tokenizer, which students can add to the pipeline to extend the capabilities of the existing toolkit.

In designing the toolkit we are mindful of two things: we want the code to be readable and approachable for students to dig into while also building in a level of abstraction that facilitates using the toolkit without fully understanding the components early in the semester. Like in earlier versions of the toolkit we plan to abstract from the implementation via basic plain text files specifying experimental material (e.g., grammatical and ungrammatical sentences) and a config file that specified pre-processing details (e.g., including puncutation) and the desired models to run the experiment on. Additionally, we will build on top of existing, and widely adopted NLP toolkits like NLTK and HuggingFace (especially for models), so that students gain some familiarity with existing industry tools.

4.4 Midterm

To scaffold the final project, the middle of the semester culminates in a midterm project, rather than a midterm exam. The intention of this project is to provide students an opportunity to concretely apply skills relevant to the final paper, but in a more structured format. Concretely, we identify 4 skills that we want to ensure students can apply going into the final project:

1. Working with existing code and/or libraries
2. Hypothesis generation and operationalizing a question
3. Interpreting and synthesizing results
4. Science communication

Development of these skills are facilitated in lab and in the production of their midterm paper. We believe it is challenging, if at the end of the semester, students are faced with two tasks, i) apply new knowledge in a new format (e.g., many other computer science courses in our department lack a final paper), and ii) develop a novel idea that excites them. The midterm project seeks to divorce these (to some extent). Rather than producing novel work, students are tasked with replicating existing work. This pre-existing structure helps guide them in the development and application of course concepts. In closely studying an existing paper, they gain familiarity with how researchers frame questions, how to synthesize results in a way that is digestible to the reader, and how to work with existing code and data.

In the following sections, we discuss how we approached selecting papers to serve as the base of student replications, and how we scaffold the skills necessary to complete it.

Types of papers and why In choosing papers, we focused on the core themes of the course and looked for papers that were (often) short, contained existing code, exposed a key methodology, and would facilitate good discussions. We settled on 5 themes: Basic Methodology, Interpretability, Experimental Design, Cross-Linguistic or Multilinguality, What's in the Data. Example papers are provided in Table 2. The Basic Methodology theme serves a particular function in scaffolding the midterm project, which we return to below. For the others, we wanted to highlight different approaches for evaluating models (Interpretability), how carefully created experiments can expose flaws in scientific reasoning (Experimental Design), how we should think broadly about language (cf. the "Bender Rule", Bender 2019; Multilinguality), and how we should think critically about what is in our training data (What's in the Data). These categories are not exclusive – papers can fall in more than one category. For example, Deas et al. (2023) invites discussion of both the contents of our training and evaluation data, but also, highlights the diversity of what is meant by English.

Scaffolds for writing the paper In writing their midterm papers, students will demonstrate their knowledge of creating research: going from data to question to experiments to results, and finally a conclusion. To scaffold the acquisition of these skills, we are relying on early labs. Students will have labs that guide them throw basic research pipelines like formatting data to work with a model. Concretely, we draw on papers from the Basic Methodology as an in-lab replication assignment. Additionally, students will present their midterm projects to us for feedback, facilitating practice with scientific communication.

4.5 Final

The course culminates in a capstone project in the form of a final project, done in small groups with individual final papers. We aim through the semester to have assessments that help ensure the students remain on track. Concretely, over the course of a few semesters of piloting this, we have settled on 5 phases:

1. Individual Ideation and Group Formation
2. Feedback Discussion
3. Pilot Presentation
4. Poster Presentation
5. Final Paper

Theme	Example 1	Example 2
Basic Methodology	Newman et al. (2021)	Warstadt and Bowman (2020)
Interpretability	Clark et al. (2019)	Hewitt and Manning (2019)
Experimental Design	McCoy et al. (2020)	Hewitt and Liang (2019)
Cross-Linguistic	Ravfogel et al. (2019)	Mueller et al. (2020)
What's in the Data	Yedetore et al. (2023)	Deas et al. (2023)

Table 2: Paper themes and examples. For the midterm paper, students will replicate papers from any category but Basic Methodology, which are used in lab.

We discuss the motivation and content of each phase below.

Ideation to Group Project In driving towards a group project, we want an opportunity for students to externalize their own interests and map it to the course content. We have an explicit assessment to target this. Students submit an individual project proposal that outlines their idea, a concrete link to a relevant dataset or a description of how they would make one, a question operationalized with an experiment or task, and their availability to work in the semester (so that groups can take into account working style/time). See Appendix A for more details. Students are asked to read all the individual project ideas and to submit a ranking of projects they would like to work on. Rather than just having students form groups immediately, we believe this facilitates better groups by allowing students to find overlapping interest with people they might not already know.

Feedback Discussion After forming groups, students are asked to put together a project proposal (similar to their individual project proposals). We review these and then have meetings with each group to help flesh out any limitations in their current proposal. This often takes the form of helping them make their project either more ambitious, or conversely, scaled down to something manageable in the remaining time of the semester. As opposed to written feedback, we find these conversations productive and useful in helping students articulate a project that is appropriate and exciting for them. In the end of the discussion, we establish what should comprise their pilot presentation.

Pilot As the class shifts to focusing on final projects, we ensure that there is time in labs for groups to make progress. We formalize this desire for making progress prior to the end of the semester with a pilot presentation. Groups are meant to implement the core part of their final project and present it to the class in the form of a short presentation. By demonstrating that their project works, at least in a limited capacity, groups can expose any issues that might arise in conducting their work (e.g., the data are not good, the model they are drawing on performs more poorly than expected). Additionally, students get practice communicating their results to a more general audience (each other). For each presentation, students submit feedback forms (see Appendix B) and drive the questions in the discussion period after the presentation.

Poster Presentation In the final week of the semester, students create and present posters about their final project. This ensures that they have a nearly complete final project prior to working on the final paper during the examination period. In the past, we have had students give feedback for each poster using a form. We have decided to have students write anonymized reviews of a subset of posters. This, we hope, encourages them to engage more substantially with the poster and helps teach them the process of science (namely, peer-review). We plan to use a reviewing form similar to that of used by ARR (e.g., highlighting the strengths, weaknesses, and key takeaway). A copy of our poster template, rubric, and prior feedback form is given in Appendix B.

Final paper Finally, each student is asked to individually write a final paper, following a template included in Appendix C. The paper mimics a typical research paper in NLP (drawing on ACL's style guide). Given the group nature of the other parts of the final project, we want to retain some way to assess the individual contributions of group members. We have found that final papers in the past have exposed both exciting differences in interpreting results but also highlight the varied contributions of group members.

4.6 Society Reflection

A core aim of this course is not only to introduce students to NLP but also produce critically engaged practitioners. The final component of the course is meant to scaffold this. In their paper on incorporating reflection on social issues in CS classes, Davis and Walker (2011) highlighted, among other things, the following two challenges: First, students are good at repeating platitudes (e.g., "it is important to address biases in models"), but find it challenging to critically think about the issues in practice. Second, formally assessing students' ability to engage with these issues can be challenging.

In our course, we hope to address these challenges by requiring students to write a 1-2 page "Society reflection" paper. For this paper, students will be asked to find and read a recent news article that discusses advances in NLP and asked to evaluate the arguments the article makes (implicitly or explicitly) about the societal implications of these advances. Since students are asked to evaluate specific arguments, merely repeating platitudes will not be sufficient; they will need to draw on their knowledge of the tools and techniques in NLP to examine the central claims, while also reflecting on the rhetorical reasons for making those claims. Students' ability to engage with the societal issues as NLP practitioners will be assessed based on their ability to identify the core claims and the soundness of their arguments when evaluating these claims.

5 Discussion

In this paper we presented two types of students NLP courses might want to train — NLP engineers and NLP scholars — and used a backwards design approach to design a capstone focused upper-level course to train the latter type of student. We started by outlining three skills we would like the NLP scholars we train to have. Then, we described six tenets and three capstone specific skills that shaped the content, organization and assessments in the course. Finally we described these different components of the course. Having taught two sections of NLP and two sections of Machine Learning in the last two years, our proposed course represents the synthesis of many conversations, both among ourselves, but also with other educators and with our students.

In designing the upperlevel course, we had to resolve a tension between the knowledge and critical thinking skills we wanted our students, as NLP scholars, to have and our desire to develop a course that fostered substantial and exciting undergraduate NLP projects. To foster a deeper understanding and appreciation of what NLP is about, we thought it was important to spend time on older material (especially since we could not assume any prior background in AI or NLP). However, to prepare our students for successful and exciting capstone projects we thought it was important to introduce them to newer tools and techniques early on.

We resolved this tension in our proposed course in the following ways.

1. We adopted a layered approach to introducing concepts where we introduce the NLP pipeline at an abstract level in the beginning, and peel away the layers as the course progresses. To accomplish this, we proposed a modular toolkit and and intentional course-lab integration.

2. We proposed a midterm replication project that provides students with an opportunity to work on larger scale projects with existing code-bases, while also giving them practice with critical thinking (e.g., reasoning about what counts as a successful replication) and science communication.

3. We proposed a highly scaffolded approach to their final capstone project involving five stages. We piloted this five-stage process in two sections of Applied Machine Learning this semester, and found that on average the student projects were more ambitious and successful. We include course materials from this pilot in the appendix.

NLP Scholar in Different Institutions and Programs While the course components we proposed are specifically designed with the constraints of our institution and program in mind, we believe aspects are applicable to training NLP Scholars in other contexts. Specifically, there are two educational environments that we would like to highlight: a computer science department at a research heavy (i.e., R1) university and other departments like linguistics or psychology where a computational linguistics course would be relevant. For both, the toolkit and societal reflection seem appropriate and useful.

The final project, as we have constructed it, requires ample one-on-one time with students, both for formal components of the grade (e.g., the project feedback and in-class presentations), but also, for helping student groups progress in their project (e.g., debugging issues). We believe these would be difficult to scale in R1 settings without relying heavily on TAs and restructuring the progression of the final projects. However, we believe the final project structure, and in particular, the replication component, would be applicable across disciplines. Having linguistics students replicate work on targeted syntactic evaluations, for example, is a good way of taking a common practice in linguistics (the construction of minimal pairs) and applying it to a computational domain. On the other hand, we think the lab/lecture structure is well suited to R1 computer science students, while it may pose challenges in being ported to other disciplinary backgrounds. We are assuming that students in our class need more time to the concepts than on the aspects of programming.

Usefulness of the NLP Engineer vs. NLP Scholar distinction Even if the goal of many NLP courses might be to train students who are a combination of an NLP Engineer and Scholar, we think the distinction can be useful when faced with conflicting goals for the course. For example, Schofield et al. (2021) advocated for a discovery based approach to teaching NLP, but concluded that students might need more guidance on/practice with aspects like File I/O, loading and saving data, manipulating numpy and spaCy objects etc. Here, the NLP Engineer vs. Scholar distinction can help instructors decide what components should students productively struggle with, and which components they are better of getting more structured guidance on.

If the goal of the course or the specific assignment is to equip students with the ability to *build* something like an NLP Engineer, then it might be helpful for students to productively struggle with components like File/IO with minimal guidance. If on the other hand, the goal is to have students *use* a tool to answer a question or explore a topic like an NLP Scholar, then students might be better off having more guidance on components of the assignment like File I/O, so they can devote more time to the exploration and analysis. This line of reasoning is applicable even for graduate level NLP courses or undergraduate courses where students come in with much stronger programming experience, and are unlikely to be challenged by programming aspects like File I/O — in these courses, instructors will need to decide the extent to which other implementational details such as GPU parallelization should be scaffolded.

Conclusion We differentiated between two types of students — NLP scholar and NLP engineer — and proposed an upper level course, with a capstone experience, designed to train the latter type of student. Ultimately, we hope that articulating the goals for an NLP scholar, and tying them back to specific components in our proposed course can facilitate broader discussions about what kinds of NLP practitioners we want to train, why, and how best to train them.

Acknowledgments

We would like to thank our colleagues in computer science and our students over the years for helping shape the course. In particular the students in NLP at Colgate in Spring 2023 and Fall 2023, the students in Applied Machine Learning at Colgate in Spring 2024, and the students in the Methods in Computational Linguistics seminar at MIT in Fall 2022. Additionally, we would like to thank our anonymous reviewers for their helpful comments and suggestions.

References

Emily M Bender. 2019. The# benderrule: On naming the languages we study and why it matters.

Kevin Clark, Urvashi Khandelwal, Omer Levy, and Christopher D. Manning. 2019. What does BERT look at? an analysis of BERT's attention. In *Proceedings of the 2019 ACL Workshop BlackboxNLP: Analyzing and Interpreting Neural Networks for NLP*, pages 276–286, Florence, Italy. Association for Computational Linguistics.

Janet Davis and Henry M Walker. 2011. Incorporating social issues of computing in a small, liberal arts college: a case study. In *Proceedings of the 42nd ACM technical symposium on Computer science education*, pages 69–74.

Nicholas Deas, Jessica Grieser, Shana Kleiner, Desmond Patton, Elsbeth Turcan, and Kathleen McKeown. 2023. Evaluation of African American language bias in natural language generation. In *Proceedings of the 2023 Conference on Empirical Methods in Natural Language Processing*, pages 6805–6824, Singapore. Association for Computational Linguistics.

Jason Eisner and Noah A. Smith. 2008. Competitive grammar writing. In *Proceedings of the Third Workshop on Issues in Teaching Computational Linguistics*, pages 97–105, Columbus, Ohio. Association for Computational Linguistics.

John Hewitt and Percy Liang. 2019. Designing and interpreting probes with control tasks. In *Proceedings of the 2019 Conference on Empirical Methods in Natural Language Processing and the 9th International Joint Conference on Natural Language Processing (EMNLP-IJCNLP)*, pages 2733–2743, Hong Kong, China. Association for Computational Linguistics.

John Hewitt and Christopher D. Manning. 2019. A structural probe for finding syntax in word representations. In *Proceedings of the 2019 Conference of the North American Chapter of the Association for Computational Linguistics: Human Language Technologies, Volume 1 (Long and Short Papers)*, pages 4129–4138, Minneapolis, Minnesota. Association for Computational Linguistics.

Patricia M King, Marie Kendall Brown, Nathan K Lindsay, and Jones R VanHecke. 2007. Liberal arts student learning outcomes: An integrated approach. *About Campus*, 12(4):2–9.

R. Thomas McCoy, Junghyun Min, and Tal Linzen. 2020. BERTs of a feather do not generalize together: Large variability in generalization across models with similar test set performance. In *Proceedings of the Third BlackboxNLP Workshop on Analyzing and Interpreting Neural Networks for NLP*, pages 217–227, Online. Association for Computational Linguistics.

Aaron Mueller, Garrett Nicolai, Panayiota Petrou-Zeniou, Natalia Talmina, and Tal Linzen. 2020. Cross-linguistic syntactic evaluation of word prediction models. In *Proceedings of the 58th Annual Meeting of the Association for Computational Linguistics*, pages 5523–5539, Online. Association for Computational Linguistics.

Benjamin Newman, Kai-Siang Ang, Julia Gong, and John Hewitt. 2021. Refining targeted syntactic evaluation of language models. In *Proceedings of the 2021 Conference of the North American Chapter of the Association for Computational Linguistics: Human Language Technologies*, pages 3710–3723, Online. Association for Computational Linguistics.

Shauli Ravfogel, Yoav Goldberg, and Tal Linzen. 2019. Studying the inductive biases of RNNs with synthetic variations of natural languages. In *Proceedings of the 2019 Conference of the North American Chapter of the Association for Computational Linguistics: Human Language Technologies, Volume 1 (Long and Short Papers)*, pages 3532–3542, Minneapolis, Minnesota. Association for Computational Linguistics.

Alexandra Schofield, Richard Wicentowski, and Julie Medero. 2021. Learning how to learn NLP: Developing introductory concepts through scaffolded discovery. In *Proceedings of the Fifth Workshop on Teaching NLP*, pages 131–137, Online. Association for Computational Linguistics.

James D Teresco, Andrea Tartaro, Amanda Holland-Minkley, Grant Braught, Jakob Barnard, and Douglas Baldwin. 2022. Cs curricular innovations with a liberal arts philosophy. In *Proceedings of the 53rd ACM Technical Symposium on Computer Science Education-Volume 1*, pages 537–543.

Alex Warstadt and Samuel R. Bowman. 2020. Linguistic analysis of pretrained sentence encoders with acceptability judgments.

Aditya Yedetore, Tal Linzen, Robert Frank, and R. Thomas McCoy. 2023. How poor is the stimulus? evaluating hierarchical generalization in neural networks trained on child-directed speech. In *Proceedings of the 61st Annual Meeting of the Association for Computational Linguistics (Volume 1: Long Papers)*, pages 9370–9393, Toronto, Canada. Association for Computational Linguistics.

A Project Proposal and Pilot Presentation Templates

Students are asked to make two project proposals. One that represents their individual idea and interest, and then later, a proposal for a group project. A verison of the proposal template is copied below.

A.1 Proposal Template

A.1.1 Introduction/ Motivation

- What is the big picture question you are trying to answer/ problem you are trying to solve? Why is this an interesting and worthwhile question to answer/ problem to work on?
- What is the specific question you will pursue? Why? (Note: you will need to pick something that is feasible to answer in 3-4 weeks)
- What are all the possible outcomes of your project? Do you think one (or few) of these outcomes are more likely than others? Why?

A.1.2 Background/Literature review

Find at least three papers related to your project. For each project write a paragraph or two summarizing:

- What were the goals of that paper? How is it related to your project?
- What methods did the paper use?
- What were the conclusions?

Google scholar (or other comparable database search) is a better place to look than standard search: you are less likely to find blogposts with unverified content on Google scholar. Note, on Google Scholar you might see a lot of preprints from arxiv, even if they were also published elsewhere. It is good practice to try and find the most recent version of a paper. The general rule of thumb you should use: peer reviewed published papers are more credible than preprints.

A.1.3 Planned methods

Describe what methods you plan to use to address your question and describe how your methods compare to prior work you describe in the background section.

- What dataset will you use? Is it already available or do you have to create it?
- What model(s)/approaches will you use?
- How will you evaluate your models? What counts as success? What conclusions can you draw (if any) if you get negative results?

A.1.4 Proposed timeline/division of labor

Breakdown your project into separate tasks. For each task, list the expected amount of time, who plans to work on it and when they expect to complete it by. For this part, it might be most straightforward to fill out a table following the format below.

One of your tasks should be "Prepare for pilot result presentation" and your timeline should highlight what work you hope to accomplish before the pilot results.

Task	Time required	Expected date of completion	Person

A.2 Pilot

After discussions between us and each group, students work towards a final project pilot presentation. This presentation demonstrates early progress on their project and showcases their question and operationalization. It takes the form of a 5-8 minute presentation with time for questions from the other students. During the presentations, students are asked to provide:

- Feedback about the content (question, methods, result interpretation, conclusion etc)
- Feedback about the presentation (framing, visuals, oral presentation etc)

B Poster Presentation Templates

At the conclusion of the semesters, groups create and present a final poster. Details on the poster template, grading rubric, and student feedback from are provided below.

B.1 Poster Template

We provide students with a final poster template (given in Figure 2) in the form of a google slide and are asked to make use of the on-campus printing services to gather their physical poster.

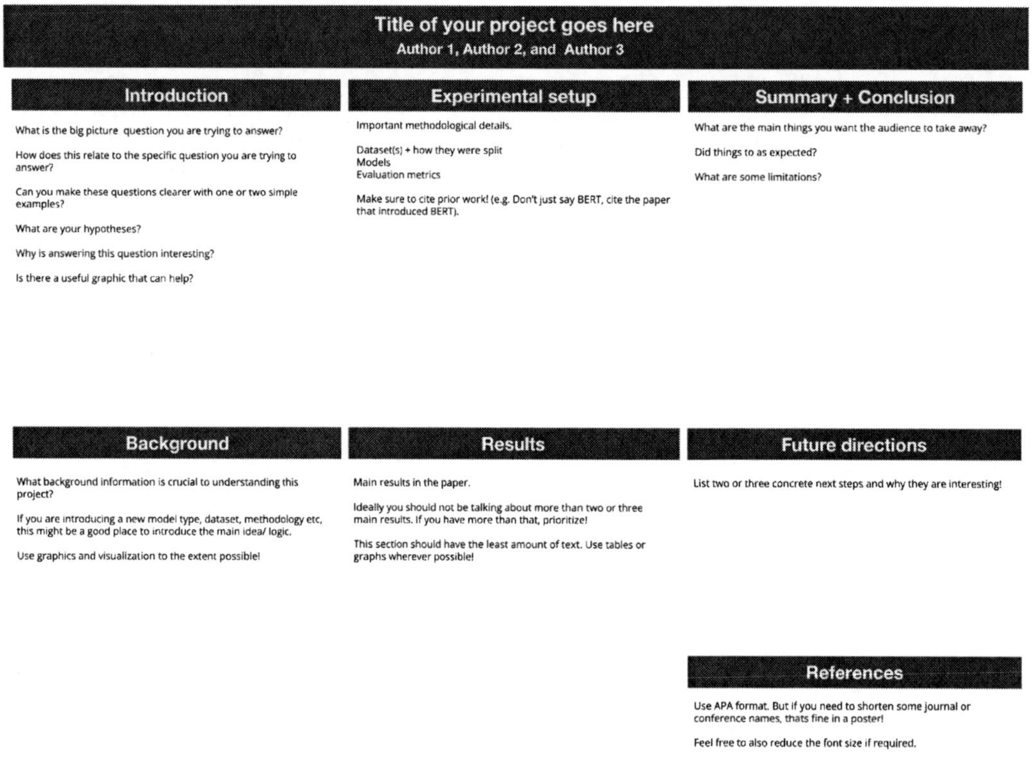

Figure 2: Final poster template

B.2 Poster Rubric

In an effort to balance listening to and grading the presentations, we settled on a brief rubric in Table 3.

Extractable from poster? (0: missing 1: yes 2: clear)			
Introduction	0	1	2
Background	0	1	2
Experimental Setup	0	1	2
Results	0	1	2
Summary + Conclusion	0	1	2
Future work	0	1	2
Clarity of presentation (0: bad 1: ok 2: exceeds expectations)			
Division of labor (ok: majority of team contributes)	0	1	2
Oral pitch (ok: leave with question, operationalization, takeaways)	0	1	2
Timing (ok: <= 5 mins)	0	1	2
Visuals (ok: informative, legible)	0	1	2
Answering Questions (ok: understand the question ask)	0	1	2

Table 3: Final poster rubric

B.3 Student Feedback on Posters

When not presenting, students are asked to engage with the other presentations and provide feedback. In prior courses, this feedback too the form of filling out a paper form. Concretely, they were asked to provide (at least) one bit of constructive feedback along each of these dimensions:

- Content
- Visualizations
- Argument presentation
- Future direction

C Final Paper Templates

Using a latex template styled on ACL's submission template, students are asked to write an individual final paper. Some guidelines we gave to students are provided below.

C.1 Final Paper Guidelines

Your final paper should have the following sections.

C.1.1 Introduction/Motivation

- What is the big picture question you are trying to answer/ problem you are trying to solve? Why is this interesting?
- What is the specific question you are pursuing? Why?

C.1.2 Background/Literature review

Find at least three papers related to your project. For each paper write a paragraph or two summarizing:

- What were the goals of that paper? How is it related to your project?
- What methods did the paper use?
- What were the conclusions?

Note, on Google Scholar you might see a lot of preprints from arxiv, even if they were also published elsewhere. It is good practice to try and find the most recent published version (i.e. conference version) of a paper.

C.1.3 Methods

Describe what methods you used to address your question and describe how your methods compare to prior work you describe in the background section.

- What dataset did you use? Was it already available or did you have to create it?
- What model(s)/approaches did you use?
- How did you evaluate your models? What counted as success? What conclusions can you draw (if any) if you got negative results?
- Include a link to a repository with your code (or similar) in the paper

C.1.4 Results

Describe what you found in your work. Put your results in a figure or a table that helps the reader synthesize what you've done.

C.1.5 Discussion

How does your work answer your question? What are the implications of your results? What are ways the work could be extended? What are the limitations of your work?

An Interactive Toolkit for Approachable NLP

AriaRay Brown[1], Julius Steuer[1], Marius Mosbach[2*], Dietrich Klakow[1]

[1]Saarland University, [2]Mila Quebec AI Institute,
{arbrown,jsteuer,dklakow}@lsv.uni-saarland.de
marius.mosbach@mila.quebec

Abstract

We present a novel tool designed for teaching and interfacing the information-theoretic modeling abilities of large language models. The Surprisal Toolkit allows students from diverse linguistic and programming backgrounds to learn about measures of information theory and natural language processing (NLP) through an online interactive tool. In addition, the interface provides a valuable research mechanism for obtaining measures of surprisal. We implement the toolkit as part of a classroom tutorial in three different learning scenarios and discuss the overall receptive student feedback. We suggest this toolkit and similar applications as resourceful supplements to instruction in NLP topics, especially for the purpose of balancing conceptual understanding with technical instruction, grounding abstract topics, and engaging students with varying coding abilities.

1 Introduction

The field of information theory has seen intriguing results in the computational modeling of human language processing. Measures of information encoded in linguistic units can be used to predict the processing difficulty, or surprisal, of language (Hale, 2001; Levy, 2008) . The topic of surprisal is relevant both to researchers who want to investigate language using measures of information density, and to students of linguistics and computer science who benefit from learning about the subject.

There is also a need for tactile, communicative, and individualized learning tools. Online tools in particular provide full flexibility for hybrid or online class environments. Visual tools that aid in understanding language model outputs, such as projects from Hoover et al. (2019); Vig (2019), are also supportive of taking steps towards interpreting models (Belinkov and Glass, 2019). Such tools for learning about abstract concepts can provide students with a conceptual intuition that they can build upon and improve.

One existing public tool, OpenAI's Playground (OpenAI, 2024), offers exploratory functionality for interacting with large language models and a modest view of token probabilities. While the Playground showcases an appealing example of a user interface, we have yet to see a toolkit available that is fitting for the goals of research and education in surprisal theory. Notably, this setting calls for a tool with payment-free usage, easily retrievable surprisal calculations, and an extendable offering of publicly available language models, ideally through a simplified user interface. With this in mind, we developed the Surprisal Toolkit as an open-source research and educational tool[1] .

The Surprisal Toolkit was built in part to exist with a suite of language modeling tools for measuring aspects of information density. As part of a larger research aim to share computational tools across related projects, the Toolkit interface enables researchers with or without programming skills to obtain and analyze surprisal. Secondly, students with an interest in learning about measures of information density or examining their importance can interact with the Toolkit as an educational tool.

We begin with the measure of surprisal and illustrate in the following sections how the web-based Toolkit supports multiple classroom environments, for a range of student profiles, in sessions taught both in person and online.

This work presents the Surprisal Toolkit, an online interface for interacting with and teaching concepts of surprisal. We demonstrate the usefulness of this tool to encourage educators and developers to consider making use of similar resources in NLP courses.

*Work done while at Saarland University.

[1]https://github.com/uds-lsv/surprisal-toolkit

Proceedings of the Sixth Workshop on Teaching NLP, pages 119–127
August 15, 2024 ©2024 Association for Computational Linguistics

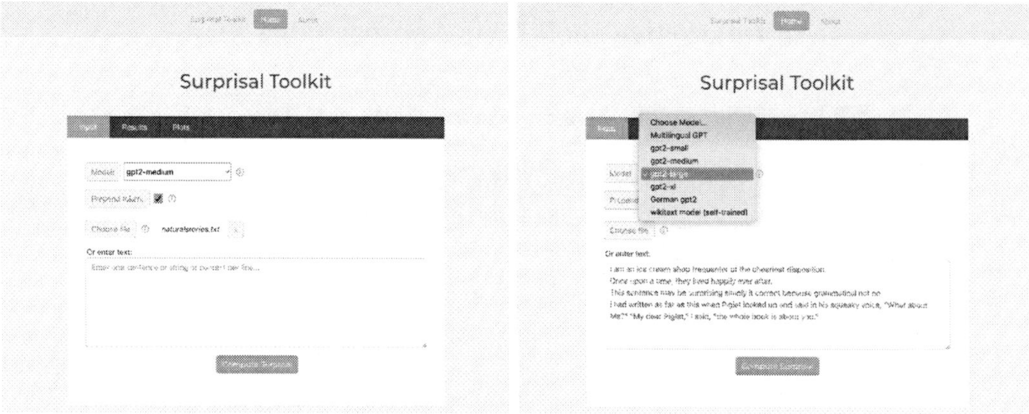

Figure 1: The Surprisal Toolkit web interface with selected user input, e.g., *Model: gpt2-medium, Prepend Token: selected, Chosen file: naturalstories.txt*, in the left window. The right window depicts text box input with 4 unique sentences separated onto new lines. Here, the open *Model* list reveals a starting selection of pretrained and self-trained models sourced from Hugging Face and *languagemodels*, respectively.

2 Learning Objectives

The tutorial we teach with the Surprisal Toolkit provides a hands-on approach to analyzing surprisal estimates from large language models. Students directly engage with applications of information theory, calculating surprisal values from model predictions and statistically comparing results in order to evaluate the alignment of machine to human language processing. The learning objectives are as follows:

1. *Learn to calculate surprisal with the Toolkit, becoming familiar with an abstract concept through concrete, visual examples.*

2. *Learn how and why to use surprisal for psycholinguistic research.* Statistically model surprisal as a predictor of human reading times using Linear Mixed Effects (LME) models. Evaluate model fit using log-likelihood and mean squared error (MSE).

3. *Learn to calculate token and word-level surprisal directly with code, machine learning libraries, and language model output.*

3 The Surprisal Toolkit

Application architecture.

The Surprisal Toolkit shown in Figure 1 is a web-based application built to interface with a language-modeling Python library, *languagemodels*, developed for information theoretic research at a large university. The *languagemodels* library supplies custom surprisal functions using PyTorch (Paszke et al., 2019) and serves as a wrapper for functionalities from Hugging Face Transformers (Wolf et al., 2019). Together with access through a browser, the Surprisal Toolkit allows for calculating and visualizing surprisal values from language models, either internally provided or externally accessed through Hugging Face Transformers.

The application was developed using Flask for back-end functionality along with ease of integration with Python in *languagemodels*, and Angular for the front-end design and user interface. We host the application on an existing web domain of the research group to allow students to directly access the Toolkit without the need for each student to build the project locally.

Purpose and benefits.

As a visual and computational tool, the Surprisal Toolkit serves two main purposes in our learning communities. First, it *simplifies access* to working with language models for students and researchers who lack experience in coding. As a stand-alone tool, it allows users to specify input, quickly obtain surprisal estimates, and allot focus to evaluating results. Thus attention is freed for assessing hypotheses or conceptually grasping adjacent learning objectives. The second purpose is to act as an interactive resource for students to *learn and experiment* with the topic of surprisal from language models. The Toolkit demonstrates both the theoretical topic of surprisal and its technical realization. The Toolkit provides a student-led introduction to the topic as well as a balance of high-level understanding. This allows it to be cohesively combined with subsequent coding instruction for implementing the processes observed in the interface.

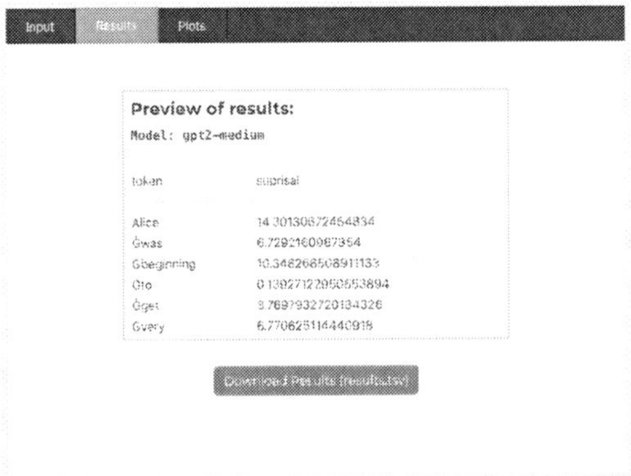

Figure 2: View of the results file preview in the Surprisal Toolkit web interface. Users can scroll through the window of token and surprisal estimates from the selected model (here, `gpt2-medium`) for the given text input. The complete *results.tsv* file can be downloaded via the button underneath.

3.1 Use Cases

We discuss several use cases for the Surprisal Toolkit as a scientific learning and research tool.

Case I: Basic usage.

The simple usage of the Toolkit is as a pre-built calculator for computing surprisal from language models across text. Surprisal is calculated on the token level (i.e., words, characters, or subwords), as word-level surprisal can be obtained by summing the retrieved surprisal values.

- Users enter text into a text box or upload a text file, select a pretrained language model, and click *Compute Surprisal*, as portrayed in Figure 1.
- In the *Results* tab of the interface shown in Figure 2, a scrolling preview of tokens and surprisal values per line of context is shown. Below it, a *Download Results (results.tsv)* button allows users to save the complete tab-separated values file with columns for `sentence_id`, `token`, `surprisal`, and `token_id`.
- To visually explore the data in the *Plots* tab (Figure 4), users select a sentence from the input text to display a plot of log base 2 surprisal across all tokens. Plot views can be adjusted by panning the window, zooming in and out, and fitting automatically. Helpful views may then be downloaded as PNG image files.

results

sentence_id	token	surprisal	token_id
0	I	6.097026824951170	40
0	Ġam	4.00877046585083	716
0	Ġan	4.898037910461430	281
0	Ġice	11.841976165771500	4771
0	Ġcream	1.0082951784133900	8566
0	Ġshop	6.462131023406980	6128
0	Ġfrequ	15.767751693725600	3593
0	enter	1.3184295892715500	9255
0	Ġof	5.436539649963380	286
0	Ġthe	2.160862445831300	262
0	Ġcheer	18.829608917236300	14042
0	iest	3.641078472137450	6386
0	Ġdisposition	15.904372215271000	24665
0	.	1.2129837274551400	13
1	Once	16.311511993408200	7454
1	Ġupon	2.119483470916750	2402

Figure 3: A cropped example of a downloaded *results.tsv* file.

Case II: Comparing language models.

The Toolkit provides an ongoing list of pretrained language models from Hugging Face of varying parameter sizes. Thus, results can be compared between them. Users may enter text or upload a text file of the same input while selecting differing models to calculate surprisal. By visualizing results in the *Plots* tab of the Toolkit, or downloading results in the *Results* tab, measures of surprisal from each model can be quickly viewed or saved for further comparison. In psycholinguistic investigations such as those in Oh and Schuler (2023); Kuribayashi et al. (2023), for example, surprisal estimates are used to compare varying models' abilities to predict human reading behavior.

Case III: Computing surprisal over text.

Surprisal values can be computed over plain text in the context of sentences, stories, or documents. Results can then be used for subsequent processing or as data to investigate research questions. As an example, in the work of Wilcox et al. (2023) the authors derive surprisal estimates for 11 languages using multilingual models such as mGPT, a variant of GPT-3 pretrained on 61 languages (Shliazhko et al., 2022), in order to assess surprisal theory cross-linguistically. mGPT, available as a pretrained model through Hugging Face, can also be selected as input in the Surprisal Toolkit.

In addition to plain text, CoNLL-U[2] formatted text files, a revised version of the CoNLL-X format (Buchholz and Marsi, 2006), can be processed through the Toolkit. Downloaded result files will include an updated CoNLL-U text file with an additional column holding surprisal values.

Case IV: Visualizing surprisal estimates.

In the *Plots* tab (see Figure 4), users can visualize surprisal values across tokens in a sentence or line of context. By comparing surprisal modulations across sentences, users can investigate hypotheses or gather quick insights. This use case is especially helpful for demonstrating to students how surprisal increases, decreases, or persists across token values.

4 Classroom Implementation

The tutorial was experienced in several learning formats for a range of student backgrounds. We describe each scenario in the following subsections with a highlight of how using the Surprisal Toolkit addressed the specific needs of the class environment.

In all classroom implementations, we presented the tutorial through online materials[3]. We began with a presentation shared on a large screen, communicating either the details of the session, as in settings 4.1 and 4.2, or a brief introduction to the topic, as in setting 4.3. In hybrid settings, online participants joined through a video meeting in which the screen was also shared. The tutorial took place over a span of 90 minutes, segmented by an introduction, group question answering, and checkpoints throughout students' self-paced learning.

The format of the tutorial was comprised of a Python Jupyter Notebook, a computational notebook with interactive code blocks for sequential documenting and visualizing of code, and a web browser for accessing the Surprisal Toolkit. The Jupyter Notebook provided four sections for students to work through independently or in pairs. Section 1 documented a guided *Surprisal Toolkit Warm-Up* in which students interacted with the web interface to familiarize with calculating surprisal over tokens. In Section 3, students used the Toolkit to quickly gather surprisal results over the Natural Stories Corpus (Futrell et al., 2020) based on probability estimates from three different GPT-2 model sizes.

The premise of the notebook was to reproduce part of the experiments in (Oh and Schuler, 2023) in order to compare statistical models of human reading time data with and without LLM surprisal values as a predictor. In other words, students were given the problem of human and neural language processing in order to explore the degree to which larger language models might be worse at predicting reading times, and why. By providing a simple interface, or input-output mechanism, for obtaining the surprisal data through the Toolkit, students were able to focus in this section on the type of research questions that could be investigated using the results. This exercise was meant in part to showcase *how* the measure of surprisal could be used in psycholinguistic research and in the analysis of large language models, thus motivating a reason to learn its calculation.

The main coding focus of the notebook was then to calculate surprisal from language model outputs, without using the Surprisal Toolkit. This section explores the technical implementation and draws attention to insights for programming directly with Transformer language models.

4.1 Course Tutorial

As part of a seminar on information theory offered at a large university, the tutorial was presented to a group of 10-15 students as a practical session. Here, students were given the opportunity to apply the information they learned in an earlier lecture about neural language models.

Student demographic.

The information theory course was offered particularly for graduate students, i.e. master's and doctoral students, as well as postdoctoral researchers with a related research focus. Thus, students were expected to be moderately informed on the subject of natural language processing, while in the midst of learning about information theory, neural language processing, and psycholinguistic research. Programming experience was not required, but students were familiar enough with running Python Jupyter Notebooks, installing dependencies, and coding functions to be able to work through technical aspects of the tutorial. The majority of students

[2]See `https://universaldependencies.org/format.html` for CoNLL-U documentation.

[3]Materials are shared as an example at: `https://github.com/uds-lsv/surprisal-toolkit-teaching-materials`

were present in person, while 3-5 engaged in the tutorial through an online meeting. Students were motivated to work and learn independently, especially as many shared the goal of being able to directly use the skills from the tutorial.

Toolkit impact: *individualized examples and theory in practice*.

For students in this scenario, the Surprisal Toolkit was useful for grounding the concept of surprisal. After learning about its calculations and implications in psycholinguistic research, students were given this tool to explore surprisal directly. This was achievable through self-guided experiments in which students expressed their hypotheses as input and inspected results through the Toolkit output. Students observed important points in the process of model selection, tokenization, and the modulation of surprisal values across a string of context.

In conjunction with lectures on the theoretical aspects of surprisal and a written tutorial describing technical implementations, the Toolkit supplemented students' learning with a hands-on approach to interacting with the concept. For example, students were able to see a range in surprisal values calculated across a sentence as in Figure 4. By clicking between sentences, the model's processing of language could be compared. When students were curious about the results they saw, they were easily able to modify the input text or model selection to gather more feedback for their question.

Each run of the Toolkit supplied an *individualized example*, of interest to the student who chose it. This was especially important for teaching the concept in a way that was relatable and accessible to every student.

4.2 Pop-up Tutorial

We next taught a tutorial on information theory, entitled "Surprisal from Large Language Models". The tutorial was open to all master's students in the university's department of Language Science and Technology who had an interest in learning more about gathering and analyzing surprisal estimates from large language models. We organized the tutorial independently of any courses in order to offer it as a distinct learning module to all interested students. For those who registered, we provided a few external readings as optional background knowledge in preparation. These included the first few pages of an introduction to information theory (Stone, 2015) and two recently published papers on the relation of surprisal from larger large language models (Oh and Schuler, 2023), as well as those from instruction-tuned models (Kuribayashi et al., 2023), and human reading behavior.

Student demographic.

A focused class size of six master's students joined the tutorial, with two participating through an online video meeting. Due to the optional nature of the session, we assume that those who took part in it were students with a special interest in learning about the topic. Most had used Python at least once previously in their courses. Background knowledge on information theory ranged from students having no formal instruction to students being generally familiar with the concept after exposure to it in courses on computational psycholinguistics. All students were either in the beginning or middle of a degree in Language Science and Technology.

Toolkit impact: *introducing and demonstrating main concepts*.

In this setting, the Surprisal Toolkit served a similar purpose of bolstering learning engagement as described in 4.1. Since students did not receive a formal lecture of instruction prior to the tutorial tasks, the Toolkit served as both an *introduction* and a *demonstration of the main concepts*. The tutorial began with a brief discussion of the learning objectives, a definition of surprisal as it relates to language processing, and research findings in the use of language model estimates to predict human reading times. Students, both online and in person, were eager to test the capabilities of the Toolkit[4].

An example interaction illustrates the benefit of having the Toolkit in this setting: While students were exploring the Toolkit, they shared several questions relating to (i) *how* the application was able to produce surprisal estimates, (ii) *what steps* were taken by the selected language model for estimation, and (iii) *what meaning* could be interpreted from the values displayed in the plot of tokens across a sentence. Essentially, all three of these questions would be answered while working through the code and instructions in the tutorial Jupyter notebook. The Toolkit thus became a precursor to the more technical and theoretical investigations within the written tutorial. Engaging with

[4]We elaborate on how to prepare for enthusiastic memory usage of web-based tools in Section 7 but ultimately were able to support the engagement.

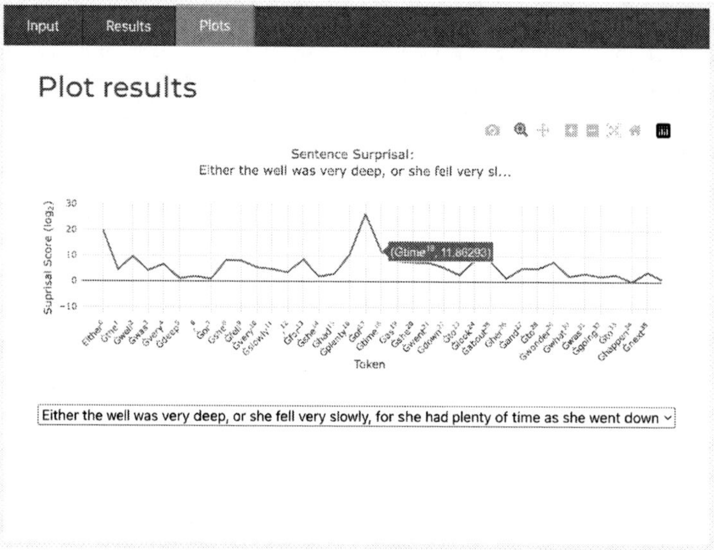

Figure 4: Plot of surprisal values from an excerpt of sentences from *Alice's Adventures in Wonderland* by Lewis Carroll. On the x-axis is the model-tokenized sentence or line of text. The Ġ symbol represents white space and, when prefixed to a token, indicates the start of an orthographic word. On the y-axis is the log base 2 surprisal score for each token. Below the plot is a drop-down menu for selecting a sentence or line of text from the input for viewing.

the Toolkit effectively directed students' attention to the information they would receive during the remaining tutorial.

4.3 Workshop

We taught the tutorial again as a workshop during a three-day computational linguistics conference designed for bachelor's and master's students of related fields. The conference was aimed at fostering knowledge exchange between students and served as both an educational and community forming event. Participants were able to attend keynote lectures given by university professors in the field of natural language processing. Lecture topics were loosely related to our tutorial topic of information theory, and may have provided interest or slight context to students who participated in the workshop. Of the day's events, students could choose to attend our workshop or opt for other talks occurring simultaneously.

Student demographic.

A group of 9 students, mostly master's, elected to participate in the workshop. We expected most participants to have little to no background knowledge on the subject of information theory, natural language processing, or computer programming. In this setting, we also could not expect participants to have prepared background knowledge outside of the classroom. Instead, we prepared a short introduction with key points for situating the tutorial. Since participants would be selecting from a full day of events to meet their intellectual interests, we aimed to create a learning environment that was direct, concise, salient, and enjoyable. Here we targeted learning through active engagement more so than through self-directed coding challenges, as offered in prior tutorials.

Toolkit impact: *engaging students and prompting student-led experiments.*

The Toolkit became a focal point for grounding concepts and engaging students in this scenario. After presenting a short series of slides with information on surprisal theory and its calculations through language models, we introduced the Surprisal Toolkit in an interactive group warm-up.

Through student-led input, we aimed to exemplify and experiment with the notions just introduced. We prompted students to come up with hypotheses that might lead to changes in surprisal values across tokens in a line of context. By comparing visualizations of plotted results, students were able to assess possible answers to their questions and experiment with further insights gained. For example, students were asked to come up with sentences that might lead to peaks or drops in surprisal values; compare output from different models; and assess the reliability of model output, along with contributing factors thereof, given their own intuitions about language. The discussion gained from using such a tool raised several interesting observations from students, whether about influences on the measure of surprisal or the processes implemented behind the interface.

5 Hybrid Classroom

One benefit of web-based learning tools is their functionality in both online and in-person settings. With the usability of the Surprisal Toolkit online, for example, we have been able to adapt our tutorial for hybrid learning with little modification. An additional advantage we observe through having taught with an interactive tool is its ability to engage remote students who are unable to physically immerse in the classroom environment.

6 Student Feedback

At the end of each tutorial, we collected optional student feedback in the form of a ten-question survey. In an effort to ensure some feedback over none, we kept questions to a minimum and included only one free response. The first question asked for confirmation that students were able to use the Surprisal Toolkit in the tutorial. Questions 2-9 were opinion questions on a 5-point Likert scale, with 5 indicating the most positive opinion. Question 10 was open-ended, allowing for optional comments or suggestions regarding the Toolkit. Students were free to fill out the survey on paper or online through a printed QR code. Those who completed the survey did so anonymously and confirmed their consent to having their answers contribute towards future research on teaching NLP. In Table 1 we present the results from the 12 student responses collected across all three tutorial sessions[5].

Overall, student feedback was positive towards using the Surprisal Toolkit as a learning tool. The majority of students gave scores of 5 in each question. All questions except for one saw scores at 3 or above. Only one question, *Did using the toolkit help you to understand more about language models or evaluating surprisal?* received a rating of 2 from a student who attended the pop-up tutorial (4.2). One possible explanation for this response could be related to reaching the memory capacity for the Toolkit server during the warm-up of this tutorial session. The experience revealed the need to manage high usage through further application development, or to carefully plan classroom scenarios to best distribute simultaneous interactions with the tool.

When asked about satisfaction with using the Toolkit as a resource and, later, satisfaction with the tutorial overall, ratings decreased slightly, with two student scores (16.7%) reducing from 4 to 3. At a minimum, we can interpret that the Toolkit did not detract from the learning environment. Even with room for improvement in the tutorial, the Toolkit provided a mostly satisfying component.

The highest-scoring question, *How interested would you be in seeing similar applications for interacting with language models in your courses?* received almost unanimous ranking of 5 for "Very interested". This result is promising, as it suggests that students enjoyed using the Toolkit enough in this instance to look positively towards further implementations of such tools in their learning environments. As educators, researchers, and developers we may be encouraged to build and share more interactive NLP tools with students who welcome the resources.

7 Discussion and Suggestions

One important consideration when developing web-based learning applications is to ensure sufficient server memory is available to handle multiple simultaneous requests. We suggest two methods for addressing this need depending on the stage of development of the tool. First, in the most ideal case, function calls to large Hugging Face models should be implemented in a way that minimizes redundant memory and allows for shared resources among user requests. Second, in the case that memory is limited, an option is to use the application in group-led activities, specifically at points in the lesson dedicated mainly to exploring the application. Shared usage, where students still have the opportunity to direct the interaction with the tool, is one way to counteract memory limitations that can be just as effective for engagement. In the workshop setting described in 4.3, we found this to positively be the case.

We suggest continuously iterating over the appli-

[5]This number represents 53% of all students who attended the tutorial sessions and stayed for the full duration of the class. Of all student responses, 16.67% originated from the course tutorial, 33.33% from the pop-up tutorial, and 50.00% from the workshop.

#	Student Feedback Question	Rating Distribution
1	How much did using the toolkit affect your learning engagement during the tutorial? *I didn't feel at all engaged...I felt very engaged*	**5** (1:0, 2:0, 3:3, 4:1, 5:8)
2	How satisfied were you with using the toolkit as a resource? *Not at all satisfied...Extremely satisfied*	**4.5** (1:0, 2:0, 3:1, 4:5, 5:6)
3	How easily were you able to interact with the toolkit? *Not at all easily...Very easily*	**5** (1:0, 2:0, 3:1, 4:2, 5:9)
4	Did using the toolkit help you to understand more about language models or evaluating surprisal? *No, strongly disagree...Yes, strongly agree*	**4.5** (1:0, 2:1, 3:2, 4:3, 5:6)
5	Did using the toolkit bring up questions about language models or surprisal that you would like to explore further? *No, strongly disagree...Yes, strongly agree*	**5** (1:0, 2:0, 3:1, 4:3, 5:8)
6	How interested would you be in using the toolkit again for a similar task? *Not at all interested...Very interested*	**5** (1:0, 2:0, 3:0, 4:5, 5:7)
7	How interested would you be in seeing similar applications for interacting with language models in your courses? *Not at all interested...Very interested*	**5** (1:0, 2:0, 3:1, 4:0, 5:11)
8	How satisfied were you with today's tutorial overall? *Not at all satisfied...Extremely satisfied*	**4.5** (1:0, 2:0, 3:3, 4:3, 5:6)

Table 1: Student feedback (N=12): distribution of responses to opinion questions on learning with the Surprisal Toolkit. Response ratings are from 1-5, with 5 being the most positive assessment. Counts are given to the right of each rating. In bold is the median response and in blue text is the most frequent.

cation of a toolkit interface, as students bring some of the most meaningful feedback for highlighting where important features can be implemented to improve learning.

A few points of interest were inquiries about (1) why `Prepend Token` was necessary when processing text with GPT-2-based language models, (2) how much context was considered when calculating token probabilities, and (3) where more information could be found about the details of the language models themselves. We addressed these points in the user interface by adding tooltips with further information to relevant areas.

The aim was not to remove the class discussion of these facets, but to reinforce the Toolkit for use by students who rely on a reiteration of the answers or may prefer independent discovery. We expect that continual integration of student feedback would bring an ongoing interchange of more informative pedagogical research tools and more empowered student users.

Based on student feedback, we also see valuable uses for making the Toolkit open-source. This could represent an additional learning opportunity and motivation for inquisitive students to investigate the concept further, and is yet to be explored in future courses.

Ongoing work on the Toolkit can provide additional features for presenting important concepts. For example, the relationship between surprisal and perplexity might be explored through the ability to calculate and compare both measures of information density.

8 Conclusion

We find the Surprisal Toolkit to balance conceptual understanding with technical implementation, providing opportunities for visual learning and efficient solutions when needed. In classroom settings, the Toolkit was able to demonstrate to students that an implementation of surprisal was possible prior to building the coding calculation themselves. The

Toolkit as a method for grounding abstract concepts provides a scaffolding for adjusting programming course content to a broader range of knowledge backgrounds. A benefit of a web-based tool is that it readily integrates into online or hybrid teaching environments. Therefore we recommend implementing such tools in further topics and courses in NLP.

Acknowledgments

Many thanks are owed to the motivated students who took part in the tutorials and offered their feedback and suggestions. We thank the organizers of the 33rd TaCoS for serendipitously contacting us with an opportunity to teach. Thank you to Zaynab Reza for helping to continue development on the Surprisal Toolkit. We also thank the reviewers for their constructive feedback. This research was supported by funding from the Deutsche Forschungsgemeinschaft (DFG, German Research Foundation), Project ID 232722074 – SFB 1102.

References

Yonatan Belinkov and James Glass. 2019. Analysis Methods in Neural Language Processing: A Survey. *Transactions of the Association for Computational Linguistics*, 7:49–72.

Sabine Buchholz and Erwin Marsi. 2006. CoNLL-X shared task on multilingual dependency parsing. In *Proceedings of the Tenth Conference on Computational Natural Language Learning (CoNLL-X)*, pages 149–164, New York City. Association for Computational Linguistics.

Richard Futrell, Edward Gibson, Harry J Tily, Idan Blank, Anastasia Vishnevetsky, Steven T Piantadosi, and Evelina Fedorenko. 2020. The natural stories corpus: a reading-time corpus of english texts containing rare syntactic constructions. *Language resources and evaluation, 55(1), 63–77.*

John Hale. 2001. A probabilistic Earley parser as a psycholinguistic model. In *Second Meeting of the North American Chapter of the Association for Computational Linguistics*.

Benjamin Hoover, Hendrik Strobelt, and Sebastian Gehrmann. 2019. exbert: A visual analysis tool to explore learned representations in transformers models. *arXiv preprint arXiv:1910.05276*.

Tatsuki Kuribayashi, Yohei Oseki, and Timothy Baldwin. 2023. Psychometric predictive power of large language models. *arXiv preprint arXiv:2311.07484*.

Roger Levy. 2008. Expectation-based syntactic comprehension. *Cognition*, 106(3):1126–1177.

Byung-Doh Oh and William Schuler. 2023. Why does surprisal from larger transformer-based language models provide a poorer fit to human reading times? *Transactions of the Association for Computational Linguistics*, 11:336–350.

OpenAI. 2024. Playground. `https://platform.openai.com/playground/complete`. Accessed: 2024-07-01.

Adam Paszke, Sam Gross, Francisco Massa, Adam Lerer, James Bradbury, Gregory Chanan, Trevor Killeen, Zeming Lin, Natalia Gimelshein, Luca Antiga, Alban Desmaison, Andreas Köpf, Edward Yang, Zach DeVito, Martin Raison, Alykhan Tejani, Sasank Chilamkurthy, Benoit Steiner, Lu Fang, Junjie Bai, and Soumith Chintala. 2019. Pytorch: An imperative style, high-performance deep learning library. *Preprint*, arXiv:1912.01703.

Oleh Shliazhko, Alena Fenogenova, Maria Tikhonova, Vladislav Mikhailov, Anastasia Kozlova, and Tatiana Shavrina. 2022. mgpt: Few-shot learners go multilingual. *arXiv preprint arXiv:2204.07580*.

James V. Stone. 2015. Information theory: A tutorial introduction. *ArXiv*, abs/1802.05968.

Jesse Vig. 2019. A multiscale visualization of attention in the transformer model. In *Proceedings of the 57th Annual Meeting of the Association for Computational Linguistics: System Demonstrations*, pages 37–42, Florence, Italy. Association for Computational Linguistics.

Ethan G. Wilcox, Tiago Pimentel, Clara Meister, Ryan Cotterell, and Roger P. Levy. 2023. Testing the Predictions of Surprisal Theory in 11 Languages. *Transactions of the Association for Computational Linguistics*, 11:1451–1470.

Thomas Wolf, Lysandre Debut, Victor Sanh, Julien Chaumond, Clement Delangue, Anthony Moi, Pierric Cistac, Tim Rault, Rémi Louf, Morgan Funtowicz, et al. 2019. Huggingface's transformers: State-of-the-art natural language processing. *arXiv preprint arXiv:1910.03771*.

Occam's Razor and Bender and Koller's Octopus

Michael Guerzhoy
University of Toronto
guerzhoy@cs.toronto.edu

Abstract

We discuss the teaching of the discussion surrounding Bender and Koller's prominent ACL 2020 paper, "Climbing toward NLU: on meaning form, and understanding in the age of data" (Bender and Koller, 2020).

We present what we understand to be the main contentions of the paper, and then recommend that the students engage with the natural counter-arguments to the claims in the paper.

We attach teaching materials that we use to facilitate teaching this topic to undergraduate students.

1 Introduction

The claim in Bender and Koller's argument in (Bender and Koller, 2020) is that a being that only has access to the form of the communication – e.g., an intelligent octopus that taps into only the submarine signals that encode accounts of the events above the sea that two people on land send each other – will not be able to "understand" what is happening above sea-level, lacking the semantics of the Morse code that was used to communicate the events transpiring above the seas. Koller and Bender argue that even if the octopus can send messages based on the patterns it sees that would be understood by the humans and the humans would be fooled into thinking they are reading messages from another human, the shallow understanding of the octopus would necessarily be revealed when trying to pretend to answer more complicated queries.

Implicit in the argument is that the intelligent octopus is analogous to a Large Language Model (LLM), akin to GPT-2 (Brown et al., 2020), GPT-4 [1], Claude 3 [2], or Meta Llama 3 [3], and that such LLMs would not be able to truly understand natural language in the same way that Bender and Koller's octopus will not.

In this paper, we present a lecture + activity that challenges Bender and Koller's argument. Students will engage with Bender and Koller's argument and with the counterargument, and come away with their own conclusions

2 Building theory form data

The scientific process itself can be analogized to a B&K octopus observing data they don't understand.

For example, astronomers observe and try to predict the motions of heavenly bodies, initially with no mechanistic understanding of why the stars appear to move the way they do. Historically, astronomers came up with multiple incorrect theories for why the heavenly bodies move the way they do (notably, the family of geocentric models). Astronomers used "epicycles" as a way to align predictions with their model, at the expense of parsimony (Duhem, 2015).

Historically, Copernicus' first models did not predict the data as well as the best epicycle-based geocentric models (Klein and Loftus, 2015).

Note that, unlike the astronomers, the octopus cannot *interact* with the world – he cannot influence what observations are made (at least before he starts communicating with the astronomers). This can influence how fast the octopus can "converge." Historically, much of the data used by Kepler was previously collected by Tycho Brahe.

2.1 Occam's razor

Occam's razor – the principle that, all things being equal, we should prefer the simpler theory – can help select the better scientific theory. For example, the B& K octopus might consider all possible theories of the world over the sea, and settle on the simplest one that explains the communications the

[1] https://openai.com/index/gpt-4-research/
[2] https://www.anthropic.com/news/claude-3-family
[3] https://llama.meta.com/llama3/

Proceedings of the Sixth Workshop on Teaching NLP, pages 128–129
August 15, 2024

octopus decodes.

3 Can the B& K octopus learn science

Every student can make their own conclusions, but ours is that it's not in principle impossible for that to happen (or if it is impossible, we don't have a clear reason to think so). The success of LLMs on tasks that require some level of world-theory-building such as the addition of integers task (Lee et al., 2023), predicted to be impossible by Bender and Koller (2020) (see Appendix B), indicates that if there are barriers to learning world models from observational data, they are not well-understood. Our view is that the prediction by B&K that a pure LLM could not learn to do arithmetic is due to insufficiently accounting for the possibility of using inductive biases to build a model of the data that corresponds to the world that the data is describing.

4 Materials

We provide slides we used in class to follow up the class's reading of Bender and Koller (2020). We also provide the following guiding questions

1. If the octopus observes different content in messages when it's dark vs. when it's light, what can the octopus possibly conclude about language?
2. Describe how the octopus might use tides to infer words that have to do with tides
3. Describe how the octopus might decode conversations about physics based on the conversations about tides – perhaps building up from observations of tides, stars, etc.
4. If you assume no "cheating" such as jointly observing tides, might you imagine conversations that involve physical and mathematical constant like G and π playing a similar role?
5. Explain why without Occam's razor, the Octopus will have a practically infinite number of theories about what the two humans could be talking about
6. What might be some insurmountable challenges for the octopus in the quest to understand the meaning of the cable signals? How
7. Consider the claim from the original paper that arithmetic is not learnable by form alone: where might that argument have gone wrong?

5 Additional materials

Julian Michael, *To Dissect An Octopus* `https://julianmichael.org/blog/2020/07/23/to-dissect-an-octopus.html` provides an excellent overview.

6 Conclusion

Many students in NLP would be familiar with Bender and Koller's argument, but have probably not engaged in the critical analysis of the arguments. We provide materials for critically analyzing the arguments made by Bender and Koller. We focus on the counterarguments since the argument itself is ably presented by the original authors. We provide slides introducing the B&K argument to the best our ability as well.

Many (though not all) students are captivated by the debate. We find that the structure provided by the guiding questions helps in our lectures.

7 Teaching materials

Slides: `https://github.com/guerzh/octopus`
Video lecture: `https://youtu.be/6QVjGF_J7I0`

References

Emily M Bender and Alexander Koller. 2020. Climbing towards nlu: On meaning, form, and understanding in the age of data. In *Proceedings of the 58th annual meeting of the association for computational linguistics*, pages 5185–5198.

Tom Brown, Benjamin Mann, Nick Ryder, Melanie Subbiah, Jared D Kaplan, Prafulla Dhariwal, Arvind Neelakantan, Pranav Shyam, Girish Sastry, Amanda Askell, et al. 2020. Language models are few-shot learners. *Advances in neural information processing systems*, 33:1877–1901.

Pierre Duhem. 2015. *To save the phenomena: An essay on the idea of physical theory from Plato to Galileo.* University of Chicago Press.

Stanley B Klein and Judith Loftus. 2015. The mental representation of trait and autobiographical knowledge about the self. *The mental representation of trait and autobiographical knowledge about the self*, pages 1–49.

Nayoung Lee, Kartik Sreenivasan, Jason D Lee, Kangwook Lee, and Dimitris Papailiopoulos. 2023. Teaching arithmetic to small transformers. In *The Twelfth International Conference on Learning Representations.*

Author Index